When Nature Turns Killer

Truly Terrifying Outdoor Adventures

Edited by Lamar Underwood

LYONS PRESS
Essex, Connecticut

LYONS PRESS

An imprint of The Globe Pequot Publishing Group, Inc.
64 South Main Street
Essex, CT 06426
www.globepequot.com

British Library Cataloguing in Publication Information available

Library of Congress Cataloging-in-Publication Data

Names: Underwood, Lamar editor
Title: When nature turns killer : truly terrifying outdoor adventures / edited by Lamar Underwood.
Description: Essex, Connecticut : Lyons Press, [2026] | Includes bibliographical references.
Identifiers: LCCN 2026004589 (print) | LCCN 2026004590 (ebook) | ISBN 9781493096046 paperback | ISBN 9781493096053 epub
Subjects: LCSH: Outdoor life | Adventure and adventurers | Nature stories, American | LCGFT: Anecdotes | Biographies
Classification: LCC GV191.24 .W54 2026 (print) | LCC GV191.24 (ebook) | DDC 796.5—dc23/eng/20260313
LC record available at https://lccn.loc.gov/2026004589
LC ebook record available at https://lccn.loc.gov/2026004590

Contents

Introduction

Lamar Underwood

No matter how cautious a wilderness traveler might be, the dangers that lurk in the trails ahead can plunge the careless or unlucky into a trap. Escaping will be difficult at best, sometimes impossible. The dangers can take many forms, beginning with the forests themselves. The trails that promised easy hiking can become virtually impenetrable tangles of brush, trees, and swamplands. Sometimes they twist and turn through hills and mountains in a never-ending maze of rivulets and short-lived paths that turn into barriers of tangled briars and vines that grab and choke and refuse to let go of your staggering lost-and-afraid body.

Of course, planning and preparation can reduce or knock out many, or most, wilderness surprises, including the biggest, most-feared one of them all: bear attacks. Black bears in the East and Midwest and grizzlies (plus black bears) in the Northwest and Rocky Mountains are very real dangers in the most remote and beautiful places in the great outdoors. Journeys that begin with confidence and determination can result in desperation and tragedy. Also, very real creatures such as poisonous snakes and swarming insects like black flies and mosquitoes can ruin your trip or put you in the hospital.

None of the wilderness threats mentioned here or any you might fear from time to time will cause the intrepid outdoor adventurer to stay home. In some cases, however, the dangers might convince some hikers or campers to revise their plans—from solo trips into deep wilderness to having a companion or two when taking on the big woods. The bears are one reason. Another is a danger I never realized existed until my computer's internet browser started landing on reports: There are some crazy people out there, and they might be dangerous.

These "crazies"—"mentally disturbed" is not strong enough—exist in shacks, caves, or anything they can find or put together in wilderness so deep that nobody ever goes there. No, I'm not saying that anybody who lives in a deep-woods shack is crazy. But some of them are, and you don't want to be the one who stumbles across them, hoping to find peace and contentment but instead finding human savages. Be aware that we're talking about places so remote and hard to reach that even law enforcement officers and professional, experienced park rangers don't go there.

The stories in the pages ahead are not about the types of lunatics I just described. Instead, they are accounts of true-life experiences as written by journalists or the people who lived them. Even the stories that are fiction—such as the tales of Jack London—are based on knowledge gleaned from actual experiences and reflect the original settings of the events. Jack London (1876–1916) did not freeze to death during his years of backcountry living in the Yukon. However, he certainly had plenty of chances to meet that fate and knew prospectors and trappers who had. He describes their battles to stay alive in such irresistible prose that, as your editor, I felt compelled to include three Jack London stories in this book.

It has been my pleasure to edit more than thirty books for the Lyons Press. You can find complete details on the Lyons internet site, run by Simon & Schuster, which now handles Lyons Press distribution. This link should take you there: https://www.simonandschuster.com/authors/Lamar-Underwood. Press the "See All" tab for the full list of thirty-six books.

No matter how short or long they may be, I hope your wilderness journeys will never take you into the dangers described in the pages ahead. Reading about such encounters should be very interesting. Living them . . . no thank you.

Chapter 1

Run for the Trees!

Lamar Underwood

As a true mountain man in 1808, John Colter was well prepared in the skills and lore needed in the Rocky Mountain wilderness—including the dangers of trapping beaver in the domain of the dreaded Blackfeet Indians. Suddenly, he and a fellow trapper found themselves surrounded by more Blackfeet than they could count. It was time to drop their rifles and perhaps live a little longer—or die right then in a torrent of arrows.

John Colter was running for his life.

His bare feet were being shredded by cactus that littered the prairie; his gasps for breath were eruptions of blood pouring over his naked body. When he broke stride to look back, his glimpse told him the main body of the Blackfeet Indians chasing him was far behind. But up close, bearing down on him in savage rage, one warrior carrying a spear was almost upon him.

The John Colter the Blackfoot warrior expected to overtake and kill with a spear was no ordinary mountain man, naked and alone on the prairie in late summer, 1808. Had the warrior known that John Colter had been with the Lewis and Clark expedition to the Pacific, and back, he might have been more cautious. Had he known that Colter had been the first mountain man to explore the Yellowstone region and had trapped and travelled over hundreds of the great Rocky Mountain streams and valleys, he might not have expected an easy kill. Perhaps he would not have taken up the chase at all. But he did not know those things. So when Colter suddenly stopped, turning to face him, the warrior was so surprised that he stumbled and fell, breaking his spear. Colter grabbed the bladed end of the weapon and thrust it into the Indian as hard as he could. The Blackfoot warrior was pinned to the prairie earth.

Now the possibility of survival swept through Colter's mind. The main body of Indians was still coming on strong. But Colter could see the line of trees marking a river. There might be places to hide there. His ruined feet carried his bloody body into new strides.

We know today that John Colter made it to the trees and hid in a brush pile in the river. He survived the desperate hours of the Blackfeet searching for him and a seven-day trek to a fort at the mouth of the Bighorn, digging up edible roots for food. Most historians today believe that Colter was literate. But he kept no diaries or journals—did not write a single word about his adventure-filled life. Everything we know about John Colter, said to be the first mountain man, comes to us from the works of writers and historians—some reliable, others speculating. On today's internet I counted eleven books about Colter, then stopped counting, turning to Hollywood instead. The movies include three major features about Colter's Run and have touched on the subject in three or four others and planned for some that were never made.

Three men actually talked to Colter about his run and wrote stories describing what he had told them. Dr. William H. Thomas wrote a brief 225-word story published in the *Pittsburgh Gazette* on July 13, 1810. Thomas James shared a trapping expedition with Colter in 1810 and penned a much longer Colter story. It is possible that the James story might have some questionable accuracy since it was not published until his 1846 book, *Three Years Among the Indians and Mexicans*. That was 40 years after he had been with Colter.

The man most quoted for his account of Colter's Run is John Bradbury, a British naturalist and scientist, who described Colter's escape in his book *Travels in the Interior of America*, published in 1817.

Bradbury placed the text of his Colter interview in footnotes on consecutive pages about his journey up the Missouri River in 1809, '10, and '11. He had met with President Thomas Jefferson at Monticello and knew to expect great discoveries on his journey up the Missouri. Here is the complete Bradbury text, unedited except for paragraphing to break up the narration:

> *This man came to St. Louis in May, 1810, in a small canoe, from the head waters of the Missouri, a distance of three thousand miles, which he traversed in thirty days. I saw him on his arrival, and received from him an account of his adventures after he had separated from Lewis and Clarke's party: one of these, from its singularity, I shall relate.*
>
> *On the arrival of the party on the head waters of the Missouri, Colter, observing an appearance of abundance of beaver*

being there, he got permission to remain and hunt for some time, which he did in company with a man of the name of Dixon. Soon after he separated from Dixon, and trapped in company with a hunter named Potts; and aware of the hostility of the Blackfeet Indians, one of whom had been killed by Lewis, they set their traps at night, and took them up early in the morning, remaining concealed during the day.

They were examining their traps early one morning, in a creek about six miles from that branch of the Missouri called Jefferson's Fork, and were ascending in a canoe, when they suddenly heard a great noise, resembling the trampling of animals; but they could not ascertain the fact, as the high perpendicular banks on each side of the river impeded their view. Colter immediately pronounced it to be occasioned by Indians, and advised an instant retreat; but was accused of cowardice by Potts, who insisted that the noise was caused by buffaloes, and they proceeded on. In a few minutes afterwards their doubts were removed, by a party of Indians making their appearance on both sides of the creek, to the amount of five or six hundred, who beckoned them to come ashore. As retreat was now impossible, Colter turned the head of the canoe to the shore; and at the moment of its touching, an Indian seized the rifle belonging to Potts; but Colter, who is a remarkably strong man, immediately retook it, and handed it to Potts, who remained in the canoe, and on receiving it pushed off into the river. He had scarcely quitted the shore when an arrow was shot at him, and he cried out, "Colter, I am wounded."

Colter remonstrated with him on the folly of attempting to escape, and urged him to come ashore. Instead of complying, he instantly levelled his rifle at an Indian, and shot him dead on the spot. This conduct, situated as he was, may appear to have been an act of madness; but it was doubtless the effect of sudden, but sound reasoning; for if taken alive, he must have expected to be tortured to death, according to their custom. He was instantly pierced with arrows so numerous, that, to use the language of Colter, "he was made a riddle of."

They now seized Colter, stripped him entirely naked, and began to consult on the manner in which he should be put to death. They were first inclined to set him up as a mark to shoot at; but the chief interfered, and seizing him by the shoulder, asked him if he could run fast? Colter, who had been some time amongst the Kee-kat-sa, or Crow Indians, had in a considerable degree acquired the Blackfeet language, and was also well acquainted with Indian customs. He knew that he had now to run for his life, with the dreadful odds of five or six hundred against him, and those armed Indians; therefore cunningly replied that he was a very bad runner, although he was considered by the hunters as remarkably swift.

The chief now commanded the party to remain stationary, and led Colter out on the prairie three or four hundred yards, and released him, bidding him to save himself if he could. At that instant the horrid war whoop sounded in the ears of poor Colter, who, urged with the hope of preserving life, ran with a speed at which he was himself surprised. He proceeded towards the Jefferson Fork [Editor's note: the Madison; he was leaving Jefferson Fork.], having to traverse a plain six miles in breadth, abounding with the prickly pear, on which he was every instant treading with his naked feet.

He ran nearly half way across the plain before he ventured to look over his shoulder, when he perceived that the Indians were very much scattered, and that he had gained ground to a considerable distance from the main body; but one Indian, who carried a spear, was much before all the rest, and not more than a hundred yards from him. A faint gleam of hope now cheered the heart of Colter: he derived confidence from the belief that escape was within the bounds of possibility; but that confidence was nearly being fatal to him, for he exerted himself to such a degree, that the blood gushed from his nostrils, and soon almost covered the fore part of his body.

He had now arrived within a mile of the river, when he distinctly heard the appalling sound of footsteps behind him, and every instant expected to feel the spear of his pursuer. Again he turned his head, and saw the savage not twenty yards from him. Determined if possible to avoid the expected blow, he suddenly stopped, turned round, and spread out his arms. The Indian, surprised by the suddenness of the action, and perhaps at the bloody appearance of Colter, also attempted to stop; but exhausted with running, he fell whilst endeavoring to throw his spear, which stuck in the ground, and broke in his hand. Colter instantly snatched up the pointed part, with which he pinned him to the earth, and then continued his flight.

The foremost of the Indians, on arriving at the place, stopped till others came up to join them, when they set up a hideous yell. Every moment of this time was improved by Colter, who, although fainting and exhausted, succeeded in gaining the skirting of the cotton wood trees, on the borders of the fork, through which he ran, and plunged into the river. Fortunately for him, a little below this place there was an island, against the upper point of which a raft of drift timber had lodged. He dived under the raft, and after several efforts, got his head above water amongst the trunks of trees, covered over with smaller wood to the depth of several feet. Scarcely had he secured himself, when the Indians arrived on the river, screeching and yelling, as Colter expressed it, "like so many devils." They were frequently on the raft during the day, and were seen through the chinks by Colter, who was congratulating himself on his escape, until the idea arose that they might set the raft on fire. In horrible suspense he remained until night, when hearing no more of the Indians, he dived from under the raft, and swam silently down the river to a considerable distance, when he landed, and travelled all night.

Although happy in having escaped from the Indians, his situation was still dreadful: he was completely naked, under a burning sun; the soles of his feet were entirely filled with the thorns of the prickly pear; he was hungry, and had no means of killing game, although he saw abundance around him, and was at least seven days journey from Lisa's Fort, on the Bighorn branch of the Roche Jaune River. These were circumstances under which almost any man but an American hunter would have despaired. He arrived at the fort in seven days, having subsisted on a root much esteemed by the Indians of the Missouri, now known by naturalists as psoralea esculenta [breadroot; Lewis and Clark's "ground potato," an Indian substitute for bread].

The maze of literature about John Colter—and the fact that he penned not a single word about his adventures—makes the search for the real John Colter and his famous escape rather daunting. The Bradbury account we have here is one of the most trusted. It was used as source material by classic writer Washington Irving in *Astoria* in 1836 and more recently was used by famous novelist A. B. Guthrie Jr. (*The Big Sky* and others) as the basis of a fictional account of Colter's Run. His story, "Mountain Madness," first appeared in the *Saturday Evening Post* magazine in 1947 and was one of the stories in Guthrie's short story collection *The Big IT* in 1960. A 1961 edition changed the title of the book to the Colter story, *Mountain Madness*.

In his foreword to the *Mountain Madness* book, Guthrie says his fictional account of Colter's Run is based on the Bradbury story. In it, he dramatically describes how Colter could have used a beaver lodge in his escape. Guthrie (1901–1991) was a Montana-born story-teller without peer. As the *New York Times* described *Mountain Madness*: "Compared to the stylized claptrap of Westerns of book, screen and TV, this book is like a frontier model Colt .45 set alongside a collection of children's cap pistols."

The three interviews with Colter are reproduced in the definitive and scholarly biography of Colter's life by Ron Anglin and Larry E. Morris. *The Mystery of John Colter, the Man Who Discovered the Yellowstone* (2014) is available on Amazon.com; I highly recommend it for Colter research. It is backed by footnotes on every reference and title used.

Out of all the varying accounts of Colter's life, these truths emerge as solid facts: After a shaky start with the Lewis and Clark Corps of Discovery in 1803, a rowdy drunken spree, he promised to never repeat such episodes. He never did, and he is mentioned in the Lewis and Clark journals for his skills and distinguished service. His hunting and trapping skills made him a valuable companion wherever he went, and he absolutely abstained from bragging or lying. The "Colter's Hell" expression was pinned on him by men who did not believe him when he described the boiling springs and geysers of the Yellowstone region, where he had been the first to visit, and similar terrain in the Shoshone River.

Other Colter solid facts: He was born in 1775 in Virginia; he was a friend of the Crow Indians and tangled with the Blackfeet on more than one occasion; his high-country routes for trapping, exploration, and survival are still debated and traced over maps that may, or may not, be accurate; no Indian arrow or tomahawk killed him; he was married and settled in a frontier home near St. Louis in Missouri when he died of jaundice in 1813. (Jaundice was a common expression for ailments caused by many things, like cancer.)

Riddles and puzzles about Colter's life—and in particular Colter's Run—still swirl through all the literature available. Was his escape run seven days, or was it much longer? Bradbury says 7; Thomas said 9; James said 11. Was the hiding place in the river a mere collection of logs, as Bradbury says, or was it a beaver dam, as the other two interviews said? The hundreds of Blackfeet Bradbury says captured Colter sound like great exaggeration. And what about those maps? Why all the debate?

You could spend a lifetime researching all this, as several have, and still end up with questions unanswered. It's better, in this writer's humble view, to remember this outstanding young pioneer when his Blackfeet captors gave him a chance. He took it. And ran into the pages of something more than legends, but the pages of real history of individual courage and determination.

Chapter 2

Terror at Land's End

George Reiger

Although best known for his years as conservation editor for Field & Stream *magazine, George Reiger is one of the most prolific writers of recent years, with numerous titles. These include* Wanderer on My Native Shore, *about his deep love of the Atlantic Coast. Excerpted from that book and appearing here with Reiger's permission, this is a true story about writing, fishing, and scuba diving in one of the most interesting places at the outermost tip of the Florida Keys, a boat ride from Key West. Be aware that many years have passed since Reiger wrote this story, and a lot of the conditions at Fort Jefferson and the surrounding waters may have changed. [Editor's Note: Many years have passed since George Reiger wrote this story, and a lot of the conditions at Fort Jefferson and the surrounding waters may have changed.]*

Key West may be the end of road, but it is not the end of the U.S. littoral zone. In fact, it is not even the end of man's habitation of those tiny coral islands stringing south from the Florida mainland which the Spanish called "cays" and the English-speaking fishermen and wreckers known as Conchs anglicized to "keys." Sixty-eight miles west of Key West is a curious monument to nineteenth-century imperialism known as Fort Jefferson. Since it is part of the national park chain of custodianship, two or more park rangers and their families live there the year-round.

Seen from the air, Fort Jefferson has all the quality of a floating toy fort dropped into the middle of an azure sea. Almost everything in the way of land lies within the fort's hexagonal walls, and only when your seaplane tilts for the landing turn do you perceive that the fort rests precariously on top of a small cay surrounded by shallow green water through which you're lucky to spot a sea turtle and then a pair of sharks languorously making their way over the sand.

Of the eleven islands discovered here by Juan Ponce de León in 1513, only seven remain, and it won't be many decades more before this cay, too, will subside under the massive weight of Fort Jefferson. A century or so from now, Spanish hogfish will swim through drowned battlements constructed to keep everything Spanish out of Florida.

Begun in 1846, the fort was originally designed to be fifty feet high with eight-foot-thick walls. It was supposed to guard the western approach to the Straits of Florida and handicap Spain's hegemony in the Caribbean. The fort was planned to house 1,500 men and 450 cannons.

After the fort was started, however, a youthful strategist in the War Department pointed out that by sailing closer to Cuba, Spanish fleets could simply bypass the fort's mighty guns, and without a sizable harbor, no significant tonnage of American warships could extend the range of the fort's stationary weapons.

Finally, how would the fort be supplied with water? Early navigators had called this cluster of islands the Dry Tortugas, implying that while it was a good area to find spawning sea turtles for food, you had to look elsewhere for water.

The young officer's observations fell on deaf ears. Bureaucracies are slow to make decisions, but once made, they require acts of God or Congress, not mere common sense, to alter. The fort would be built, and as if to underline the government's commitment to faith over facts, the island on which it would sit was renamed Garden Key with, perhaps, the childish hope that wishing would make it so.

Sixteen million bricks were eventually mortared into walls around the perimeter of Garden Key, but the War Department's original design was never finished. Only 141 guns were mounted, and fewer than 500 men were ever garrisoned at the fort. The island's wells were soon salty, and today visitors who want to camp overnight must bring their own fresh water.

Although the War Department eventually realized it had a white elephant on its hands, it was not able to unload Fort Jefferson onto a sister agency until 1935 when President Franklin D. Roosevelt declared it to be a national monument. The Interior Department has even less money to maintain the fort than the War Department had. However, the Park Service does not try to explain this to visitors who complain of the increasing number of areas of the fort closed to them because stairs and walls are decaying and have become dangerous. Instead, the rangers tell visitors that the Park Service is using the fort as a living laboratory of the ocean's effect on man-made structures—as though we ever had any other choice.

Most visitors come out of curiosity. A few want to see the cell where Dr. Samuel A. Mudd was wrongfully incarcerated for having rightfully given medical aid to a disguised John Wilkes

Booth after he had murdered Abraham Lincoln. Dr. Mudd was eventually pardoned after valiantly working during a yellow fever epidemic to save many of the garrison and his fellow prisoners when fifty-eight men, including the fort's surgeon, died. However, rather than maintain his memory as a martyr, his memory fell into the too-common practice of assigning guilt based solely on association. His name—except in the pejorative expression "his name is Mudd"—has been largely forgotten. Most biographical dictionaries no longer carry him.

However, they do carry Ernest Hemingway, whose life and art have a vital connection with Fort Jefferson. In 1928 Hemingway met Carlos Gutiérrez, the owner of a Cuban fishing smack, in Fort Jefferson's tiny harbor. Hemingway was there to catch marlin in the blue water beyond the reefs; Gutiérrez was there to catch bait so he could return to Cuba where he fished for marlin off Coijimar, a coastal village about ten miles east of Havana. Gutiérrez had been following this routine since 1884 when he went to sea with his father at the age of six.

Naturally Hemingway, the tyro, was fascinated by Carlos' marlin fishing stories. Two in particular stuck in Hemingway's mind. One was about a huge white marlin which Carlos hooked but which was seized in turn by another unknown marlin over which Carlos had no control. After a long while, the greater fish let go, and Carlos brought his 150-pound catch, crushed and dead, to the surface.

The other story concerned an old man who went out fishing alone and hooked a big fish which dragged him far out to sea. Two days later, the old man was picked up with the head and tail of an enormous blue marlin lashed to his skiff. He had fought the fish for two days and two nights with a handline, finally bringing it close enough to harpoon. Then, finding the marlin too large to pull into his small boat, the old man tied it alongside. Sharks arrived, and despite stubborn resistance with clubs and gaffs, the old man lost half his catch. When he was picked up, sharks still circled the boat, and the old man was sobbing in frustration and exhaustion. The marlin's scant remains weighed eight hundred pounds.

Thus, on a still tropic night anchored off Fort Jefferson's derelict coaling dock, while fish splashed and rolled in the shallows, Ernest Hemingway first heard the tale that he would one day refine into a Pulitzer Prize–winning book called *The Old Man and the Sea*. Hemingway eventually fished in Cuba, looked up Carlos, and made him his guide, and from him and his own observations learned enough about billfish to write a twenty-six-page scientific treatise, "Marlin Off Cuba," which was published the year Fort Jefferson became a national monument.

However, the story of the old man and a victory that transcended inevitable defeat was something that Hemingway had to wrestle with and nurture for twenty-four years before it was finished in his mind.

Then *The Old Man and the Sea* took just eight weeks to complete with practically no rewriting.

Yet, earlier than Hemingway's fateful meeting with Gutiérrez, and even earlier than the injustice done Dr. Mudd, Fort Jefferson served as the site for a major contribution to marine biology. In 1843, Charles Darwin published his first monograph, *The Structure and Distribution of Coral-Reefs*, which theorized that all reefs begin by growing next to an island or continental platform (fringing reefs), that they continue growing upon themselves while the land mass begins to subside (barrier reefs), and that they still continue growing after the land mass, usually an island, has long since sunk beneath the waves (atolls). The core of Darwin's thesis assumed an adaptability and relatively fast growth rate for coral reefs that most scientists of his day were unwilling to credit.

To test Darwin's theory, Louis Agassiz and Spencer Fullerton Baird asked their mutual friend, Joseph Bassett Holder, in 1859 to collect specimens and to study the growth of corals near Key West where Dr. Holder was surgeon-in-charge of the government's engineering facilities. When the Civil War broke out and Dr. Holder became the health officer for the military prison at Fort Jefferson, he delegated his marine scientific work to his precocious son, Charles Frederick, who took measurements of the coral growing in the sea-water moat which nearly surrounds the fort.

Young Holder learned that while massive brain corals do grow slowly, branched corals grow much faster than had previously been realized—as much as 12.5 centimeters per year in the warm, shallow, and protected waters of the moat. He further found that some, particularly younger, corals can double their diameters within six months to a year. Although Joseph Bassett Holder continued to supervise the scientific correspondence that sailed between Garden Key and Agassiz's Museum of Comparative Zoology at Harvard and Baird's Smithsonian Institution, both scientists in the North knew that the fieldwork was being done by a ten-year-old boy. Nonetheless, Agassiz and Baird revised their estimates on the development of barrier reefs and coral atolls which they had formerly assumed grew from the bottom up rather than merely being relicts of fringing reefs.

Well over a century later, some of the same corals that young Holder studied still grow at Fort Jefferson. Periodic hurricanes have done less damage to these intricate animal colonies than to the fort itself. Left to their own devices and barring an unexpected plague of coral-eating fishes, sponges, or echinoderms (starfishes and sea urchins), or a catastrophe of cold water, there is no reason why these same corals might not outlive the fort.

At my campsite, I put on my mask, snorkel, and flippers and enter the water between Fort Jefferson's new dock and the pilings of the old.

I have largely given up spear fishing, which is prohibited in the waters around the fort, and shell collecting, also prohibited, because such physical contact with my surroundings ruins the dreamlike quality of being underwater. My hands, gloved to protect them from inadvertent contact with red fire sponges and stinging corals, seem to belong to somebody else or, perhaps, to nobody at all.

Twenty years ago, I dived the way film addicts go to the movies. The spectacle of the sea became more important to me than anything in my terrestrial existence. Then a would-be assassin swam off the screen and shocked me out of my reverie. In June 1964, I was diving solo over a ledge in about thirty-five feet of water. In those days I had undamaged ears and a lung capacity that allowed me to free-dive to such depths. I was pursuing a snapper with my spear gun when the shadow of a large fish passed over me. I looked up and saw that the nine-foot, requiem-type shark above me lacked the penis-like appendages known as claspers which trail from the male shark's pelvic fins and which are used to hold the female and insert semen. By observing such details, I tried to avoid thinking about the fact that the shark was interested in me.

I surfaced and began a slow retreat toward the beach several hundred yards away. The shark turned and came within ten feet before veering off and disappearing into the blue haze of deep water. A moment or so elapsed and she was suddenly there again, this time coming from the beach directly behind me. Again and again, she disappeared in one direction and reappeared from another. She was a cat and I was her mouse. Each time she reappeared, she seemed to swim a little faster and turn away a little closer.

As I got into shallower water, the shark could only approach from the offshore side, but she also came toward me after increasingly shorter intervals which took her only to the limit of my underwater vision before she turned and with a flick of the tail sped toward me. Finally, she came so close I used the butt of my spear gun and my gloved right hand to shear her away. At that point, my carefully calculated retreat turned into a rout. I turned and stumbled the remaining yards from the water to the sand, expecting at any instant to feel the shark bite into one of my legs!

But she was gone—possibly as startled by the contact as I was. Up until the moment I actually put my hands on the shark, she had been only a forbidding character in an underwater scenario in which the hero (me) could always wake up (come ashore) when the suspense became unbearable. At the moment of contact, however, I felt an intimation of my own mortality.

René Tillich, my partner on that camping trip who had taken a siesta while I had recklessly dived by myself, was unable to find enough clothes and blankets in our combined duffels to stop my violent trembling. He suggested we move up the coast a few miles, and we did, but it was a day before I could swim much beyond where I could stand.

Chapter 3

When Lewis and Clark First Met Grizzlies!

From the Journals of Lewis and Clark

Your editor always finds himself reading The Journals of Lewis and Clark *with two mindsets. In one I am sharing and feeling the wonder of their second year (1805) on the high plains and mountains of the undiscovered American West. Every day they see teeming bison (buffalo) herds, elk, deer, antelope, beaver, birds, and waterfowl. William Clark estimated one buffalo herd to number ten thousand. This idyllic life described in* The Journals *is interrupted by visions of the toil and hardships of the journey—the raging rivers, virtually impossible mountain passes, hailstorms and snow, the demands of moving camps of men and supplies. The unedited versions of* The Journals *are difficult to read, with misspellings and gaps, but well worth the effort. In the excerpts we have here, we're focusing on the pages that describe encounters with beasts larger and more ferocious than ever seen before: grizzly bears. At one point, Meriwether Lewis wrote in his journal, "I would rather face 2 Indians than one grizzly bear." The Corps of Discovery had many "firsts" that would be recorded in American history. One of them was grizzly bear attacks. While the excerpts from* The Journals *I have included focus mostly on the bears, I have also included references to abundant game and wildlife and interesting daily activities. Editor's note: The text refers frequently to "brown" or "blonde" bears. These are grizzlies, as explained by Lewis in* The Journal *entries to come.*

[Lewis, April 13, 1805]
Saturday April 13th

. . . we found a number of carcases of the Buffaloe lying along shore, which had been drowned by falling through the ice in winter and lodged on shore by the high water when the river broke up about the first of this month. we saw also many tracks of the white bear of enormous size, along the river shore and about the carcases of the Buffaloe, on which I presume they feed. we have not as yet seen one of these anamals, tho their tracks are so abundant and recent. the men as well as ourselves are anxious to meet with some of these bear. the Indians give a very formidable account of the strength and ferocity of this anamal, which they never dare to attack but in parties of six eight or ten persons; and are even then frequently defeated with the loss of one or more of their party. the savages attack this anamal with their bows and arrows and the indifferent guns with which the traders furnish them, with these they shoot with such uncertainty and at so short a distance, that they frequently mis their aim & fall a sacrefice to the bear. two Minetaries were killed during the last winter in an attack on a white bear. this anamall is said more frequently to attack a man on meeting with him, than to flee from him. When the Indians are about to go in quest of the white bear, previous to their departure, they paint themselves and perform all those superstitious rights commonly observed when they are about to make war uppon a neighbouring nation.

[Lewis, April 29, 1805]
Monday April 29th 1805.

Set out this morning at the usual hour; the wind was moderate; I walked on shore with one man. about 8 A.M. we fell in with two brown or yellow bear; both of which we wounded; one of them made his escape, the other after my firing on him pursued me seventy or eighty yards, but fortunately had been so badly wounded that he was unable to pursue so closely as to prevent my charging my gun; we again repeated our fir and killed him. it was a male not fully grown, we estimated his weight at 300 lbs. not having the means of ascertaining it precisely. The legs of this bear are somewhat longer than those of the black, as are it's tallons and tusks incomparably larger and longer. the testicles, which in the black bear are placed pretty well back between the thyes and contained in one pouch like those of the dog and most quadrupeds, are in the yellow or brown bear placed much further forward, and are suspended in seperate pouches from two to four inches asunder; it's colour is yellowish brown, the eyes small, black, and piercing; the front of the fore legs near the feet is usually black; the fur is finer thicker and deeper than that of the black bear. these are all the particulars in which this anamal appeared to me to differ from the black bear; it is a much more furious and formidable anamal, and will frequently pursue the hunter when wounded. it is asstonishing to see the wounds they will bear before they can be put to death. the Indians may well fear this anamal equiped as they generally are with their bows and arrows or indifferent fuzees, but in the hands of skillfull riflemen they are by no means as formidable or dangerous as they have been represented. game is still very abundant we can scarcely cast our eyes in any direction without percieving deer Elk Buffaloe or Antelopes. The quantity of wolves appear to increase in the same proportion; they generally hunt in parties of six eight or ten; they kill a great number of the Antelopes at this season; the Antelopes are yet meagre and the females are big with young; the wolves take them most generally in attempting to swim the river; in this manner my dog caught one drowned it and brought it on shore; they are but clumsey swimers, tho on land when in good order, they are extreemly fleet and dureable. we have frequently seen the wolves in pursuit of the Antelope in the plains; they appear to decoy a single one from a flock, and then pursue it, alturnately relieving each other untill they take it. on joining Capt Clark he informed me that he had seen a female and faun of the bighorned anamal; that they ran for some distance with great aparent ease along the side of the river bluff where it was almost perpendicular; two of the party fired on them while in motion without effect. we took the flesh of the bear on board and proceeded. Capt. Clark walked on shore this evening, killed a deer, and saw several of the bighorned anamals. there is more appearance of coal today than we have yet seen, the stratas are 6 feet thick in some instances; the earth has been birnt in many places, and always appears in stratas on the same level with the stratas of coal. we came too this evening in the mouth of a little river, which falls in on the Stard. side. This stream is about 50 yards wide from bank to bank; the water occupyes about 15 yards. the banks are of earth only, abrupt, tho not high—the bed, is of mud principally. Capt Clark, who was up this streeam about three miles, informed me that it continued about the same width, that it's current was gentle and it appeared navigable for perogus it meanders through an extensive, fertile, and beautifull vally as far as could bee seen about N. 30°W. there was but one solitary tree to be seen on the banks of this river after it left the bottom of the Missouri. the water of this river is clear, with a brownish yelow tint. here the highlands receede from the Missouri, leaving the vally formed by the river from seven to eight miles wide, and reather lower then usual.—This stream my friend Capt. C. named Marthas river.

[Lewis, May 5, 1805]
Sunday May 5th 1805

Capt. Clark and Drewyer killed the largest brown bear this evening which we have yet seen. it was a most tremendious looking anamal, and extreemly hard to kill notwithstanding he had five balls through his lungs and five others in various parts he swam more than half the distance across the river to a sandbar & it was at least twenty minutes before he died; he did not attempt to attact, but fled and made the most tremendous roaring from the moment he was shot. We had no means of weighing this monster; Capt. Clark thought he would weigh 500 lbs. for my own part I think the estimate too small by 100 lbs. he measured 8 Feet 7 1/2 Inches from the nose to the extremety of the hind feet, 5 F. to 1/2 Inch arround the breast, 1 F. 11 I. arround the middle of the arm, & 3 F. 11 I. arround the neck; his tallons which were five in number on each foot were 4 1/8 Inches in length. he was in good order, we therefore divided him among the party and made them boil the oil and put it in a cask for future uce; the oil is as hard as hogs lard when cool, much more so than that of the black bear. this bear differs from the common black bear in several respects; it's tallons are much longer and more blont, it's tale shorter, it's hair which is of a redish or bey brown, is longer thicker and finer than that of the black bear; his liver lungs and heart are much larger even in proportion with his size; the heart particularly was as large as that of a large Ox. his maw was also ten times the size of black bear, and was filled with flesh and fish. his testicles were pendant from the belly and placed four inches assunder in seperate bags or pouches.—this animal also feeds on roots and almost every species of wild fruit.

[Lewis, May 11, 1805]

About 5 P.M. my attention was struck by one of the Party runing at a distance towards us and making signs and hollowing as if in distress, I ordered the perogues to put too, and waited untill he arrived; I now found that it was Bratton the man with the soar hand whom I had permitted to walk on shore, he arrived so much out of breath that it was several minutes before he could tell what had happened; at length he informed me that in the woody bottom on the Lard. side about 1 1/2 below us he had shot a brown bear which immediately turned on him and pursued him a considerable distance but he had wounded it so badly that it could not overtake him; I immediately turned out with seven of the party in quest of this monster, we at length found his trale and persued him about a mile by the blood through very thick brush of rosbushes and the large leafed willow; we finally found him concealed in some very thick brush and shot him through the skull with two balls; we proceeded to dress him as soon as possible, we found him in good order; it was a monstrous beast, not quite so large as that we killed a few days past but in all other rispects much the same the hair is remarkably long fine and rich tho he appears parshally to have discharged his winter coat; we now found that Bratton had shot him through the center of the lungs, notwithstanding which he had pursued him near half a mile and had returned more than double that distance and with his tallons had prepared himself a bed in the earth of about 2 feet deep and five long and was perfectly alive when we found him which could not have been less than 2 hours after he received the wound; these bear being so hard to die reather intimedates us all; I must confess that I do not like the gentlemen and had reather fight two Indians than one bear; there is no other chance to conquer them by a single shot but by shooting them through the brains, and this becomes difficult in consequence of two large muscles which cover the sides of the forehead and the sharp projection of the center of the frontal bone, which is also of a pretty good thickness. the flece and skin were as much as two men could possibly carry. by the time we returned the sun had set and I determined to remain here all night, and directed the cooks to render the bear's oil and put it in the kegs which was done. there was about eight gallons of it.

[Lewis, May 13, 1805]
13th of May Monday 1805

Capt Clark walked on shore and killed a very fine buffaloe cow. I felt an inclination to eat some veal and walked on shore and killed a very fine buffaloe calf and a large woolf, much the whitest I had seen, it was quite as white as the wool of the common sheep. one of the party wounded a brown bear very badly, but being alone did not think proper to pursue him. In the evening the men in two of the rear canoes discovered a large brown bear lying in the open grounds about 300 paces from the river, and six of them went out to attack him, all good hunters; they took the advantage of a small eminence which concealed them and got within 40 paces of him unperceived, two of them reserved their fires as had been previously conscerted, the four others fired nearly at the same time and put each his bullet through him, two of the balls passed through the bulk of both lobes of his lungs, in an instant this monster ran at them with open mouth, the two who had reserved their fires discharged their pieces at him as he came towards them, boath of them struck him, one only slightly and the other fortunately broke his shoulder, this however only retarded his motion for a moment only, the men unable to reload their guns took to flight, the bear pursued and had very nearly overtaken them before they reached the river; two of the party betook themselves to a canoe and the others seperated an concealed themselves among the willows, reloaded their pieces, each discharged his piece at him as they had an opportunity they struck him several times again but the guns served only to direct the bear to them, in this manner he pursued two of them seperately so close that they were obliged to throw aside their guns and pouches and throw themselves into the river altho the bank was nearly twenty feet perpendicular; so enraged was this anamal that he plunged into the river only a few feet behind the second man he had compelled take refuge in the water, when one of those who still remained on shore shot him through the head and finally killed him; they then took him on shore and butched him when they found eight balls had passed through him in different directions; the bear being old the flesh was indifferent, they therefore only took the skin and fleece, the latter made us several gallons of oil.

[Lewis, May 19, 1805]
Sunday May 19th 1805.

The last night was disagreeably cold; we were unable to set out untill 8 oclock A.M. in consequence of a heavy fogg, which obscured the river in such a manner that we could not see our way; this is the first we have experienced in any thing like so great a degree; there was also a fall of due last evening, which is the second we have experienced since we have entered this extensive open country. at eight we set out and proceeded as yesterday by means of the cord principally, the hills are high and the country similar to that of yesterday. Capt Clark walked on shore with two of the hunters and killed a brown bear; notwithstanding that it was shot through the heart it ran at it's usual pace near a quarter of a mile before it fell. one of the party wounded a beaver, and my dog as usual swam in to catch it; the beaver bit him through the hind leg and cut the artery; it was with great difficulty that I could stop the blood; I fear it will yet prove fatal to him.

[Lewis, May 22, 1805]
Wednesday May 22nd, 1805.

We encamped earlyer this evening than usual in order to render the oil of a bear which we killed. I do not believe that the Black bear common to the lower part of this river and the Atlantic States, exists in this quarter; we have neither seen one of them nor their tracks which would be easily distinguished by it's shortness of tallons when compared with the brown grizly or white bear. I believe that it is the same species or family of bears which assumes all those colours at different ages and seasons of the year.

[Lewis, June 12, 1805]
Wednesday June 12th 1805.

This morning I felt myself quite revived, took another portion of my decoction and set out at sunrise. I now boar out from the river in order to avoid the steep ravines of the river which usually make out in the plain to the distance of one or two miles; after gaining the leavel plain my course was a little to the West of S.W.—having traveled about 12 miles by 9 in the morning, the sun became warm, and I boar a little to the south in order to gain the river as well to obtain water to allay my thirst as to kill something for breakfast; for the plain through which we had been passing possesses no water and is so level that we cannot approach the buffaloe within shot before they discover us and take to flight. we arrived at the river about 10 A.M. having traveled about 15 m. at this place there is a handsom open bottom with some cottonwood timber, here we met with two large bear, and killed them boath at the first fire, a circumstance which I beleive has never happend with the party in killing the brown bear before. we dressed the bear, breakfasted on a part of one of them and hung the meat and skins on the trees out of the reach of the wolves. I left a note on a stick near the river for Capt. Clark, informing him of my progress &c. narrow leafed cottonwood grows here in common with the other species of the same tree.

[Lewis, June 13, 1805]
Thursday June 13th 1805.

I am induced to believe that the Brown, the white and the Grizly bear of this country are the same species only differing in colour from age or more probably from the same natural cause that many other anamals of the same family differ in colour. one of those which we killed yesterday was of a creemcoloured white while the other in company with it was of the common bey or rdish brown, which seems to be the most usual colour of them. the white one appeared from it's tallons and teath to be the youngest; it was smaller than the other, and although a monstrous beast we supposed that it had not yet attained it's growth and that it was a little upwards of two years old. the young cubs which we have killed have always been of a brownish white, but none of them as white as that we killed yesterday. one other that we killed sometime since which I mentioned sunk under some driftwood and was lost, had a white stripe or list of about eleven inches wide entirely arround his body just behind the shoalders, and was much darker than these bear usually are. the grizly bear we have never yet seen. I have seen their tallons in possession of the Indians and from their form I am perswaded if there is any difference between this species and the brown or white bear it is very inconsiderable. There is no such anamal as a black bear in this open country or of that species generally denominated the black bear my fare is really sumptuous this evening; buffaloe's humps, tongues and marrowbones, fine trout parched meal pepper and salt, and a good appetite; the last is not considered the least of the luxuries.

[Lewis, June 14, 1805]
Friday June 14th 1805.

This morning at sunrise I dispatched Joseph Fields with a letter to Capt. Clark and ordered him to keep sufficiently near the river to observe it's situation in order that he might be enabled to give Capt. Clark an idea of the point at which it would be best to halt to make our portage. I set one man about preparing a saffold and collecting wood to dry the meat. Sent the others to bring in the ballance of the buffaloe meat, or at least the part which the wolves had left us, for those fellows are ever at hand and ready to partake with us the moment we kill a buffaloe; and there is no means of puting the meat out of their reach in those plains; the two men shortly after returned with the meat and informed me that the wolves had devoured the greater part of the meat. about ten OClock this morning while the men were engaged with the meat I took my Gun and espontoon and thought I would walk a few miles and see where the rappids termineated above, and return to dinner. accordingly I set out and proceeded up the river about S.W. after passing one continued rappid and three small cascades of abut four or five feet each at the distance of about five miles I arrived at a fall of about 19 feet; the river is hereabout 400 yds. wide. This pitch which I called the crooked falls occupys about three fourths of the width of the river, commencing on the South side, extends obliquly upwards about 150 yds. then forming an accute angle extends downwards nearly to the commencement of four small Islands lying near the N. shore; among these Islands and between them and the lower extremity of the perpendicular pitch being a distance of 100 yards or upwards, the water glides down the side of a sloping rock with a volocity almost equal to that of it's perpendicular decent. just above this rappid the river makes a suddon bend to the right or Northwardly. I should have returned from hence but hearing a tremendious roaring above me I continued my rout across the point of a hill a few hundred yards further and was again presented by one of the most beatifull objects in nature, a cascade of about fifty feet perpendicular streching at rightangles across the river from side to side to the distance of at least a quarter of a mile. here the river pitches over a shelving rock, with an edge as regular and as streight as if formed by art, without a nich or brake in it; the water decends in one even and uninterupted sheet to the bottom wher dashing against the rocky bottom rises into foaming billows of great hight and rappidly glides away, hising flashing and sparkling as it departs the sprey rises from one extremity to the other to 50 f. I now thought that if a skillfull painter had been asked to make a beautifull cascade that he would most probably have pesented the precise immage of this one; nor could I for some time determine on which of those two great cataracts to bestoe the palm, on this or that which I had discovered yesterday; at length I determined between these two great rivals for glory that this was pleasingly beautifull, while the other was sublimely grand. I had scarcely infixed my eyes from this pleasing object before I discovered another fall above at the distance of half a mile; thus invited I did not once think of returning but hurried thither to amuse myself with this newly discovered object. I found this to be a cascade of about 14 feet possessing a perpendicular pitch of about 6 feet. this was tolerably regular streching across the river from bank to bank where it was about a quarter of a mile wide; in any other neighbourhood but this, such a cascade would probably be extoled for it's beaty and magniffìcence, but here I passed it by with but little attention, determining as I had proceded so far to continue my rout to the head of the rappids if it should even detain me all night. at every rappid cateract and cascade I discovered that the bluffs grew lower or that the bed of the river rose nearer to a level with the plains. still pursuing the river with it's course about S.W. passing a continued sene of rappids and small cascades, at the distance of 2 1/2 miles I arrived at another cataract of 26 feet. this is not immediately perpendicular, a rock about 1/3 of it's decent seems to protrude to a small distance and receives the water in it's passage downwards and gives a curve to the water tho it falls mostly with a regular and smoth sheet. the river is near six hundred yards wide at this place, a beatifull level plain on the S. side only a few feet above the level of the pitch; on the N. side where I am the country is More broken and immediately behind me near the river a high hill. below this fall at a little distance a beatifull little Island well timbered is situated about the middle of the river. in this Island on a Cottonwood tree an Eagle has placed her nest; a more inaccessable spot I beleive she could not have found; for neither man nor beast dare pass those gulphs which seperate her little domain from the shores. the water is also broken in such manner as it decends over this pitch that the mist or sprey rises to a considerable hight. this fall is certainly much the greatest I ever behald except those two which I have mentioned below. it is incomparably a greater cataract and a more noble interesting object than the celibrated falls of Potomac or Soolkiln &c. just above this is another cascade of about 5 feet, above which the water as far as I could see began to abate of it's valosity, and I therefore determined to ascend the hill behind me which promised a fine prospect of the adjacent country, nor was I disappointed on my arrival at it's summit. from hence I overlooked a most beatifull and extensive plain reaching from the river to the base of the Snowclad mountains to the S. and S. West; I also observed the missoury streching it's meandering course to the South through this plain to a great distance filled to it's even and grassey brim; another large river flowed in on it's Western side about four miles above me and extended itself through a level and fertile valley of 3 miles in width a great distance to the N.W. rendered more conspicuous by the timber which garnished it's borders. in these plains and more particularly in the valley just below me immence herds of buffaloe are feeding. the missouri just above this hill makes a bend to the South where it lies a smoth even and unruffled sheet of water of nearly a mile in width bearing on it's watry bosome vast flocks of geese which feed at pleasure in the delightfull pasture on either border. the young geese are now completely feathered except the wings which both in the young and old are yet deficient. after feasting my eyes on this ravishing prospect and resting myself a few minutes I determined to procede as far as the river which I saw discharge itself on the West side of the Missouri convinced that it was the river which the Indians call medicine river and which they informed us fell into the Missouri just above the falls I decended the hills and directed my course to the bend of the Missouri near which there was a herd of at least a thousand buffaloe; here I thought it would be well to kill a buffaloe and leave him untill my return from the river and if I then found that I had not time to get back to camp this evening to remain all night here there being a few sticks of drift wood lying along shore which would answer for my fire, and a few smattering cottonwood trees a few hundred yards below which would afford me at least a semblance of a shelter. under this impression I scelected a fat buffaloe and shot him very well, through the lungs; while I was gazeing attentively on the poor anamal discharging blood in streams from his mouth and nostrils, expecting him to fall every instant, and having entirely forgotton to reload my rifle, a large white, or reather brown bear, had perceived and crept on me within 20 steps before I discovered him; in the first moment I drew up my gun to shoot, but at the same instant recolected that she was not loaded and that he was too near for me to hope to perform this opperation before he reached me, as he was then briskly advancing on me; it was an open level plain, not a bush within miles nor a tree within less than three hundred yards of me; the river bank was sloping and not more than three feet above the level of the water; in short there was no place by means of which I could conceal myself from this monster untill I could charge my rifle; in this situation I thought of retreating in a brisk walk as fast as he was advancing untill I could reach a tree about 300 yards below me, but I had no sooner terned myself about but he pitched at me, open mouthed and full speed, I ran about 80 yards and found he gained on me fast, I then run into the water the idea struk me to get into the water to such debth that I could stand and he would be obliged to swim, and that I could in that situation defend myself with my espontoon; accordingly I ran haistily into the water about waist deep, and faced about and presented the point of my espontoon, at this instant he arrived at the edge of the water within about 20 feet of me; the moment I put myself in this attitude of defence he sudonly wheeled about as if frightened, declined the combat on such unequal grounds, and retreated with quite as great precipitation as he had just before pursued me. as soon as I saw him run off in that manner I returned to the shore and charged my gun, which I had still retained in my hand throughout this curious adventure. I saw him run through the level open plain about three miles, till he disappeared in the woods on medecine river; during the whole of this distance he ran at full speed, sometimes appearing to look behind him as if he expected pursuit. I now began to reflect on this novil occurrence and indeavoured to account for this sudden retreat of the bear. I at first thought that perhaps he had not smelt me before he arrived at the waters edge so near me, but I then reflected that he had pursued me for about 80 or 90 yards before I took the water and on examination saw the grownd toarn with his tallons immediately on the impression of my steps; and the cause of his allarm still remains with me misterious and unaccountable.—so it was and I feelt myself not a little gratifyed that he had declined the combat. My gun reloaded I felt confidence once more in my strength; and determined not to be thwarted in my design of visiting medicine river, but determined never again to suffer my peice to be longer empty than the time she necessarily required to charge her. I passed through the plain nearly in the direction which the bear had run to Medecine River, found it a handsome stream, about 200 yds. wide with a gentle current, apparently deep, it's waters clear, and banks which were formed principally of darkbrown and blue clay were about the hight of those of the Missouri or from 3 to 5 feet; yet they had not the appearance of ever being overflown, a circumstance, which I did not expect so immediately in the neighbourhood of the mountains, from whence I should have supposed, that sudden and immence torrants would issue at certain seasons of the year; but the reverse is absolutely the case. I am therefore compelled to beleive that the snowey mountains yeald their warters slowly, being partially effected every day by the influence of the sun only, and never suddonly melted down by haisty showers of rain. having examined Medecine river I now determined to return, having by my estimate about 12 miles to walk. I looked at my watch and found it was half after six P.M.—in returning through the level bottom of Medecine river and about 200 yards distant from the Missouri, my direction led me directly to an anamal that I at first supposed was a wolf; but on nearer approach or about sixty paces distant I discovered that it was not, it's colour was a brownish yellow; it was standing near it's burrow, and when I approached it thus nearly, it couched itself down like a cat looking immediately at me as if it designed to spring on me. I took aim at it and fired, it instantly disappeared in it's burrow; I loaded my gun and examined the place which was dusty and saw the track from which I am still further convinced that it was of the tiger kind. whether I struck it or not I could not determine, but I am almost confident that I did; my gun is true and I had a steady rest by means of my espontoon, which I have found very serviceable to me in this way in the open plains. It now seemed to me that all the beasts of the neighbourhood had made a league to distroy me, or that some fortune was disposed to amuse herself at my expence, for I had not proceded more than three hundred yards from the burrow of this tyger cat, before three bull buffaloe, which wer feeding with a large herd about half a mile from me on my left, seperated from the herd and ran full speed towards me, I thought at least to give them some amusement and altered my direction to meet them; when they arrived within a hundred yards they mad a halt, took a good view of me and retreated with precipitation. I then continued my rout homewards passed the buffaloe which I had killed, but did not think it prudent to remain all night at this place which really from the succession of curious adventures wore the impression on my mind of inchantment; at sometimes for a moment I thought it might be a dream, but the prickley pears which pierced my feet very severely once in a while, particularly after it grew dark, convinced me that I was really awake, and that it was necessary to make the best of my way to camp. it was sometime after dark before I returned to the party; I found them extremely uneasy for my safety; they had formed a thousand conjectures, all of which equally forboding my death, which they had so far settled among them, that they had already agreed on the rout which each should take in the morning to surch for me. I felt myself much fortiegued, but eat a hearty supper and took a good night's rest.—the weather being warm I had left my leather over shirt and had woarn only a yellow flannin one.

[Lewis, June 25, 1805]
Tuesday June 25th 1805.

This morning early I sent the party back to the lower camp; dispatched Frazier down with the canoe for Drewyer and the meat he had collected, and Joseph Fields up the Missouri to hunt Elk. at eight OClk. sent Gass and Sheilds over to the large Island for bark and timber. about noon Fields returned and informed me that he had seen two white bear near the river a few miles above and in attempting to shoot them had stumbled uppon a third which immediately made at him being only a few steps distant; that in runing in order to escape from the bear he had leaped down a steep bank of the river on a stony bar where he fell cut his hand bruised his knees and bent his gun. that fortunately for him the bank hid him from the bear when he fell and that by that means he had escaped. this man has been truly unfortunate with these bear, this is the second time that he has narrowly escaped from them.

[Clark, June 25, 1805]
June 25th Tuesday 1805

A fair warm morning, Clouded & a few drops of rain at 5 oClock A.M. fair I feel my Self a little unwell with a looseness &c. &c. put out the Stores to dry & Set Chabonah &c to Cook for the party against their return—he being the only man left on this Side with me I had a little Coffee for brackfast which was to me a rarity as I had not tasted any Since last winter.—It may be here worthy of remark that the Sales were hoised in the Canoes as the men were drawing them and the wind was great relief to them being Sufficiently Strong to move the Canoes on the Trucks, this is Saleing on Dry land in every Sence of the word, Serjeant N Pryor Sick, the party amused themselves with danceing untill 10 oClock all Chearfullness and good humer, they all tied up their loads to make an early Start in the morning.

[Lewis, June 27, 1805]
Thursday June 27th 1805.

The party returned early this morning for the remaining canoe and baggage; Whitehouse was not quite well this morning I therefore detained him and about 10 A.M. set him at work with Frazier sewing the skins together for the boat; Shields and Gass continued the operation of shaving and fiting the horizontall bars of wood in the sections of the boat; the timber is so crooked and indifferent that they make but little progress, for myself I continued to act the part of cook in order to keep all hands employed. some Elk came near our camp and we killed 2 of them at 1 P.M. a cloud arrose to the S.W. and shortly after came on attended with violent Thunder Lightning and hail &c. (see notes on diary of the weather for June). soon after this storm was over Drewyer and J. Fields returned. they were about 4 miles above us during the storm, the hail was of no uncommon size where they were. They had killed 9 Elk and three bear during their absence; one of the bear was the largest by far that we have yet seen; the skin appear to me to be as large as a common ox. while hunting they saw a thick brushey bottom on the bank of the river where from the tracks along shore they suspected that there were bare concealed; they therefore landed without making any nois and climbed a leaning tree and placed themselves on it's branches about 20 feet above the ground, when thus securely fixed they gave a hoop and this large bear instantly rushed forward to the place from whence he had heard the human voice issue, when he arrived at the tree he made a short paus and Drewyer shot him in the head. it is worthy of remark that these bear never climb. the fore feet of this bear measured nine inches across and the hind feet eleven and—3/4 in length & exclusive of the tallons and seven inches in width. a bear came within thirty yards of our camp last night and eat up about thirty weight of buffaloe suit which was hanging on a pole. my dog seems to be in a constant state of alarm with these bear and keeps barking all night. soon after the storm this evening the water on this side of the river became of a deep crimson colour which I presume proceeded from some stream above and on this side. there is a kind of soft red stone in the bluffs and bottoms of the gullies in this neighbourhood which forms this colouring matter.—At the lower camp. Capt. Clark completed a draught of the river with the couses and distances from the entrance of the Missouri to Ft. Mandan, which we intend depositing here in order to guard against accedents. Sergt. Pryor is somewhat better this morning. at 4 P.M. the party returned from the upper camp; Capt. C. gave them a drink of grog; they prepared for the labour of the next day. soon after the party returned it began to rain accompanyed by some hail and continued a short time; a second shower fell late in the evening accompanyed by a high wind from N.W.—the mangled carcases of several buffaloe pass down the river today which had no doubt perished in the falls.

[Lewis, July 2, 1805]
Tuesday July 2nd, 1805

A shower of rain fell very early this morning after which we dispatched the men for the remaining baggage at the 6 mile stake. Shields and Bratton seting their tarkiln, Sergts. Pryor and Gass at work on the waystrips and myself and all other hands engaged in puting the boat together which we accomplished in about 3 hours and I then set four men at work sewing the leather over the cross bars of Iron on the inner side of the boat, which form the ends of the sections. about 2 P.M. the party returned with the baggage, all well pleased that they had completed the laborious task of the portage. The Musquetoes uncommonly troublesome the wind hard from the S.W. all day I think it possible that these almost perpetual S.W. winds proceede from the agency of the Snowey Mountains and the wide level and untimbered plains which streach themselves along their bases for an immence distance (i e) that the air comeing in contact with the snow is suddonly chilled and condenced, thus becoming heavier than the air beneath in the plains, it glides down the sides of these mountains & decends to the plains, where by the constant action of the sun on the face of an untimbered country there is a partial vacuum formed for it's reception. I have observed that the winds from this quarter are always the coldest and most violent which we experience, yet I am far from giving full credit to my own hypothesis on this subject; if hoever I find on the opposite side of these mountains that the winds take a contrary direction I shall then have more faith. After I had completed my observation of Equal Altitudes today Capt. Clark Myself and 12 men passed over to the large island to hunt bear. the brush in that part of it where the bear frequent is an almost impenetrable thicket of the broad leafed willow; this brush we entered in small parties of 3 or four together and surched in every part. we found one only which made at Drewyer and he shot him in the brest at the distance of about 20 feet, the ball fortunately passed through his heart, the stroke knocked the bear down and gave Drewyer time to get out of his sight; the bear changed his course we pursued him about a hundred yards by the blood and found him dead; we surched the thicket in every part but found no other, and therefore returned. this was a young male and would weigh about 400 lbs.

Chapter 4

All-Gold Canyon

Jack London

The prose skills of Jack London (1876–1916) are evident in a list of short stories and novels too lengthy to include here. This story of a lone prospector hoping to strike it rich in the vast Yukon is one of London's best. It was first published in Moon-Face and Other Stories. *Well known to London addicts, like your editor, the story remained in relative obscurity until it was filmed for the big screen in amazing color by renowned American filmmakers the Coen Brothers. Released in 2018, titled* The Ballad of Buster Scruggs, *the film is a collection of six individual stories of Western adventures. "All-Gold Canyon," as produced and filmed by the Coen Brothers, is one of the six stories and is one of the best ever made about the high country and its pioneers.*

It was the green heart of the canyon, where the walls swerved back from the rigid plan and relieved their harshness of line by making a little sheltered nook and filling it to the brim with sweetness and roundness and softness. Here all things rested. Even the narrow stream ceased its turbulent down-rush long enough to form a quiet pool. Knee-deep in the water, with drooping head and half-shut eyes, drowsed a red-coated, many-antlered buck.

On one side, beginning at the very lip of the pool, was a tiny meadow, a cool, resilient surface of green that extended to the base of the frowning wall. Beyond the pool a gentle slope of earth ran up and up to meet the opposing wall. Fine grass covered the slope—grass that was spangled with flowers, with here and there patches of color, orange and purple and golden. Below, the canyon was shut in. There was no view. The walls leaned together abruptly and the canyon ended in a chaos of rocks, moss-covered and hidden by a green screen of vines and creepers and boughs of trees. Up the canyon rose far hills and peaks, the big foothills, pine-covered and remote. And far beyond, like clouds upon the border of the sky, towered minarets of white, where the Sierra's eternal snows flashed austerely the blazes of the sun.

There was no dust in the canyon. The leaves and flowers were clean and virginal. The grass was young velvet. Over the pool three cottonwoods sent their snowy fluffs fluttering down the quiet air. On the slope the blossoms of the wine-wooded manzanita filled the air with springtime odors, while the leaves, wise with experience, were already beginning their vertical twist against the coming aridity of summer. In the open spaces on the slope, beyond the farthest shadow-reach of the manzanita, poised the mariposa lilies, like so many flights of jewelled moths suddenly arrested and on the verge of trembling into flight again. Here and there that woods harlequin, the madrone, permitting itself to be caught in the act of changing its pea-green trunk to madder-red, breathed its fragrance into the air from great clusters of waxen bells. Creamy white were these bells, shaped like lilies-of-the-valley, with the sweetness of perfume that is of the springtime.

There was not a sigh of wind. The air was drowsy with its weight of perfume. It was a sweetness that would have been cloying had the air been heavy and humid. But the air was sharp and thin. It was as starlight transmuted into atmosphere, shot through and warmed by sunshine, and flower-drenched with sweetness.

An occasional butterfly drifted in and out through the patches of light and shade. And from all about rose the low and sleepy hum of mountain bees—feasting Sybarites that jostled one another good-naturedly at the board, nor found time for rough discourtesy. So quietly did the little stream drip and ripple its way through the canyon that it spoke only in faint and occasional gurgles. The voice of the stream was as a drowsy whisper, ever interrupted by dozings and silences, ever lifted again in the awakenings.

The motion of all things was a drifting in the heart of the canyon. Sunshine and butterflies drifted in and out among the trees. The hum of the bees and the whisper of the stream were a drifting of sound. And the drifting sound and drifting color seemed to weave together in the making of a delicate and intangible fabric which was the spirit of the place.

It was a spirit of peace that was not of death, but of smooth-pulsing life, of quietude that was not silence, of movement that was not action, of repose that was quick with existence without being violent with struggle and travail. The spirit of the place was the spirit of the peace of the living, somnolent with the easement and content of prosperity, and undisturbed by rumors of far wars.

The red-coated, many-antlered buck acknowledged the lordship of the spirit of the place and dozed knee-deep in the cool, shaded pool. There seemed no flies to vex him and he was languid with rest. Sometimes his ears moved when the stream awoke and whispered; but they moved lazily, with foreknowledge that it was merely the stream grown garrulous at discovery that it had slept.

But there came a time when the buck's ears lifted and tensed with swift eagerness for sound. His head was turned down the canyon. His sensitive, quivering nostrils scented the air. His eyes could not pierce the green screen through which the stream rippled away, but to his ears came the voice of a man. It was a steady, monotonous, singsong voice. Once the buck heard the harsh clash of metal upon rock. At the sound he snorted with a sudden start that jerked him through the air from water to meadow, and his feet sank into the young velvet, while he pricked his ears and again scented the air. Then he stole across the tiny meadow, pausing once and again to listen, and faded away out of the canyon like a wraith, soft-footed and without sound.

The clash of steel-shod soles against the rocks began to be heard, and the man's voice grew louder. It was raised in a sort of chant and became distinct with nearness, so that the words could be heard:

Tu'n around an' tu'n yo' face
Untoe them sweet hills of grace
(D' pow'rs of sin yo' am scornin'!).
Look about an' look aroun'
Fling yo' sin-pack on d' groun'
(Yo' will meet wid d' Lord in d' mornin'!).

A sound of scrambling accompanied the song, and the spirit of the place fled away on the heels of the red-coated buck. The green screen was burst asunder, and a man peered out at the meadow and the pool and the sloping side-hill. He was a deliberate sort of man. He took in the scene with one embracing glance, then ran his eyes over the details to verify the general impression. Then, and not until then, did he open his mouth in vivid and solemn approval:

"Smoke of life an' snakes of purgatory! Will you just look at that! Wood an' water an' grass an' a side-hill! A pocket-hunter's delight an' a cayuse's paradise! Cool green for tired eyes! Pink pills for pale people ain't in it. A secret pasture for prospectors and a resting-place for tired burros. It's just booful!"

He was a sandy-complexioned man in whose face geniality and humor seemed the salient characteristics. It was a mobile face, quick-changing to inward mood and thought. Thinking was in him a visible process. Ideas chased across his face like wind-flaws across the surface of a lake. His hair, sparse and unkempt of growth, was as indeterminate and colorless as his complexion. It would seem that all the color of his frame had gone into his eyes, for they were startlingly blue. Also, they were laughing and merry eyes, within them much of the naiveté and wonder of the child; and yet, in an unassertive way, they contained much of calm self-reliance and strength of purpose founded upon self-experience and experience of the world.

From out the screen of vines and creepers he flung ahead of him a miner's pick and shovel and gold-pan. Then he crawled out himself into the open. He was clad in faded overalls and black cotton shirt, with hobnailed brogans on his feet, and on his head a hat whose shapelessness and stains advertised the rough usage of wind and rain and sun and camp-smoke. He stood erect, seeing wide-eyed the secrecy of the scene and sensuously inhaling the warm, sweet breath of the canyon-garden through nostrils that dilated and quivered with delight. His eyes narrowed to laughing slits of blue, his face wreathed itself in joy, and his mouth curled in a smile as he cried aloud:

"Jumping dandelions and happy hollyhocks, but that smells good to me! Talk about your attar o' roses an' cologne factories! They ain't in it!"

He had the habit of soliloquy. His quick-changing facial expressions might tell every thought and mood, but the tongue, perforce, ran hard after, repeating, like a second Boswell.

The man lay down on the lip of the pool and drank long and deep of its water. "Tastes good to me," he murmured, lifting his head and gazing across the pool at the side-hill, while he wiped his mouth with the back of his hand. The side-hill attracted his attention. Still lying on his stomach, he studied the hill formation long and carefully. It was a practised eye that traveled up the slope to the crumbling canyon-wall and back and down again to the edge of the pool. He scrambled to his feet and favored the side-hill with a second survey.

"Looks good to me," he concluded, picking up his pick and shovel and gold-pan.

He crossed the stream below the pool, stepping agilely from stone to stone. Where the side-hill touched the water he dug up a shovelful of dirt and put it into the gold-pan. He squatted down, holding the pan in his two hands, and partly immersing it in the stream. Then he imparted to the pan a deft circular motion that sent the water sluicing in and out through the dirt and gravel. The larger and the lighter particles worked to the surface, and these, by a skillful dipping movement of the pan, he spilled out and over the edge. Occasionally, to expedite matters, he rested the pan and with his fingers raked out the large pebbles and pieces of rock.

The contents of the pan diminished rapidly until only fine dirt and the smallest bits of gravel remained. At this stage he began to work very deliberately and carefully. It was fine washing, and he washed fine and finer, with a keen scrutiny and delicate and fastidious touch. At last the pan seemed empty of everything but water; but with a quick semi-circular flirt that sent the water flying over the shallow rim into the stream, he disclosed a layer of black sand on the bottom of the pan.

So thin was this layer that it was like a streak of paint. He examined it closely. In the midst of it was a tiny golden speck. He dribbled a little water in over the depressed edge of the pan. With a quick flirt he sent the water sluicing across the bottom, turning the grains of black sand over and over. A second tiny golden speck rewarded his effort.

The washing had now become very fine—fine beyond all need of ordinary placer-mining. He worked the black sand, a small portion at a time, up the shallow rim of the pan. Each small portion he examined sharply, so that his eyes saw every grain of it before he allowed it to slide over the edge and away. Jealously, bit by bit, he let the black sand slip away. A golden speck, no larger than a pin-point, appeared on the rim, and by his manipulation of the water it returned to the bottom of the pan. And in such fashion another speck was disclosed, and another. Great was his care of them. Like a shepherd he herded his flock of golden specks so that not one should be lost. At last, of the pan of dirt nothing remained but his golden herd. He counted it, and then, after all his labor, sent it flying out of the pan with one final swirl of water.

But his blue eyes were shining with desire as he rose to his feet. "Seven," he muttered aloud, asserting the sum of the specks for which he had toiled so hard and which he had so wantonly thrown away. "Seven," he repeated, with the emphasis of one trying to impress a number on his memory.

He stood still a long while, surveying the hillside. In his eyes was a curiosity, new-aroused and burning. There was an exultance about his bearing and a keenness like that of a hunting animal catching the fresh scent of game.

He moved down the stream a few steps and took a second panful of dirt.

Again came the careful washing, the jealous herding of the golden specks, and the wantonness with which he sent them flying into the stream.

"Five," he muttered, and repeated, "five."

He could not forbear another survey of the hill before filling the pan farther down the stream. His golden herds diminished. "Four, three, two, two, one," were his memory tabulations as he moved down the stream. When but one speck of gold rewarded his washing, he stopped and built a fire of dry twigs. Into this he thrust the gold-pan and burned it till it was blue-black. He held up the pan and examined it critically. Then he nodded approbation. Against such a color-background he could defy the tiniest yellow speck to elude him.

Still moving down the stream, he panned again. A single speck was his reward. A third pan contained no gold at all. Not satisfied with this, he panned three times again, taking his shovels of dirt within a foot of one another. Each pan proved empty of gold, and the fact, instead of discouraging him, seemed to give him satisfaction. His elation increased with each barren washing, until he arose, exclaiming jubilantly:

"If it ain't the real thing, may God knock off my head with sour apples!"

Returning to where he had started operations, he began to pan up the stream. At first his golden herds increased—increased prodigiously. "Fourteen, eighteen, twenty-one, twenty-six," ran his memory tabulations. Just above the pool he struck his richest pan—thirty-five colors.

"Almost enough to save," he remarked regretfully as he allowed the water to sweep them away.

The sun climbed to the top of the sky. The man worked on. Pan by pan, he went up the stream, the tally of results steadily decreasing.

"It's just booful, the way it peters out," he exulted when a shovelful of dirt contained no more than a single speck of gold. And when no specks at all were found in several pans, he straightened up and favored the hillside with a confident glance.

"Ah, ha! Mr. Pocket!" he cried out, as though to an auditor hidden somewhere above him beneath the surface of the slope. "Ah, ha! Mr. Pocket! I'm a-comin', I'm a-comin', an' I'm shorely gwine to get yer! You heah me, Mr. Pocket? I'm gwine to get yer as shore as punkins ain't cauliflowers!"

He turned and flung a measuring glance at the sun poised above him in the azure of the cloudless sky. Then he went down the canyon, following the line of shovel-holes he had made in filling the pans. He crossed the stream below the pool and disappeared through the green screen. There was little opportunity for the spirit of the place to return with its quietude and repose, for the man's voice, raised in ragtime song, still dominated the canyon with possession.

After a time, with a greater clashing of steel-shod feet on rock, he returned. The green screen was tremendously agitated. It surged back and forth in the throes of a struggle. There was a loud grating and clanging of metal. The man's voice leaped to a higher pitch and was sharp with imperativeness. A large body plunged and panted. There was a snapping and ripping and rending, and amid a shower of falling leaves a horse burst through the screen. On its back was a pack, and from this trailed broken vines and torn creepers. The animal gazed with astonished eyes at the scene into which it had been precipitated, then dropped its head to the grass and began contentedly to graze. A second horse scrambled into view, slipping once on the mossy rocks and regaining equilibrium when its hoofs sank into the yielding surface of the meadow. It was riderless, though on its back was a high-horned Mexican saddle, scarred and discolored by long usage.

The man brought up the rear. He threw off pack and saddle, with an eye to camp location, and gave the animals their freedom to graze. He unpacked his food and got out frying-pan and coffee-pot. He gathered an armful of dry wood, and with a few stones made a place for his fire.

"My!" he said, "but I've got an appetite. I could scoff iron-filings an' horseshoe nails an' thank you kindly, ma'am, for a second helpin'."

He straightened up, and, while he reached for matches in the pocket of his overalls, his eyes traveled across the pool to the side-hill. His fingers had clutched the match-box, but they relaxed their hold and the hand came out empty. The man wavered perceptibly. He looked at his preparations for cooking and he looked at the hill.

"Guess I'll take another whack at her," he concluded, starting to cross the stream.

"They ain't no sense in it, I know," he mumbled apologetically. "But keepin' grub back an hour ain't goin' to hurt none, I reckon."

A few feet back from his first line of test-pans he started a second line. The sun dropped down the western sky, the shadows lengthened, but the man worked on. He began a third line of test-pans. He was cross-cutting the hillside, line by line, as he ascended. The center of each line produced the richest pans, while the ends came where no colors showed in the pan. And as he ascended the hillside the lines grew perceptibly shorter. The regularity with which their length diminished served to indicate that somewhere up the slope the last line would be so short as to have scarcely any length at all, and that beyond could come only a point. The design was growing into an inverted "V." The converging sides of this "V" marked the boundaries of the gold-bearing dirt.

The apex of the "V" was evidently the man's goal. Often he ran his eye along the converging sides and on up the hill, trying to divine the apex, the point where the gold-bearing dirt must cease. Here resided "Mr. Pocket"—for so the man familiarly addressed the imaginary point above him on the slope, crying out:

"Come down out o' that, Mr. Pocket! Be right smart an' agreeable, an' come down!"

"All right," he would add later, in a voice resigned to determination. "All right, Mr. Pocket. It's plain to me I got to come right up an' snatch you out bald-headed. An' I'll do it! I'll do it!" he would threaten still later.

Each pan he carried down to the water to wash, and as he went higher up the hill the pans grew richer, until he began to save the gold in an empty baking powder can which he carried carelessly in his hip-pocket. So engrossed was he in his toil that he did not notice the long twilight of oncoming night. It was not until he tried vainly to see the gold colors in the bottom of the pan that he realized the passage of time. He straightened up abruptly. An expression of whimsical wonderment and awe overspread his face as he drawled:

"Gosh darn my buttons! if I didn't plumb forget dinner!"

He stumbled across the stream in the darkness and lighted his long-delayed fire. Flapjacks and bacon and warmed-over beans constituted his supper. Then he smoked a pipe by the smouldering coals, listening to the night noises and watching the moonlight stream through the canyon. After that he unrolled his bed, took off his heavy shoes, and pulled the blankets up to his chin. His face showed white in the moonlight, like the face of a corpse. But it was a corpse that knew its resurrection, for the man rose suddenly on one elbow and gazed across at his hillside.

"Good night, Mr. Pocket," he called sleepily. "Goodnight."

He slept through the early gray of morning until the direct rays of the sun smote his closed eyelids, when he awoke with a start and looked about him until he had established the continuity of his existence and identified his present self with the days previously lived.

To dress, he had merely to buckle on his shoes. He glanced at his fireplace and at his hillside, wavered, but fought down the temptation and started the fire.

"Keep yer shirt on, Bill; keep yer shirt on," he admonished himself. "What's the good of rushin'? No use in gettin' all het up an' sweaty. Mr. Pocket'll wait for you. He ain't a-runnin' away before you can get your breakfast. Now, what you want, Bill, is something fresh in yer bill o' fare. So it's up to you to go an' get it."

He cut a short pole at the water's edge and drew from one of his pockets a bit of line and a draggled fly that had once been a royal coachman.

"Mebbe they'll bite in the early morning," he muttered, as he made his first cast into the pool. And a moment later he was gleefully crying:

"What'd I tell you, eh? What'd I tell you?"

He had no reel, nor any inclination to waste time, and by main strength, and swiftly, he drew out of the water a flashing ten-inch trout. Three more, caught in rapid succession, furnished his breakfast. When he came to the stepping-stones on his way to his hillside, he was struck by a sudden thought, and paused.

"I'd just better take a hike down-stream a ways," he said. "There's no tellin' who may be snoopin' around."

But he crossed over on the stones, and with a "I really oughter take that hike," the need of the precaution passed out of his mind and he fell to work.

At nightfall he straightened up. The small of his back was stiff from stooping toil, and as he put his hand behind him to soothe the protesting muscles, he said:

"Now what d'ye think of that? I clean forgot my dinner again! If I don't watch out, I'll sure be degeneratin' into a two-meal-a-day crank."

"Pockets is the hangedest things I ever see for makin' a man absent-minded," he communed that night, as he crawled into his blankets. Nor did he forget to call up the hillside, "Good night, Mr. Pocket! Good night!"

Rising with the sun, and snatching a hasty breakfast, he was early at work. A fever seemed to be growing in him, nor did the increasing richness of the test-pans allay this fever. There was a flush in his cheek other than that made by the heat of the sun, and he was oblivious to fatigue and the passage of time. When he filled a pan with dirt, he ran down the hill to wash it; nor could he forbear running up the hill again, panting and stumbling profanely, to refill the pan.

He was now a hundred yards from the water, and the inverted "V" was assuming definite proportions. The width of the pay-dirt steadily decreased, and the man extended in his mind's eye the sides of the "V" to their meeting place far up the hill. This was his goal, the apex of the "V," and he panned many times to locate it.

"Just about two yards above that manzanita bush an' a yard to the right," he finally concluded.

Then the temptation seized him. "As plain as the nose on your face," he said, as he abandoned his laborious cross-cutting and climbed to the indicated apex. He filled a pan and carried it down the hill to wash. It contained no trace of gold. He dug deep, and he dug shallow, filling and washing a dozen pans, and was unrewarded even by the tiniest golden speck. He was enraged at having yielded to the temptation, and berated himself blasphemously and pridelessly. Then he went down the hill and took up the cross-cutting.

"Slow an' certain, Bill; slow an' certain," he crooned. "Short-cuts to fortune ain't in your line, an' it's about time you know it. Get wise, Bill; get wise. Slow an' certain's the only hand you can play; so go to it, an' keep to it, too."

As the cross-cuts decreased, showing that the sides of the "V" were converging, the depth of the "V" increased. The gold-trace was dipping into the hill. It was only at thirty inches beneath the surface that he could get colors in his pan. The dirt he found at twenty-five inches from the surface, and at thirty-five inches yielded barren pans. At the base of the "V," by the water's edge, he had found the gold colors at the grass roots. The higher he went up the hill, the deeper the gold dipped. To dig a hole three feet deep in order to get one test-pan was a task of no mean magnitude; while between the man and the apex intervened an untold number of such holes to be dug. "An' there's no tellin' how much deeper it'll pitch," he sighed, in a moment's pause, while his fingers soothed his aching back.

Feverish with desire, with aching back and stiffening muscles, with pick and shovel gouging and mauling the soft brown earth, the man toiled up the hill. Before him was the smooth slope, spangled with flowers and made sweet with their breath. Behind him was devastation. It looked like some terrible eruption breaking out on the smooth skin of the hill. His slow progress was like that of a slug, befouling beauty with a monstrous trail.

Though the dipping gold-trace increased the man's work, he found consolation in the increasing richness of the pans. Twenty cents, thirty cents, fifty cents, sixty cents, were the values of the gold found in the pans, and at nightfall he washed his banner pan, which gave him a dollar's worth of gold-dust from a shovelful of dirt.

"I'll just bet it's my luck to have some inquisitive one come buttin' in here on my pasture," he mumbled sleepily that night as he pulled the blankets up to his chin.

Suddenly he sat upright. "Bill!" he called sharply. "Now, listen to me, Bill; d'ye hear! It's up to you, to-morrow mornin', to mosey round an' see what you can see. Understand? To-morrow morning, an' don't you forget it!"

He yawned and glanced across at his side-hill. "Good night, Mr. Pocket," he called.

In the morning he stole a march on the sun, for he had finished breakfast when its first rays caught him, and he was climbing the wall of the canyon where it crumbled away and gave footing. From the outlook at the top he found himself in the midst of loneliness. As far as he could see, chain after chain of mountains heaved themselves into his vision. To the east his eyes, leaping the miles between range and range and between many ranges, brought up at last against the white-peaked Sierras—the main crest, where the backbone of the Western world reared itself against the sky. To the north and south he could see more distinctly the cross-systems that broke through the main trend of the sea of mountains. To the west the ranges fell away, one behind the other, diminishing and fading into the gentle foothills that, in turn, descended into the great valley which he could not see.

And in all that mighty sweep of earth he saw no sign of man nor of the handiwork of man—save only the torn bosom of the hillside at his feet. The man looked long and carefully. Once, far down his own canyon, he thought he saw in the air a faint hint of smoke. He looked again and decided that it was the purple haze of the hills made dark by a convolution of the canyon wall at its back.

"Hey, you, Mr. Pocket!" he called down into the canyon. "Stand out from under! I'm a-comin', Mr. Pocket! I'm a-comin'!"

The heavy brogans on the man's feet made him appear clumsy-footed, but he swung down from the giddy height as lightly and airily as a mountain goat. A rock, turning under his foot on the edge of the precipice, did not disconcert him. He seemed to know the precise time required for the turn to culminate in disaster, and in the meantime he utilized the false footing itself for the momentary earth-contact necessary to carry him on into safety. Where the earth sloped so steeply that it was impossible to stand for a second upright, the man did not hesitate. His foot pressed the impossible surface for but a fraction of the fatal second and gave him the bound that carried him onward. Again, where even the fraction of a second's footing was out of the question, he would swing his body past by a moment's hand-grip on a jutting knob of rock, a crevice, or a precariously rooted shrub. At last, with a wild leap and yell, he exchanged the face of the wall for an earth-slide and finished the descent in the midst of several tons of sliding earth and gravel.

His first pan of the morning washed out over two dollars in coarse gold. It was from the centre of the "V." To either side the diminution in the values of the pans was swift. His lines of cross-cutting holes were growing very short. The converging sides of the inverted "V" were only a few yards apart. Their meeting-point was only a few yards above him. But the pay-streak was dipping deeper and deeper into the earth. By early afternoon he was sinking the test-holes five feet before the pans could show the gold-trace.

For that matter, the gold-trace had become something more than a trace; it was a placer mine in itself, and the man resolved to come back after he had found the pocket and work over the ground. But the increasing richness of the pans began to worry him. By late afternoon the worth of the pans had grown to three and four dollars. The man scratched his head perplexedly and looked a few feet up the hill at the manzanita bush that marked approximately the apex of the "V." He nodded his head and said oracularly:

"It's one o' two things, Bill: one o' two things. Either Mr. Pocket's spilled himself all out an' down the hill, or else Mr. Pocket's so rich you maybe won't be able to carry him all away with you. And that'd be an awful shame, wouldn't it, now?" He chuckled at contemplation of so pleasant a dilemma.

Nightfall found him by the edge of the stream, his eyes wrestling with the gathering darkness over the washing of a five-dollar pan.

"Wisht I had an electric light to go on working," he said.

He found sleep difficult that night. Many times he composed himself and closed his eyes for slumber to overtake him; but his blood pounded with too strong desire, and as many times his eyes opened and he murmured wearily, "Wisht it was sun-up." Sleep came to him in the end, but his eyes were open with the first paling of the stars, and the gray of dawn caught him with breakfast finished and climbing the hillside in the direction of the secret abiding-place of Mr. Pocket.

The first cross-cut the man made, there was space for only three holes, so narrow had become the pay-streak and so close was he to the fountainhead of the golden stream he had been following for four days.

"Be ca'm, Bill; be ca'm," he admonished himself, as he broke ground for the final hole where the sides of the "V" had at last come together in a point.

"I've got the almighty cinch on you, Mr. Pocket, an' you can't lose me," he said many times as he sank the hole deeper and deeper.

Four feet, five feet, six feet, he dug his way down into the earth. The digging grew harder. His pick grated on broken rock. He examined the rock. "Rotten quartz," was his conclusion as, with the shovel, he cleared the bottom of the hole of loose dirt. He attacked the crumbling quartz with the pick, bursting the disintegrating rock asunder with every stroke.

He thrust his shovel into the loose mass. His eye caught a gleam of yellow. He dropped the shovel and squatted suddenly on his heels. As a farmer rubs the clinging earth from fresh-dug potatoes, so the man, a piece of rotten quartz held in both hands, rubbed the dirt away.

"Sufferin' Sardanopolis!" he cried. "Lumps an' chunks of it! Lumps an' chunks of it!"

It was only half rock he held in his hand. The other half was virgin gold. He dropped it into his pan and examined another piece. Little yellow was to be seen, but with his strong fingers he crumbled the rotten quartz away till both hands were filled with glowing yellow. He rubbed the dirt away from fragment after fragment, tossing them into the gold-pan. It was a treasure-hole. So much had the quartz rotted away that there was less of it than there was of gold. Now and again he found a piece to which no rock clung—a piece that was all gold. A chunk, where the pick had laid open the heart of the gold, glittered like a handful of yellow jewels, and he cocked his head at it and slowly turned it around and over to observe the rich play of the light upon it.

"Talk about yer Too Much Gold diggin's!" the man snorted contemptuously. "Why, this diggin' 'd make it look like thirty cents. This diggin' is All Gold. An' right here an' now I name this yere canyon 'All Gold Canyon,' b' gosh!"

Still squatting on his heels, he continued examining the fragments and tossing them into the pan. Suddenly there came to him a premonition of danger. It seemed a shadow had fallen upon him. But there was no shadow. His heart had given a great jump up into his throat and was choking him. Then his blood slowly chilled and he felt the sweat of his shirt cold against his flesh.

He did not spring up nor look around. He did not move. He was considering the nature of the premonition he had received, trying to locate the source of the mysterious force that had warned him, striving to sense the imperative presence of the unseen thing that threatened him. There is an aura of things hostile, made manifest by messengers too refined for the senses to know; and this aura he felt, but knew not how he felt it. His was the feeling as when a cloud passes over the sun. It seemed that between him and life had passed something dark and smothering and menacing; a gloom, as it were, that swallowed up life and made for death—his death.

Every force of his being impelled him to spring up and confront the unseen danger, but his soul dominated the panic, and he remained squatting on his heels, in his hands a chunk of gold. He did not dare to look around, but he knew by now that there was something behind him and above him. He made believe to be interested in the gold in his hand. He examined it critically, turned it over and over, and rubbed the dirt from it. And all the time he knew that something behind him was looking at the gold over his shoulder.

Still feigning interest in the chunk of gold in his hand, he listened intently and he heard the breathing of the thing behind him. His eyes searched the ground in front of him for a weapon, but they saw only the uprooted gold, worthless to him now in his extremity. There was his pick, a handy weapon on occasion; but this was not such an occasion. The man realized his predicament. He was in a narrow hole that was seven feet deep. His head did not come to the surface of the ground. He was in a trap.

He remained squatting on his heels. He was quite cool and collected; but his mind, considering every factor, showed him only his helplessness. He continued rubbing the dirt from the quartz fragments and throwing the gold into the pan. There was nothing else for him to do. Yet he knew that he would have to rise up, sooner or later, and face the danger that breathed at his back.

The minutes passed, and with the passage of each minute he knew that by so much he was nearer the time when he must stand up, or else—and his wet shirt went cold against his flesh again at the thought—or else he might receive death as he stooped there over his treasure.

Still he squatted on his heels, rubbing dirt from gold and debating in just what manner he should rise up. He might rise up with a rush and claw his way out of the hole to meet whatever threatened on the even footing above ground. Or he might rise up slowly and carelessly, and feign casually to discover the thing that breathed at his back. His instinct and every fighting fibre of his body favored the mad, clawing rush to the surface. His intellect, and the craft thereof, favored the slow and cautious meeting with the thing that menaced and which he could not see. And while he debated, a loud, crashing noise burst on his ear. At the same instant he received a stunning blow on the left side of the back, and from the point of impact felt a rush of flame through his flesh. He sprang up in the air, but halfway to his feet collapsed. His body crumpled in like a leaf withered in sudden heat, and he came down, his chest across his pan of gold, his face in the dirt and rock, his legs tangled and twisted because of the restricted space at the bottom of the hole. His legs twitched convulsively several times. His body was shaken as with a mighty ague. There was a slow expansion of the lungs, accompanied by a deep sigh. Then the air was slowly, very slowly, exhaled, and his body as slowly flattened itself down into inertness.

Above, revolver in hand, a man was peering down over the edge of the hole. He peered for a long time at the prone and motionless body beneath him. After a while the stranger sat down on the edge of the hole so that he could see into it, and rested the revolver on his knee. Reaching his hand into a pocket, he drew out a wisp of brown paper. Into this he dropped a few crumbs of tobacco. The combination became a cigarette, brown and squat, with the ends turned in. Not once did he take his eyes from the body at the bottom of the hole. He lighted the cigarette and drew its smoke into his lungs with a caressing intake of the breath. He smoked slowly. Once the cigarette went out and he relighted it. And all the while he studied the body beneath him.

In the end he tossed the cigarette stub away and rose to his feet. He moved to the edge of the hole. Spanning it, a hand resting on each edge, and with the revolver still in the right hand, he muscled his body down into the hole. While his feet were yet a yard from the bottom he released his hands and dropped down.

At the instant his feet struck bottom he saw the pocket-miner's arm leap out, and his own legs knew a swift, jerking grip that overthrew him. In the nature of the jump his revolver hand was above his head. Swiftly as the grip had flashed about his legs, just as swiftly he brought the revolver down. He was still in the air, his fall in process of completion, when he pulled the trigger. The explosion was deafening in the confined space. The smoke filled the hole so that he could see nothing. He struck the bottom on his back, and like a cat's the pocket-miner's body was on top of him. Even as the miner's body passed on top, the stranger crooked in his right arm to fire; and even in that instant the miner, with a quick thrust of elbow, struck his wrist. The muzzle was thrown up and the bullet thudded into the dirt of the side of the hole.

The next instant the stranger felt the miner's hand grip his wrist. The struggle was now for the revolver. Each man strove to turn it against the other's body. The smoke in the hole was clearing. The stranger, lying on his back, was beginning to see dimly. But suddenly he was blinded by a handful of dirt deliberately flung into his eyes by his antagonist. In that moment of shock his grip on the revolver was broken. In the next moment he felt a smashing darkness descend upon his brain, and in the midst of the darkness even the darkness ceased.

But the pocket-miner fired again and again, until the revolver was empty. Then he tossed it from him and, breathing heavily, sat down on the dead man's legs.

The miner was sobbing and struggling for breath. "Measly skunk!" he panted; "a-campin' on my trail an' lettin' me do the work, an' then shootin' me in the back!"

He was half crying from anger and exhaustion. He peered at the face of the dead man. It was sprinkled with loose dirt and gravel, and it was difficult to distinguish the features.

"Never laid eyes on him before," the miner concluded his scrutiny. "Just a common an' ordinary thief, hang him! An' he shot me in the back! He shot me in the back!"

He opened his shirt and felt himself, front and back, on his left side.

"Went clean through, and no harm done!" he cried jubilantly. "I'll bet he aimed all right all right; but he drew the gun over when he pulled the trigger—the cur! But I fixed 'm! Oh, I fixed 'm!"

His fingers were investigating the bullet-hole in his side, and a shade of regret passed over his face. "It's goin' to be stiffer'n hell," he said. "An' it's up to me to get mended an' get out o'here."

He crawled out of the hole and went down the hill to his camp. Half an hour later he returned, leading his pack-horse. His open shirt disclosed the rude bandages with which he had dressed his wound. He was slow and awkward with his left-hand movements, but that did not prevent his using the arm.

The bight of the pack-rope under the dead man's shoulders enabled him to heave the body out of the hole. Then he set to work gathering up his gold. He worked steadily for several hours, pausing often to rest his stiffening shoulder and to exclaim:

"He shot me in the back, the measly skunk! He shot me in the back!"

When his treasure was quite cleaned up and wrapped securely into a number of blanket-covered parcels, he made an estimate of its value.

"Four hundred pounds, or I'm a Hottentot," he concluded. "Say two hundred in quartz an' dirt—that leaves two hundred pounds of gold. Bill! Wake up! Two hundred pounds of gold! Forty thousand dollars! An' it's yourn—all yourn!"

He scratched his head delightedly and his fingers blundered into an unfamiliar groove. They quested along it for several inches. It was a crease through his scalp where the second bullet had ploughed.

He walked angrily over to the dead man.

"You would, would you!" he bullied. "You would, eh? Well, I fixed you good an' plenty, an' I'll give you decent burial, too. That's more'n you'd have done for me."

He dragged the body to the edge of the hole and toppled it in. It struck the bottom with a dull crash, on its side, the face twisted up to the light. The miner peered down at it.

"An' you shot me in the back!" he said accusingly.

With pick and shovel he filled the hole. Then he loaded the gold on his horse. It was too great a load for the animal, and when he had gained his camp he transferred part of it to his saddle-horse. Even so, he was compelled to abandon a portion of his outfit—pick and shovel and gold-pan, extra food and cooking utensils, and divers odds and ends.

The sun was at the zenith when the man forced the horses at the screen of vines and creepers. To climb the huge boulders the animals were compelled to uprear and struggle blindly through the tangled mass of vegetation. Once the saddle-horse fell heavily and the man removed the pack to get the animal on its feet. After it started on its way again the man thrust his head out from among the leaves and peered up at the hillside.

"The measly skunk!" he said, and disappeared.

There was a ripping and tearing of vines and boughs. The trees surged back and forth, marking the passage of the animals through the midst of them. There was a clashing of steel-shod hoofs on stone, and now and again a sharp cry of command. Then the voice of the man was raised in song:—

Tu'n around an' tu'n yo' face
Untoe them sweet hills of grace
(D' pow'rs of sin yo' am scornin'!).
Look about an' look aroun'
Fling yo' sin-pack on d' groun'
(Yo'-will meet wid d' Lord in d' mornin'!).

The song grew faint and fainter, and through the silence crept back the spirit of the place. The stream once more drowsed and whispered; the hum of the mountain bees rose sleepily. Down through the perfume-weighted air fluttered the snowy fluffs of the cottonwoods. The butterflies drifted in and out among the trees, and over all blazed the quiet sunshine. Only remained the hoof-marks in the meadow and the torn hillside to mark the boisterous trail of the life that had broken the peace of the place and passed on.

Chapter 5

A Grip on Death

Archibald Rutledge

The author of this tale is one of the greatest ever produced by the South Carolina low country. A poet laureate of South Carolina and author of many books about growing up and living in the Santee River region, Archibald Rutledge (1883–1973) wrote almost all of his stories in the first person, in which the narrator is telling the story. In this tale, he steps back and uses third-person narration, telling the story as if watching it happen. The main character is a man named Norman Milstead, who knows and loves the low country with a passion that radiates from Rutledge's prose. Under the title "Milstead Ropes One," the story first appeared in Field & Stream *magazine in 1926, and its popularity carried it into the book anthology* The Field and Stream Reader *(Doubleday, 1946).*

The whole thing probably started on the day Vincente Blasco's motorboat ran out of gas when it was in the river opposite Norman Milstead's plantation. "I thought something would happen to you on your pleasure jaunts one of these days, Vincente," Milstead was saying as he met the little Italian down on the decrepit plantation wharf.

Beneath Vincente's piratic mustache gleamed white teeth. He could smile engagingly. "I need de gas," he explained. "My tank, heem is dry."

"Can't you burn moonshine?"

"Too much expense," Vincente explained seriously, with a gesture somewhat Oriental and certainly comprehensive.

"I can let you have five gallons. Will you bring it back to me next week?"

"Yes, and bring you six for your favor."

"Look here, Vincente," said Milstead, a sudden thought coming to him, "I want to show you something. While your man is getting the gas, just come over here with me by this big oak."

Milstead led the Italian down a short stretch of river-bank, over-arched with jasmine vines, dimmed by myrtle that exhaled fragrance as they brushed the bushes. They emerged upon an open glade under a monster live-oak—a vast tree that must have stood there for nearly two centuries. Over it clambered huge manbodied vines; and growing on the marvelously long limbs, some of them parallel with the ground and not more than five feet from it, were fairy forests of vivid green ferns. Near the base of the oak the plantation owner paused.

They made an interesting contrast in manhood as they stood there together: the Italian, short, stout, swarthy, radiating a certain charm which came from quick apprehension, alert interest, deft precision in adjusting himself to any situation. Milstead was tall, grave, clean-shaven; a powerful figure, but spare. His hair was black, and inclined to curl a little; his eyes were dark blue. They looked rather piercingly from under beetle brows. Such eyes can be tender; but they can also be vindictive.

It was hard to get at the age of Vincente; possibly fifty, though his flair for living always made him appear younger than he was. But certainly he was older than Milstead, by ten, possibly fifteen, years.

"Some tree," said Vincente, his quick black eyes appraising the majesty of the monarch.

"I didn't bring you here to look at a tree," Milstead said; "you have seen plenty of big ones in Italy. But, Vincente, I want you to see what came my way yesterday. You're interested in natural history."

He stepped around the tree, leading Blasco by the arm. Pausing, he pointed to something hung against the rugged bark of the old patriarch. Another patriarch it was, and apparently of another world. Milstead expected an exclamation of awe from his visitor. But all he got was a chirpy whistle, perhaps of mild surprise.

"I killed it and brought it in," Milstead explained. "There is a den out near a place called Jones' Pond. One was killed there two years ago; now this one; a third has been seen. I fastened this one up here this morning to photograph him. Seven feet, nine inches he measures; and his weight is thirty-four pounds. He had eighteen rattles. It is what we call a diamondback. You aren't seeing things, Vincente. Bet you didn't leave anything like that in Italy."

If Vincente was impressed by these words, his reaction was singular indeed. "Ah," he breathed, as if he hadn't really heard Milstead at all; and he stepped forward toward the snake and touched it with a delicate forefinger, "Ah, my friend," he went on, "it is a pity that he is dead. If he was alive, I could make you an offer for heem."

"Offer?" asked Milstead. "What in the world would you do in the city with a monster like that? The whole police department would raid your fruit shop."

"A serpent like this—deadly, terrible—he is what the people like to see. 'Oh,'" he mimicked, "'have you seen what Vincente Blasco has in his store on Broad Street? It is one of the wonders of the world. It is a sea-serpent. It is a chimera. It frightened me, but I am glad I saw it.' So they would talk," Vincente explained. "They would come. That means trade. I hear, too," he added, "that rats have a fear of such a snake. I have too many rats. It would be nice arrangement."

"Perhaps I can get you one," Milstead said. "What would he be worth? But I don't vouch for the nice arrangement part of it."

"I am no dealer in such pretties," Vincente answered; "but if he is as large as this one, and full of life, I give you feefty dollars."

"Next week," Milstead answered, "when you come by here on one of your trips, leave those six gallons of gas for me, and have fifty dollars handy in your rompers."

It was the first week in October when all this occurred; and it happened that at the time Milstead had little work on his hands. To ride the woods, to locate a big diamondback, and to capture him for Blasco this seemed an easy and rather an interesting way to make fifty dollars. Besides, he would be ridding his own place of a creature that was a somewhat constant menace to man and to stock. Only the month before he had lost a Jersey heifer from snake-bite. The thing was worth trying at any rate. Besides, he could take his gun along and round up a covey or two. It was the first of the season, and his old setter was sick for a hunt.

Two days after Vincente's visit, Milstead made an early start for what he believed to be the rendezvous of a fine covey of quail, and possibly of a diamondback as well. The nature of the morning did not appear quite in keeping with so curious and grim an enterprise. An autumn haze hung over the river, where the long hat lances of light from the rising sun made the mists sparkle. Into the purple tops of towering yellow pines stole the radiant beams; and from those crests were raveled away streamers of light.

Mocking-birds, returning to their lyric mood after a long silence, were warbling from smilax-crowned hollies and cedars. Carolina wrens called with wild, sweet abandon to one another. Milstead heard one quite near him, and another answering from across the river, a full half-mile away.

The world was steeped in a mellow peace, a balmy serenity. Mystical airs breathed through the quiet forest, in the circling arms of which Milstead's home lay. It seemed a morning for almost any other kind of an undertaking than the one that was afoot.

But perhaps, thought Milstead, Poe was wrong in giving dismal settings for his dismal tales. The effect of tragedy may be heightened by contrast; there is something satiric in the peril that is encountered in beautiful sunshine, with birds happily warbling, and with the sky gazing calmly down with eyes of fathomless azure.

"I believe I can locate one of these things for Vincente," Milstead told himself as he journeyed out through the scented wood land. "The old dog can take care of himself all right. He knows a snake."

As the forest glimmered in the dawn, it was a radiant, dewy world into which the plantation-owner rode. The pine-trash on the road exhaled a spicy odor of freshness and wild cleanliness. High in the lustral morning heavens the giant yellow pines soared, choiring softly to the rising sun. The wild-woods glinted, shimmered, seemed aware of the miracle that they themselves were. It did not appear the kind of world that might hold peril and tragedy. It appeared made for love and peace, for song and joy.

Milstead knew where certain great diamondbacks had their haunt. During the preceding summer his neighbor, Claude Marlowe, a woodsman of the pineland, had killed one that was little short of eight feet. Milstead had wondered at it; had examined it as it had hung on a persimmon bush beside the public road. And one of his hounds, happening to pass the place, began to show signs of extreme caution and mistrust; finally located the thing; backed away with the glint of ancient wisdom in his sagacious eyes, and, ere he left the scene, howled lugubriously.

Paris Green Washington, a plantation negro of a singular dearth of imagination, had reported that he had seen, near the same locality, a snake of the same species and apparently of the same proportions. Several other persons had had the dubious privilege of seeing one of these serpent-wonders; and each person had apparently made his discovery in the neighborhood of Jones' Pond, a strange cypressed lagoon that lay on Milstead's place, not two miles from the house. He had reason to believe these negroes and their stories, especially since each one admitted that his attitude toward the chimera in question had been one of extreme conciliation. Then, of course, there was this late serpent that Milstead had shown to his friend Vincente Blasco.

"I'll get him one," he repeated; "and he'll be as welcome to it as fifty dollars will be to me. Besides, I've a sneaking interest in these babies that love so to play with their rattles."

He had tied behind his saddle a big burlap sack. Stopping by a group of young hickories, he cut one with a stout fork in its end. He had caught snakes before. Pinning one's head to the ground with the fork, he would hold him tight until he could get his hand around the thing's neck. Then it could be lifted and thrust down into the bag. The sack tied shut, he would leave his catch until he could return to the plantation for a wagon and a big box.

It may be thrilling, but it isn't exactly delicately discreet to carry a diamondback in a flimsy bag. A mere scratch from an inch-long fang may do damage that no amount of caution and effort can repair.

Out of the plantation's far gateway and into the lonely woods the man rode. The baby-branches, drenched in fragrant dew, glistened, and exhaled a winy fragrance. The sunshine filtered shyly into these remote solitudes.

Milstead saw a buck, thin strips of velvet hanging in tatters from his horns, slide into a myrtle thicket. Woodpeckers were hammering in assiduous fashion, calling stridently whenever they let up on their carpentering. Cicadas began to shrill, but not so aridly as they would later in the day.

A half-mile from the gate, Milstead turned off the road, literally taking to the woods. He had a curious feeling that the rare exotic beauty of the world which surrounded him had about it something sinister, something ironic, something satiric. He attributed his sensation to the eerie grimness of his mission. And it was the anticipation that caused his feeling. When he actually came on the snake, all would be well. All would be well . . . began to wonder if it would.

Afar off now, in the open pinelands, appeared the lagoon, marked by its magical gleam of black waters, its moss-hung bald cypresses, its aspect of perpetual, mournful beauty. In those giant trees snowy egrets nested, so spectral in their loveliness as to be like spirits of the place. In the dark waters alligators lived their solitary, treacherous lives; and large-mouth bass of unbelievable size managed to exist there by reason of their swiftness as dodgers of the huge reptiles. Wood-ducks nested in the low forks of the cypresses; and often they were seen, as placid and as beautiful as the waters themselves, floating on that mirror-like surface.

To the right of the lagoon was a long savanna—a green plain of many acres in extent, where flag-flowers grew, and gaudy flytraps, and alluring orchid flowers. It had a certain air of faerie peril, a beauty not quite of earth, an eerie loveliness not quite familiar, not quite smiling. It was toward this glimmering stretch of country that Milstead headed his horse.

It was the horse that gave him the first intimation that he had found what he was after. For a few yards Milstead noticed that his animal—a little red pony that he enjoyed riding because of his sure-footedness in the woods—began to show a gingerly sort of stepping that his rider interpreted to mean that the creature did not like the lush, quaking footing that the savanna afforded. Milstead idly recalled that the pony had one spring bogged down in a ricefield; and now he thought it possible that that far recollection had returned to him.

But then the horse stopped. His head went up high. He trembled. His ears were cocked. He gave vent to a shocked and mighty snort, as if blowing spasmodically from him some dreadful odor. Probably that was precisely what the red pony was doing.

He next began to quiver violently; and his whole attitude gave his rider to understand that they had both better be moving out of that place.

"It may be a snake," the man said slowly. "Well," he added half aloud, "that's what I've come after."

He decided to dismount. There were no trees near. A strange, scrubby, little live-oak growing forlornly on the edge of a ridge of sand that crossed the savanna seemed the only place where he could tie his horse. That he must tie him was evident, for by now the animal was positive that his life depended upon his immediate departure for somewhere else.

His rider slipped from him, leading him with much persuasion to the oak bush, where he tied him securely. The morning was warm. Milstead slipped off his coat, tying it to the saddle. Then he began to look about cautiously.

He whistled for his setter. Then, for the first time, he noticed the dog standing. Could it be a covey of quail? Could it be a woodcock, migrated early? It might be a snake. That it was Milstead grew more certain as he watched how fidgety the dog was, and with what a curious gleam in his eyes he stared at the bushes ahead of him. Down the ridge of sand he went, peering ahead under the sparse growth of huckleberry bushes. A curious odor assailed him. He knew it must be animal. Suddenly but it seemed vegetable. It was like cucumber; yet its pungency was like that of bear-scent. Milstead knew what it was. If he had been flamboyant in his way of thinking, he would have called it the odor of Sudden Death.

"I see it now," he said to himself. "It's about the kind that Vincente wants, too. It's rather larger than any I've ever picked up. It certainly is no plaything,"

Under the bronzing huckleberry bushes lay the great serpent, a regal reptile. He had lately shed his skin, and in his tawny gold phase he looked almost gaudy. Black and yellow and brown he gleamed on the white sand, lying there indolently in a huge shape. Milstead caught the glint from his cold unlidded eyes.

But, after all, a man is a man, and a snake is of a creation infinitely and remotely inferior. Against a sensible man, even the hugest diamondback, lacking the tremendous advantage of surprise, is helpless.

Milstead strode forward softly, his forked stick held before him. The snake saw the weapon coming; he seemed to bulge. Thrillingly his rattles began to sing their arid warning. Preliminary to taking his coil, the serpent foreshortened himself. His bulk seemed amazing.

Milstead could not help marking the thin, contemptuous lips of his antagonist; his baleful spade-head; his massive jaws, powerfully articulated. The Seminoles used to call him "The Great King"; and this specimen justified that proud appellation.

The man had a curious feeling that he was intruding; though perhaps that is a somewhat natural emotion that any man may experience upon encountering a deadly serpent in the wilds. Really, Milstead thought, this was the diamondback's home, this lush savanna, this dreamy stealthy place; the dim shores of this lonely lagoon—they were the serpent's by right of eminent domain.

"I'll have to get the dog out of the way first," he said to himself. "This is strictly my little affair."

Jerking a chain from his pocket, he walked around cautiously, fastened the snap to a ring in the setter's collar, and then led him to a safe distance, where he tied him to a stout bush. Returning, he found that the great serpent had not moved. Milstead extended his forked stick, parting the bushes. A man must be sure that he's dealing with only one snake. These beauties often come in pairs.

Now the forked stick was close to the snake's massive head. There was a chance that the reptile would strike at it. Milstead did not want to infuriate it more than was necessary, though capture would assuredly madden it. With a deft maneuver, avoiding the spade-shaped head, he thrust the fork down strongly behind the massive jaws. The pointed ends of the stick were buried in the sand. The diamondback was securely caught.

As Milstead expected, the body of the snake writhed weirdly out of the bushes, his rattles whirring wildly. The powerful muscular body, contorted into fearsome coils of frantic maneuvers, turned and twisted above the copper-colored huckleberry leaves. Keeping the fork tightly thrust downward, the man approached. He had done this thing before. But something now told him to beware. . . . Several times in his life he had had what appeared to be premonitions. He certainly felt one now. But there was Vincente, and his fifty dollars.

Stooping now, with his stick held tighter than ever, Milstead thrust his left hand down under the bushes. It touched the snake's back. It slipped down that gorgeous broad hide until the fingers were just behind the forked stick. Then they closed like a vise about the snake's throat. Milstead had the thing by the neck. He released the stick, and tossed it aside into the savanna. Then he tried to rise from his stooped position.

The effort caused him to stagger. He found himself suddenly struggling with main power to hold his grip on the diamondback's neck; and he staggered when he lifted that massive writhing weight. But he steadied himself. He was apparent master of the situation after all. Then he took a step toward his horse.

The red pony had witnessed the whole singular performance; and there was no denying that he understood the entire affair everything save what he believed his master's arrant folly. He now stood quite ready and also quite determined to make a bolt. This

Milstead evidently did not perceive—or was too busy with another matter to take much account of.

The body of the diamondback writhed upward. Almost before his captor realized what was happening, the snake had coiled its immense body about his left arm; and partly because of pain, partly certainly because of anger, and wholly because it was struggling for its freedom, the reptile began to constrict the man's arm. At first Milstead, his eye now on the pony, was not exactly aware of what was really happening. Other serpents had done precisely the same thing before.

He was walking slowly toward his horse, talking to it to make it calm. He glanced down at his left hand, extended now away from him, and to his horror he saw that the rattler's head was moving; it seemed to have some purchase that the man could not control. At the same time, Milstead felt a certain dim but of his left arm.

The diamondback was tightening his coil about the man's bare arm; that grip was deadening. It meant that the man's grasp of the snake's neck would inevitably weaken. It was loosening now. Milstead knew it. The great serpent appeared to know it, for he continued slowly but remorselessly to tighten his deadly coil.

Unless he could do something quickly, the sure thing to happen would be that the snake, freeing his head, would strike the man. Already that grim head was moving in the man's grasp. Milstead dared not reach round with his right hand; for, not knowing just what liberty the reptile had, he did not know whether he might not launch himself forward for an inch or two, sufficiently far for a fatal strike.

He thought of stooping down and laying the snake's head on the sand, and trying to crush it with his heel. But such a maneuver, with a serpent of this size and strength, would likely mean bungling—the rattler's pulling loose, and striking surely and with deadly effect.

Then there was the chance that the man might hold his grip until he could ride in to the plantation for help. It would take only a matter of a few minutes. That seemed the best way out if he could hold on. But that was the question. Milstead had encountered something too formidable for him. He felt himself outmaneuvered and, physically, almost overpowered.

Few people realize the sheer animal strength of a serpent of this size. Milstead began to realize it. He would have to get help. The thing seemed to have him.

But he had forgotten for the moment that the horse was fully aware of the nature of the thing the man was carrying. As his master approached, the red pony backed away, snorting, straining at the buck-hide thong that tied him. Even the stubborn live-oak bush was bent almost over with the frantic pulling of the tethered mount.

While Milstead was still five yards away, he saw that he would never ride home on that horse with that snake. There are some things that simply cannot be done. The man doubted if he could get up to the red pony, much less mount it and ride away. Clearly the horse considered that to approach was his master's intent; and with equal clearness he considered that such an intent was an imposition.

Milstead paused, talking to the pony the while. Well a horse knows the tone of fear; and it fills him with apprehension. There was the red pony, his head and neck extended, the thong that tied him taut as a bowstring. There was his would-be rider, a horrible thing in his hand, his arm banded by the cold coils of a chimera—a tortured man, trying to speak words of assurance. There was the diamondback, momentarily insinuating himself out of the man's nerve-wrung grasp.

There seemed no help near for Milstead. He thought of the oily Vincente Blasco, and he cursed him in his heart.

Milstead looked about him for a moment, trying to locate a weapon of some sort. The long, sandy ridge spanning the pale green savanna offered nothing. The beauty of the bright woodland mocked the man. Flocks of bluebirds were warbling like aerial rivulets. The sunshine made the lovely savanna twinkle with myriads of lustrous lights. There was a fragrant, meadowy scent of dew and lush foliage and rare flowers awaft in the air.

But all this was irony. Here was a man fighting for his life.

There was a half-hitch tying the red pony to the oak bush. The same kind of tie fastened the thong to the bridle. Milstead felt a sudden overpowering need for that tough, pliable piece of buckskin. But whether he could get it was the question. Undoubtedly the pony was about to break away. Whether the thong would break, or whether it would pull off at one end or the other, who could tell? The man had to have a part of that thong. He stepped forward toward the horse.

Of course, the red pony now knew that his master was demented. He reared, plunged. Milstead walked toward him, but now he held his fettered left arm behind him, away from him. It dropped with exhaustion and with the dead weight of the diamondback. He was almost to the horse now. The red pony blew out his breath in a long, amazed snort. He pawed bickeringly. His eyes were bulging large, and showed much white. His ears were shot straight forward at an angle that expressed both acute astonishment and vivid alertness.

Milstead reached his right hand forward to get it on the dangling loose tip of the half-hitch. He had, of course, to loose it at the bridle. The horse tried to bolt. The thong held. The horse curvetted until he almost ran around Milstead. With a deft lunge the man leaped forward, caught the tip of the thong, and gave it a jerk.

The red pony was free; and he appeared to appreciate marvelously his freedom. He flashed through the edge of the savanna, snorting loudly; he dashed away frantically, yet unwilling to lose any sight of what might be happening. With stirrups flying and clanking, he galloped off, looking back first from one side, then from the other, his head wildly high, his mane and tail streaming. A ship is by no means the only thing that sets its sails when it lifts anchor.

Milstead's horse was gone. But he had the buck-hide thong. The other end of it was still tied to the stout oak bush. With his right hand, with fingers which trembled and appeared woefully bungling, he painfully made a slip-knot in the end of the buckskin. With his teeth he tightened a ball-knot on the end of the lithe, strong string.

He made no attempt to loose the other end from the bush. Rather he edged away from it until the thong was taut once more the bush bending. Then with infinite caution, he lifted the open slip-knot, dropped it neatly over the serpent's head, saw that the loop tightened in place. Then he got down on his knees, so that the stretched thong would be parallel with the ground. It was an awkward stance, but an effective one.

He backed slowly away. The noose tightened, the strangling diamondback writhed; the bush bent low. Milstead felt the constricting bands on his arm relaxing. He was aware of breathing more easily. In another moment the pull of the bush whipped the snake, heavy as it was, clear away from him, throwing it on the sand in the little oak's sultry shadow.

The man regained his feet, breathing heavily, looking down on the writhing chimera that but a moment before had literally had him in its grasp. In the high pines near the lagoon, pines that now murmured and waved in an ecstasy of morning gladness, parula warblers chanted their elfin melodies. The sun gleamed and glinted across the savanna as if nothing had happened.

Milstead thought bitterly that the same melodies would have been lyrically chanted, the same sunlight lustrally gleamed, had the great reptile made an end of him. He had long since learned what every true woodsman knows: that under the beauteous garb of nature beats a heart that is relentless; for to him who sees aright, the countenance of nature has always about it something not quite intimate, not quite safe.

"He'll stay there, I think, for a while," said Milstead, eying the massive convolutions of the huge serpent turning and wallowing in the dry sand beside the oak bush. Then, having gone over and loosed the setter, he turned and started toward the glimmering lagoon.

On the borders of this he caught the red pony. From behind the saddle he unstrapped the heavy burlap bag. Retracing his steps, he was soon again on the ridge of sand spanning the savanna. It was now no task to lift the half-strangled snake by the heavy thong and drop it in the sack. The mouth of this he tied shut. Then he carried his burden rather gingerly out toward the road, where he laid it in a heavy bed of gallberry bushes.

To ride back to the plantation, returning with a wagon and a box for the captive, were matters of only a half hour. And in an hour Milstead had the huge diamondback free of sack and of buckskin thong, safely in a commodious box with a wire front. But he built a little extension and put a second wire front protecting the first—or protecting those who were curious enough to investigate. The whole dread arrangement he put in an empty feedhouse, awaiting the coming of Vincente Blasco.

In a few days' time the familiar spluttering of the Italian's motorboat engine was heard on the river; and, true to his promise, he delivered at Milstead's wharf six gallons of gasoline. He found Milstead somewhat grim and silent.

"How 'bout da beeg snake?" he asked. "You cannot catch so easy, I know. Maybe next week, next month?"

"You can get him today," Milstead replied in a most disinterested fashion.

"You got heem? 'Live? Beeg one?"

"Big enough," the other admitted. Vincente drew out his wallet. "I have feefty for you," he said, peeling off the tens from an astonishing assortment.

"Now, Vincente," Milstead said, "this thing you are getting is a dangerous thing, you understand?"

"I want him dang'rous," the little Italian answered.

"But no monkeying with him will do," the other warned. "You must keep people away from him, and you must stay away yourself."

"He not much to handle," Vincente said easily. "You catch heem, is it not?"

"Yes, I caught him."

"Oh, yes," Milstead responded dryly. "I just lassoed him and dropped him in a sack."

Vincente, always a bit of an actor, suddenly made the deft motions of throwing a lariat, then of lifting with it something heavy that he had caught. "Like dat?" he queried, his white teeth flashing.

"Well, yes," Milstead admitted, grudgingly, "but with a good deal less effort."

"I will get heem now," the Italian said. "You ought to go into the business," he advised, his sharp black eyes gleaming. "Easy money."

"Thanks."

"You could catcha many beeg snake."

"I rather think, Vincente," Milstead answered, with a certain depth of meaning that the other could not fully appreciate, "that perhaps there are some things in this world not meant to be caught."

Chapter 6

Tembo!

Carl Akeley

One of our most famous portrayers of African wildlife—in impressive sculpture, paintings, and books—started out as a lad wanting to become a taxidermist. That desire led Carl Akeley (1864–1926) from familiar American birds and animals to trailing the fearsome lords of the jungle with camera and gun in their native habitat. His name is commemorated in the great Akeley Hall of African Mammals at New York's American Museum of Natural History.

Huge gray shadows are creeping through the forest, but there is not even an echo of a footfall. The feathery foliage is stirring overhead. But there is no sound. You are only dimly conscious that something is happening in the great mysterious jungle. Something is living, breathing, moving vaguely, in the awesome gloom. A faint whisper—"Tembo!" The black gun boy has seen! His eyes are a hundred times keener than a white man's will ever be. Cold steel—your heavy gun barrel—is slipping through your cold fingers. They shake a little as you grasp your rifle and bring it to your shoulder. Suddenly you are face to face with the greatest mammal in the world. The elephant! Free and fearless, quick and powerful almost beyond comprehension, he fixes his small wicked-looking eyes upon those who have dared to cross his trail. With ease and grace his long, prehensile trunk, so near and so menacing, may reach out and smite, finishing an earthly career forever. The herd has been disturbed; it stands tensely silent, while the scales of life and death balance and a coin spins at the feet of the gods.

Now, with scarcely a murmur, the great elephant herd shifts and ebbs and flows. It has seen you, but the dawn breeze has been favorable. Tembo has not smelled you. He glides noiselessly into the inner recesses of the great dark forest. The lord of the land has spoken and his word is "peace."

The sun breaks through a piled up cloud, its rays filtering through the tree tops to the trail beneath. A tiny bird twitters bursts into song high up on a moss-draped bough. The silence is shattered. Something relaxes the whole length and breadth of your nervous system. Tembo has retreated to the remote feeding grounds of his jungle home.

The elephant always may be trusted to provide the hunter with plenty of excitement. His great size, colossal strength and magnificent courage are qualities that make him stand out as one of the most interesting as well as one of the most dangerous of beasts, often he appears when least expected and frequently does the totally unexpected. Walking unprepared into his presence is like stepping out of a quiet home into No Man's Land—it may be perfectly safe but the odds are considerably against it.

One day in Uganda we followed the trail of two old bull elephants for five hours. We were in a big feeding ground and the elephant tracks crossed, intermingled and circled in a bewildering maze. I had told Bill, my faithful Kikuyu gun bearer, to follow them more to test his ability than in the hope that he would succeed in bringing me to the herd. But I underrated Bill. Suddenly the boy stopped short and held up his cane as a signal for caution. Not more than twenty feet from us stood the two old bulls. They had not heard our approach nor had they caught our scent, but as I studied them from the shelter of a dense bush I realized that we were in a very dangerous position.

I had no desire to kill an elephant, except one for my museum group—and that meant only an unusually fine specimen; but I had even less desire to be killed by an elephant. So, with two of them as close to me as if we had been in the same room, and with nothing between us but a flimsy screen of bushes, I could take no chances. I hesitated, trying to convince myself that the tusks were fine enough to justify a shot. Then, without warning, my decision was made for me. A great gray trunk was thrust inquiringly forward—forward until it nearly touched my gun barrel. The movement may have been an attempt to catch my scent. I do not know. I had one glimpse of angry eyes set in a solid wall-like head—and I fired. The animal, wounded in the neck, swung around and bolted. I could not watch him nor gauge the effect of my shot, as his companion was right in front of me. He paused for a moment; then, apparently familiar with the deadly language of the rifle, he made a quick retreat.

Bill and I followed for about a hundred yards. The wounded bull scented us, turned and charged. I took aim, but there was no need to press the trigger, for the giant had made his last stand. His column-like legs swayed, crumpled beneath his weight, and the tremendous body lay outstretched on the ground. My bullet had pierced the jugular vein—a quick death. It had been a chance shot but, fired from such a short distance, it was much more effective than such shots usually are.

I had luck that day. Not, however, until some years later, when I talked with other hunters in Nairobi, did I realize how good my luck really was. I talked with men there who had had experiences similar to my own but who had not had my good fortune in escaping without injury. Great hunters who had been tossed and trampled—and lived to tell the tale.

Outram by keeping cool in a great emergency saved himself from a most unpleasant death. He had shot an elephant and the beast had fallen. Believing it finished, Outram approached. "Suddenly," he said, "to my surprise and horror the dead elephant rose and rushed at me. He caught me with his trunk and I went spinning through the air. I don't know whether in that brief flight I thought at all, but by the time I landed rather hard in the grass, amazement had given way to fear and I was sure that something had to be done and done quickly.

"I could see the elephant coming after me to trample me into the ground. Fortunately he paused for a second to crush my helmet, which had fallen off during the attack. That second saved me. I got under the beast's tail and there I clung while he wheeled and circled in a vicious attempt to get me in reach of trunk or tusks or feet. After a few moments of this sport, my injuries began to tell on me. The unequal contest could not have lasted much longer. Fortunately at the crucial moment my companion arrived and killed the elephant."

Hutchinson's story was similar to Outram's. An elephant caught him in the same way, wiped up the ground with him and then threw him into the trampled vegetation; but he had presence of mind enough to mix himself up in the animal's legs until his gun boy could fire.

The angry beast that caught Alan Black more nearly carried his charge to a finish. The method of attack was the same; but when the elephant discarded him, Black landed in a bush that broke his fall. The elephant followed and stepped on him, returning two or three times to step on him again, but the bush into which Black had fallen served as a cushion and saved his life.

The elephant's trunk is the most remarkable organ any animal possesses. The arm of a man is notable because it may be swung about at any angle from the shoulder, but the elephant's trunk may be twisted and turned in any direction and at any point in its entire length. It is just as powerful in one position as in another. It is without bone—a great flexible cable of muscles and sinew, so tough that the sharpest knife will scarcely cut it. It is so delicate that the elephant may pluck the tenderest blade of grass, yet so strong that he may lift a tree weighing a ton and toss it about easily. With his great height and short, thick neck, the elephant would find it difficult indeed to feed if it were not for his trunk. However it enables him to secure the choicest morsels on the ground or in the tree tops and to strip a whole forest of bark and branches, if he feels like it. With his trunk he has a most extraordinary ability to detect the faintest scent and to punish or kill an enemy.

Since the elephant has something like a fair chance, elephant hunting, unlike a good deal of the shooting that is done in the name of sport, always seems to me a legitimate game. This splendid animal wields a pair of heavy weapons—his mighty tusks—each one of which may weigh as much as the average man; and they are backed by several tons of brute strength. With an agility and a sagacity not to be rivaled by any other beast of his size today, he is a worthy opponent for any sportsman. Elephant hunting is always a game full of interest and excitement, because the elephant is such a wise old fellow that the hunter never learns all of his tricks.

Swiftly and surely the white man and the white man's rifles are getting the better of old Tembo. Everywhere is he compelled to retreat before the advance of civilization. But occasionally the African elephant has his innings; and when he does, he winds up the episode with a dramatic flourish of trunk and tusks that the most spectacular handling of a gun cannot rival.

Every elephant hunter has known moments of nerve-torturing suspense—moments when his wits, his courage and his skill with a gun have stood between him and an open grave. His opponent is adroit, fearless, resourceful, and possessed of tremendous strength. Of course, no one can put himself in the elephant's place and imagine the animal's feeling when it faces a rifle, but I am convinced that this great beast's attitude is one of supreme confidence. A man is handicapped, when he confronts a charging elephant, by his own state of mind. He knows he has "picked the fight." He knows he is the intruder. And he has a guilty feeling that creates in him a demoralizing fear that could never affect one who enters a contest with an absolute conviction of right. "Here's something about half as big as one of my legs," says Tembo to himself. "A dwarfed thing equally objectionable to my eyes and nose. He's trying to frighten me with that little stick he's carrying but I'll trample the runt and gore him and perhaps sit on him afterwards."

Then, when the "stick" emits a roar and a flash, if death is not instantaneous, the elephant is thoroughly angered and becomes more dangerous than before. To the hunter it is a different story.

He is not overconfident, through ignorance of his antagonist's power. Instead, he is handicapped by the knowledge that if his gun or his wits or his nerves fail him he will be quickly finished by the charging beast.

If the man keeps his head, he has slightly more than half a chance in any combat with elephants; but if the elephant gets his man, it is fairly certain that there will be no need for the services of a doctor. There are exceptions to this rule—once in a while the victim survives—as I can testify.

I had been on a collecting expedition for the museum, and had obtained all the necessary specimens, when an old bull who tried the quiet waiting game "got" me. Descending from the ice fields of Mount Kenya, that snow-capped peak on the equator, we had made a temporary camp, intending to rest until our base camp could be portered to us. The interlude gave me an opportunity to make some pictures of the typical elephant country all about us. With a party of fifteen, including gun boys and a few porters, I went back up the mountain to an elevation of nine thousand feet at the edge of the dense bamboo forest.

Probably all would have gone well, and I might have obtained some valuable photographs, had we not run across the spoor of three large bulls. It was an old trail and I knew it would take time to follow it, but the tracks were so unusual in size that I could not resist the temptation. There was always the chance that the trail might be crossed by a fresher one made as the bulls circled about feeding, but instead it led us on from noon until sundown without bringing us to any new sign.

The night on the mountain was so bitterly cold that we were glad to be up and on the move again at daybreak. There was frost in the air and the morning was still misty when we entered a great elephant feeding ground. It was an open space where the rank growth attained eight or ten feet in height and where the animals milled about eating the vegetation and trampling it down until there was very little left. The place itself was a labyrinth of trails, and from it, as the spokes of a wheel radiate from a hub, were the clear and definite tracks of the departing elephants. Soon after we left this feeding ground I came upon the fresh tracks of my three old bulls, so fresh that they must have been in that very spot an hour before.

But the network of paths led nowhere. For some time we wandered about in an attempt to follow the elephants; then, growing impatient, I left the clearing, intending to circle about it in the hope of finding on its outskirts the trail which the tuskers had taken. I had gone but a short distance when I found more fresh tracks. I stopped to examine them, and, as I did so, the crackling of bamboo not two hundred yards ahead caught my attention. The bulls were almost within rifle shot and were giving me the signal for the final stalk.

I waited while one of my trackers ran silently along the trail to a point about fifty yards away where it made an abrupt turn. He indicated the direction the animals had taken. Then I turned my attention to the porters, watching them select a place to lay down their loads in a clump of trees where they would be somewhat protected in case of a stampede. The second gun boy presented his rifle for inspection. I examined it, found everything in order, and sent the boy to a safe distance with the porters. The first gun boy presented his gun; I took it, handing him the rifle I had already examined. The second gun was now ready. I leaned it against my body and stood, my back to the wall of the forest, blowing upon my hands numbed by the cold and chafing them in order to have at a moment's notice a supple trigger finger. At the same time the first gun boy was taking the cartridges from his bandolier and holding them up so that I could be sure that each was a full steel-jacketed bullet—the only kind that will penetrate an elephant's head. There was no reason to suppose that the animals suspected our presence, and I prepared for the stalk with my customary caution and with more than my usual deliberation.

I was standing with my gun leaning against my hip, still warming my hands and still looking at the cartridges one after another. In a flash, one of the calmest moments of my hunting experience changed to the most profoundly intense moment of my entire life. I suddenly knew that an elephant was right behind me. I grabbed my gun, and as I wheeled around I tried to shove the safety catch forward. It would not budge. I wanted desperately to look at it, but there was no time. I remember thinking that I must pull the trigger hard enough to fire. Then something struck me a staggering blow. I saw the point of a tusk right at my chest. Instinctively I seized it in my left hand, reached out for the other tusk with my right, and went to the ground between them as the great body bore down upon me. One merciless little eye gleamed savagely above me as the elephant drove his tusks into the ground on either side of me, his rolled-up trunk against my chest. I heard a wheezy grunt as the great bull plunged forward, and I realized vaguely that I was being crushed beneath him. Then the light went out.

It was evening before I recovered consciousness, in a dazed sort of way. I was dimly aware of seeing a fire. I was lying where the old bull had left me, in a cold mountain rain, while my superstitious black boys, believing that I was dead, refused to touch me. I tried to shout, and I must have succeeded after a fashion, for a little later I felt myself being carried away by my legs and shoulders.

Later I had another lucid interval, in which I realized that I was in one of the porters' tents. Then I tried to piece together the events that had led to my accident. I supposed that my back was broken because I could not move. I felt no pain. I was miserably cold and numb, and that reminded me of a bottle of brandy, carried for emergencies. I ordered the boys to bring it to me and pour it down my throat. I also had them prepare for me some hot bovril, and gradually the numbness left me. Then I discovered that I could move my arm a little. I tried the same experiment with my leg and was successful. Though the effort brought pain, it told me that I had at least a chance for recovery.

When morning came, my mind was clear enough to inquire for my white companions at the camp below, and the boys told me that soon after the elephant knelt on me they had dispatched a messenger asking for help. At that rate, assistance should have been close at hand. Fearing that the rescue party was lost on the mountain, I ordered my heavy gun to be fired every fifteen minutes, and within an hour my boys heard an answering shot from a smaller rifle. When relief arrived I was a sorry looking spectacle. The blow from the elephant's trunk which had stunned me had also skinned my forehead, blackened and closed an eye, broken my nose and torn open one cheek so that my teeth were exposed. Several of my ribs were broken and my lungs were punctured. I was covered with mud and splashed with blood. But apparently it was my face that was the awful sight. Just why I was not crushed completely, I shall never know. Beneath the old bull's weight, or even under the pressure of his enormous trunk, my body would have offered about as much resistance as a soda cracker. My only explanation—and I think it is the correct one—is that a root or rock under the surface of the ground must have stopped his tusks, and that seeing me unconscious he must have thought he had killed me. He had then left me and had charged about the clearing after the black boys.

My experience is just one more illustration of my idea that a combat between a man and an elephant is still a fairly equal contest. Even the express rifles of the twentieth century have not given the hunter an overwhelming advantage over this mighty beast.

Chapter 7

The Man-Eaters of Tsavo: The Most Dangerous Ever!

John Henry Patterson

There is so much to say about this book that an editor like myself could easily find himself writing "a book about the book." I will not attempt to do that, while hoping you will enjoy this excerpt from the original book, The Man-Eaters of Tsavo. *The author, John Henry Patterson, had been a lieutenant colonel in the British military when his civilian job as an engineer sent him to East Africa in 1898 to supervise the building of a railroad bridge over the Tsavo River. In what is Kenya today, the job was daunting as an engineering feat, but two man-eating lions turned it into a drama that has endured for decades since.*

The internet site Wikipedia says, "Several publications about and studies of man-eating lions of Tsavo have been inspired by Patterson's account." These include a British monochrome version, a 1952 3-D version called Bwana Devil, *and the huge 1996* The Ghost and the Darkness, *which has the superb performance of Val Kilmer before his tragic death by a rare disease in 2024.*

As The Ghost and the Darkness *reveals, the two lions today can be seen at the Field Museum in Chicago, with their actual skins preserved by a taxidermist's skills. It is hard to realize that they killed thirty or more people and shut down the building of a railroad. When you see the lions at the Field Museum, however, in their actual skins, in a frozen moment of realism, you will appreciate even more Patterson's story of the man-eaters. You can see photos of the lions at the Field Museum on the internet by searching for "Field Museum Tsavo Lions." Be aware that due to briars and genetic influences, these famous lions do not have the huge and colorful features of most lions seen today, like the MGM lion.*

Now, to Patterson's story.

The Reign of Terror

The lions seemed to have got a bad fright the night Brock and I sat up in wait for them in the goods-wagon, for they kept away from Tsavo and did not molest us in any way for some considerable time—not, in fact, until long after Brock had left me and gone on safari (a caravan journey) to Uganda. In this breathing space which they vouchsafed us, it occurred to me that should they renew their attacks, a trap would perhaps offer the best chance of getting at them, and that if I could construct one in which a couple of coolies might be used as bait without being subjected to any danger, the lions would be quite daring enough to enter it in search of them and thus be caught. I accordingly set to work at once, and in a short time managed to make a sufficiently strong trap out of wooden sleepers, tram-rails, pieces of telegraph wire, and a length of heavy chain. It was divided into two compartments—one for the men and one for the lion. A sliding door at one end admitted the former, and once inside this compartment they were perfectly safe, as between them and the lion, if he entered the other, ran a cross wall of iron rails only three inches apart, and embedded both top and bottom in heavy wooden sleepers. The door which was to admit the lion was, of course, at the opposite end of the structure, but otherwise the whole thing was very much on the principle of the ordinary rat-trap, except that it was not necessary for the lion to seize the bait in order to send the door clattering down. This part of the contrivance was arranged in the following manner. A heavy chain was secured along the top part of the lion's doorway, the ends hanging down to the ground on either side of the opening; and to these were fastened, strongly secured by stout wire, short lengths of rails placed about six inches apart. This made a sort of flexible door which could be packed into a small space when not in use, and which abutted against the top of the doorway when lifted up. The door was held in this position by a lever made of a piece of rail, which in turn was kept in its place by a wire fastened to one end and passing down to a spring concealed in the ground inside the cage. As soon as the lion entered sufficiently far into the trap, he would be bound to tread on the spring; his weight on this would release the wire, and in an instant down would come the door behind him; and he could not push it out in any way, as it fell into a groove between two rails firmly embedded in the ground.

In making this trap, which cost us a lot of work, we were rather at a loss for want of tools to bore holes in the rails for the doorway, so as to enable them to be fastened by the wire to the chain. It occurred to me, however, that a hard-nosed bullet from my .303 would penetrate the iron, and on making the experiment I was glad to find that a hole was made as cleanly as if it had been punched out.

When the trap was ready I pitched a tent over it in order further to deceive the lions, and built an exceedingly strong boma round it.

One small entrance was made at the back of the enclosure for the men, which they were to close on going in by pulling a bush after them; and another entrance just in front of the door of the cage was left open for the lions. The wiseacres to whom I showed my invention were generally of the opinion that the man-eaters would be too cunning to walk into my parlour; but, as will be seen later, their predictions proved false. For the first few nights I baited the trap myself, but nothing happened except that I had a very sleepless and uncomfortable time, and was badly bitten by mosquitoes.

As a matter of fact, it was some months before the lions attacked us again, though from time to time we heard of their depredations in other quarters. Not long after our night in the goods-wagon, two men were carried off from railhead, while another was taken from a place called Engomani, about ten miles away. Within a very short time, this latter place was again visited by the brutes, two more men being seized, one of whom was killed and eaten, and the other so badly mauled that he died within a few days. As I have said, however, we at Tsavo enjoyed complete immunity from attack, and the coolies, believing that their dreaded foes had permanently deserted the district, resumed all their usual habits and occupations, and life in the camps returned to its normal routine.

At last we were suddenly startled out of this feeling of security. One dark night the familiar terror-stricken cries and screams awoke the camps, and we knew that the "demons" had returned and had commenced a new list of victims. On this occasion a number of men had been sleeping outside their tents for the sake of coolness, thinking, of course, that the lions had gone for good, when suddenly in the middle of the night one of the brutes was discovered forcing its way through the boma. The alarm was at once given, and sticks, stones and firebrands were hurled in the direction of the intruder. All was of no avail, however, for the lion burst into the midst of the terrified group, seized an unfortunate wretch amid the cries and shrieks of his companions, and dragged him off through the thick thorn fence. He was joined outside by the second lion, and so daring had the two brutes become that they did not trouble to carry their victim any further away, but devoured him within thirty yards of the tent where he had been seized. Although several shots were fired in their direction by the jemadar of the gang to which the coolie belonged, they took no notice of these and did not attempt to move until their horrible meal was finished. The few scattered fragments that remained of the body I would not allow to be buried at once, hoping that the lions would return to the spot the following night; and on the chance of this I took up my station at nightfall in a convenient tree. Nothing occurred to break the monotony of my watch, however, except that I had a visit from a hyena, and the next morning I learned that the lions had attacked another camp about two miles from Tsavo—for by this time the camps were again scattered, as I had works in progress all up and down the line. There the man-eaters had been successful in obtaining a victim, whom, as in the previous instance, they devoured quite close to the camp. How they forced their way through the bomas without making a noise was, and still is, a mystery to me; I should have thought that it was next to impossible for an animal to get through at all. Yet they continually did so, and without a sound being heard.

After this occurrence, I sat up every night for over a week near likely camps, but all in vain. Either the lions saw me and then went elsewhere, or else I was unlucky, for they took man after man from different places without ever once giving me a chance of a shot at them. This constant night watching was most dreary and fatiguing work, but I felt that it was a duty that had to be undertaken, as the men naturally looked to me for protection. In the whole of my life I have never experienced anything more nerve-shaking than to hear the deep roars of these dreadful monsters growing gradually nearer and nearer, and to know that some one or other of us was doomed to be their victim before morning dawned. Once they reached the vicinity of the camps, the roars completely ceased, and we knew that they were stalking for their prey. Shouts would then pass from camp to camp, "Khabar dar, bhaieon, shaitan ata" ("Beware, brothers, the devil is coming"), but the warning cries would prove of no avail, and sooner or later agonising shrieks would break the silence, and another man would be missing from roll-call next morning.

I was naturally very disheartened at being foiled in this way night after night, and was soon at my wits' end to know what to do; it seemed as if the lions were really "devils" after all and bore a charmed life.

As I have said before, tracking them through the jungle was a hopeless task; but as something had to be done to keep up the men's spirits, I spent many a weary day crawling on my hands and knees through the dense undergrowth of the exasperating wilderness around us. As a matter of fact, if I had come up with the lions on any of these expeditions, it was much more likely that they would have added me to their list of victims than that I should have succeeded in killing either of them, as everything would have been in their favour. About this time, too, I had many helpers, and several officers—civil, naval and military—came to Tsavo from the coast and sat up night after night in order to get a shot at our daring foes. All of us, however, met with the same lack of success, and the lions always seemed capable of avoiding the watchers, while succeeding, at the same time in obtaining a victim.

I have a very vivid recollection of one particular night when the brutes seized a man from the railway station and brought him close to my camp to devour. I could plainly hear them crunching the bones, and the sound of their dreadful purring filled the air and rang in my ears for days afterwards. The terrible thing was to feel so helpless; it was useless to attempt to go out, as of course the poor fellow was dead, and in addition it was so pitch dark as to make it impossible to see anything. Some half a dozen workmen, who lived in a small enclosure close to mine, became so terrified on hearing the lions at their meal that they shouted and implored me to allow them to come inside my boma.

This I willingly did, but soon afterwards I remembered that one man had been lying ill in their camp, and on making enquiry I found that they had callously left him behind alone. I immediately took some men with me to bring him to my boma, but on entering his tent I saw by the light of the lantern that the poor fellow was beyond need of safety. He had died of shock at being deserted by his companions.

From this time matters gradually became worse and worse. Hitherto, as a rule, only one of the man-eaters had made the attack and had done the foraging, while the other waited outside in the bush; but now they began to change their tactics, entering the bomas together and each seizing a victim. In this way two Swahili porters were killed during the last week of November, one being immediately carried off and devoured. The other was heard moaning for a long time, and when his terrified companions at last summoned up sufficient courage to go to his assistance, they found him stuck fast in the bushes of the boma, through which for once the lion had apparently been unable to drag him.

He was still alive when I saw him next morning, but so terribly mauled that he died before he got to the hospital.

Within a few days of this the two brutes made a most ferocious attack on the largest camp in the section, which for safety's sake was situated within a stone's throw of Tsavo Station and close to a Permanent Way Inspector's iron hut. Suddenly in the dead of night the two man-eaters burst in among the terrified workmen, and even from my boma, some distance away, I could plainly hear the panic-stricken shrieking of the coolies. Then followed cries of "They've taken him; they've taken him," as the brutes carried off their unfortunate victim and began their horrible feast close beside the camp. The inspector, Mr. Dalgairns, fired over fifty shots in the direction in which he heard the lions, but they were not to be frightened and calmly lay there until their meal was finished. After examining the spot in the morning, we at once set out to follow the brutes, Mr. Dalgairns feeling confident that he had wounded one of them, as there was a trail on the sand like that of the toes of a broken limb. After some careful stalking, we suddenly found ourselves in the vicinity of the lions, and were greeted with ominous growlings. Cautiously advancing and pushing the bushes aside, we saw in the gloom what we at first took to be a lion cub; closer inspection, however, showed it to be the remains of the unfortunate coolie, which the man-eaters had evidently abandoned at our approach. The legs, one arm and half the body had been eaten, and it was the stiff fingers of the other arm trailing along the sand which had left the marks we had taken to be the trail of a wounded lion. By this time the beasts had retired far into the thick jungle where it was impossible to follow them, so we had the remains of the coolie buried and once more returned home disappointed.

Now the bravest men in the world, much less the ordinary Indian coolie, will not stand constant terrors of this sort indefinitely. The whole district was by this time thoroughly panic-stricken, and I was not at all surprised, therefore, to find on my return to camp that same afternoon (December 1) that the men had all struck work and were waiting to speak to me. When I sent for them, they flocked to my boma in a body and stated that they would not remain at Tsavo any longer for anything or anybody; they had come from India on an agreement to work for the government, not to supply food for either lions or "devils." No sooner had they delivered this ultimatum than a regular stampede took place. Some hundreds of them stopped the first passing train by throwing themselves on the rails in front of the engine, and then, swarming on to the trucks and throwing in their possessions anyhow, they fled from the accursed spot.

After this the railway works were completely stopped; and for the next three weeks practically nothing was done but build "lion-proof" huts for those workmen who had had sufficient courage to remain. It was a strange and amusing sight to see these shelters perched on the top of water-tanks, roofs and girders—anywhere for safety—while some even went so far as to dig pits inside their tents, into which they descended at night, covering the top over with heavy logs of wood.

Every good-sized tree in the camp had as many beds lashed on to it as its branches would bear—and sometimes more. I remember that one night when the camp was attacked, so many men swarmed on to one particular tree that down it came with a crash, hurling its terror-stricken load of shrieking coolies close to the very lions they were trying to avoid. Fortunately for them, a victim had already been secured, and the brutes were too busy devouring him to pay attention to anything else.

The District Officer's Narrow Escape

Some little time before the flight of the workmen, I had written to Mr. Whitehead, the District Officer, asking him to come up and assist me in my campaign against the lions, and to bring with him any of his askaris (native soldiers) that he could spare. He replied accepting the invitation, and told me to expect him about dinner-time on December 2, which turned out to be the day after the exodus. His train was due at Tsavo about six o'clock in the evening, so I sent my "boy" up to the station to meet him and to help in carrying his baggage to the camp. In a very short time, however, the "boy" rushed back trembling with terror, and informed me that there was no sign of the train or of the railway staff, but that an enormous lion was standing on the station platform. This extraordinary story I did not believe in the least, as by this time the coolies—never remarkable for bravery—were in such a state of fright that if they caught sight of a hyena or a baboon, or even a dog, in the bush, they were sure to imagine it was a lion; but I found out next day that it was an actual fact, and that both stationmaster and signalman had been obliged to take refuge from one of the man-eaters by locking themselves in the station building.

I waited some little time for Mr. Whitehead, but eventually, as he did not put in an appearance, I concluded that he must have postponed his journey until the next day, and so had my dinner in my customary solitary state. During the meal I heard a couple of shots, but paid no attention to them, as rifles were constantly being fired off in the neighbourhood of the camp. Later in the evening, I went out as usual to watch for our elusive foes, and took up my position in a crib made of sleepers which I had built on a big girder close to a camp which I thought was likely to be attacked. Soon after settling down at my post, I was surprised to hear the man-eaters growling and purring and crunching up bones about seventy yards from the crib. I could not understand what they had found to eat, as I had heard no commotion in the camps, and I knew by bitter experience that every meal the brutes obtained from us was announced by shrieks and uproar. The only conclusion I could come to was that they had pounced upon some poor unsuspecting native traveller. After a time I was able to make out their eyes glowing in the darkness, and I took as careful aim as was possible in the circumstances and fired; but the only notice they paid to the shot was to carry off whatever they were devouring and to retire quietly over a slight rise, which prevented me from seeing them. There they finished their meal at their ease.

As soon as it was daylight, I got out of my crib and went towards the place where I had last heard them. On the way, whom should I meet but my missing guest, Mr. Whitehead, looking very pale and ill, and generally dishevelled.

"Where on earth have you come from?" I exclaimed. "Why didn't you turn up to dinner last night?"

"A nice reception you give a fellow when you invite him to dinner," was his only reply.

"Why, what's up?" I asked.

"That infernal lion of yours nearly did for me last night," said Whitehead.

"Nonsense, you must have dreamed it!" I cried in astonishment.

For answer he turned round and showed me his back. "That's not much of a dream, is it?" he asked.

His clothing was rent by one huge tear from the nape of the neck downwards, and on the flesh there were four great claw marks, showing red and angry through the torn cloth. Without further parley, I hurried him off to my tent, and bathed and dressed his wounds; and when I had made him considerably more comfortable, I got from him the whole story of the events of the night.

It appeared that his train was very late, so that it was quite dark when he arrived at Tsavo Station, from which the track to my camp lay through a small cutting. He was accompanied by Abdullah, his sergeant of askaris, who walked close behind him carrying a lighted lamp. All went well until they were about half-way through the gloomy cutting, when one of the lions suddenly jumped down upon them from the high bank, knocking Whitehead over like a ninepin, and tearing his back in the manner I had seen. Fortunately, however, he had his carbine with him, and instantly fired. The flash and the loud report must have dazed the lion for a second or two, enabling Whitehead to disengage himself; but the next instant the brute pounced like lightning on the unfortunate Abdullah, with whom he at once made off. All that the poor fellow could say was: "Eh, Bwana, simba" ("Oh, Master, a lion"). As the lion was dragging him over the bank, Whitehead fired again, but without effect, and the brute quickly disappeared into the darkness with his prey. It was of course, this unfortunate man whom I had heard the lions devouring during the night. Whitehead himself had a marvellous escape; his wounds were happily not very deep, and caused him little or no inconvenience afterwards.

On the same day, December 3, the forces arrayed against the lions were further strengthened. Mr. Farquhar, the Superintendent of Police, arrived from the coast with a score of sepoys to assist in hunting down the man-eaters, whose fame had by this time spread far and wide, and the most elaborate precautions were taken, his men being posted on the most convenient trees near every camp. Several other officials had also come up on leave to join in the chase, and each of these guarded a likely spot in the same way, Mr. Whitehead sharing my post inside the crib on the girder. Further, in spite of some chaff, my lion trap was put in thorough working order, and two of the sepoys were installed as bait.

Our preparations were quite complete by nightfall, and we all took up our appointed positions. Nothing happened until about nine o'clock, when to my great satisfaction the intense stillness was suddenly broken by the noise of the door of the trap clattering down. "At last," I thought, "one at least of the brutes is done for." But the sequel was an ignominious one.

The bait-sepoys had a lamp burning inside their part of the cage, and were each armed with a Martini rifle, with plenty of ammunition. They had also been given strict orders to shoot at once if a lion should enter the trap. Instead of doing so, however, they were so terrified when he rushed in and began to lash himself madly against the bars of the cage, that they completely lost their heads and were actually too unnerved to fire. Not for some minutes—not, indeed, until Mr. Farquhar, whose post was close by, shouted at them and cheered them on—did they at all recover themselves. Then when at last they did begin to fire, they fired with a vengeance—anywhere, anyhow. Whitehead and I were at right angles to the direction in which they should have shot, and yet their bullets came whizzing all round us. Altogether they fired over a score of shots, and in the end succeeded only in blowing away one of the bars of the door, thus allowing our prize to make good his escape. How they failed to kill him several times over is, and always will be, a complete mystery to me, as they could have put the muzzles of their rifles absolutely touching his body. There was, indeed, some blood scattered about the trap, but it was small consolation to know that the brute, whose capture and death seemed so certain, had only been slightly wounded.

Still we were not unduly dejected, and when morning came, a hunt was at once arranged. Accordingly we spent the greater part of the day on our hands and knees following the lions through the dense thickets of thorny jungle, but though we heard their growls from time to time, we never succeeded in actually coming up with them. Of the whole party, only Farquhar managed to catch a momentary glimpse of one as it bounded over a bush. Two days more were spent in the same manner, and with equal unsuccess; and then Farquhar and his sepoys were obliged to return to the coast. Mr. Whitehead also departed for his district, and once again I was left alone with the man-eaters.

Death of the First Man-Eater

A day or two after the departure of my allies, as I was leaving my boma soon after dawn on December 9, I saw a Swahili running excitedly towards me, shouting out "Simba! Simba!" ("Lion! Lion!"), and every now and again looking behind him as he ran. On questioning him I found that the lions had tried to snatch a man from the camp by the river, but being foiled in this had seized and killed one of the donkeys, and were at that moment busy devouring it not far off. Now was my chance.

I rushed for the heavy rifle which Farquhar had kindly left with me for use in case an opportunity such as this should arise, and, led by the Swahili, I started most carefully to stalk the lions, who, I devoutly hoped, were confining their attention strictly to their meal. I was getting on splendidly, and could just make out the outline of one of them through the dense bush, when unfortunately my guide snapped a rotten branch. The wily beast heard the noise, growled his defiance, and disappeared in a moment into a patch of even thicker jungle close by. In desperation at the thought of his escaping me once again, I crept hurriedly back to the camp, summoned the available workmen and told them to bring all the tom-toms, tin cans, and other noisy instruments of any kind that could be found. As quickly as possible I posted them in a half-circle round the thicket, and gave the head jemadar instructions to start a simultaneous beating of the tom-toms and cans as soon as he judged that I had had time to get round to the other side. I then crept round by myself and soon found a good position and one which the lion was most likely to retreat past, as it was in the middle of a broad animal path leading straight from the place where he was concealed. I lay down behind a small ant hill, and waited expectantly. Very soon I heard a tremendous din being raised by the advancing line of coolies, and almost immediately, to my intense joy, out into the open path stepped a huge maneless lion. It was the first occasion during all these trying months upon which I had had a fair chance at one of these brutes, and my satisfaction at the prospect of bagging him was unbounded.

Slowly he advanced along the path, stopping every few seconds to look round. I was only partially concealed from view, and if his attention had not been so fully occupied by the noise behind him, he must have observed me. As he was oblivious to my presence, however, I let him approach to within about fifteen yards of me, and then covered him with my rifle. The moment I moved to do this, he caught sight of me, and seemed much astonished at my sudden appearance, for he stuck his forefeet into the ground, threw himself back on his haunches and growled savagely. As I covered his brain with my rifle, I felt that at last I had him absolutely at my mercy, but . . . never trust an untried weapon! I pulled the trigger, and to my horror heard the dull snap that tells of a misfire.

Worse was to follow. I was so taken aback and disconcerted by this untoward accident that I entirely forgot to fire the left barrel, and lowered the rifle from my shoulder with the intention of reloading—if I should be given time. Fortunately for me, the lion was so distracted by the terrific din and uproar of the coolies behind him that instead of springing on me, as might have been expected, he bounded aside into the jungle again. By this time I had collected my wits, and just as he jumped I let him have the left barrel. An answering angry growl told me that he had been hit; but nevertheless he succeeded once more in getting clear away, for although I tracked him for some little distance, I eventually lost his trail in a rocky patch of ground.

Bitterly did I anathematise the hour in which I had relied on a borrowed weapon, and in my disappointment and vexation I abused owner, maker, and rifle with fine impartiality. On extracting the unexploded cartridge, I found that the needle had not struck home, the cap being only slightly dented; so that the whole fault did indeed lie with the rifle, which I later returned to Farquhar with polite compliments.

Seriously, however, my continued ill-luck was most exasperating; and the result was that the Indians were more than ever confirmed in their belief that the lions were really evil spirits, proof against mortal weapons. Certainly, they did seem to bear charmed lives.

After this dismal failure there was, of course, nothing to do but to return to camp. Before doing so, however, I proceeded to view the dead donkey, which I found to have been only slightly devoured in the quarters. It is a curious fact that lions always begin at the tail of their prey and eat upwards towards the head. As their meal had thus been interrupted evidently at the very beginning, I felt pretty sure that one or other of the brutes would return to the carcass at nightfall. Accordingly, as there was no tree of any kind close at hand, I had a staging erected some ten feet away from the body. This machan was about twelve feet high and was composed of four poles stuck into the ground and inclined towards each other at the top, where a plank was lashed to serve as a seat. Further, as the nights were still pitch dark, I had the donkey's carcase secured by strong wires to a neighbouring stump, so that the lions might not be able to drag it away before I could get a shot at them.

At sundown, therefore, I took up my position on my airy perch, and much to the disgust of my gun-bearer, Mahina, I decided to go alone. I would gladly have taken him with me, indeed, but he had a bad cough, and I was afraid lest he should make any involuntary noise or movement which might spoil all. Darkness fell almost immediately, and everything became extraordinarily still. The silence of an African jungle on a dark night needs to be experienced to be realised; it is most impressive, especially when one is absolutely alone and isolated from one's fellow creatures, as I was then. The solitude and stillness, and the purpose of my vigil, all had their effect on me, and from a condition of strained expectancy I gradually fell into a dreamy mood which harmonised well with my surroundings. Suddenly I was startled out of my reverie by the snapping of a twig: and, straining my ears for a further sound, I fancied I could hear the rustling of a large body forcing its way through the bush. "The man-eater," I thought to myself; "surely to-night my luck will change and I shall bag one of the brutes." Profound silence again succeeded; I sat on my eyrie like a statue, every nerve tense with excitement. Very soon, however, all doubt as to the presence of the lion was dispelled. A deep long-drawn sigh—sure sign of hunger—came up from the bushes, and the rustling commenced again as he cautiously advanced. In a moment or two a sudden stop, followed by an angry growl, told me that my presence had been noticed; and I began to fear that disappointment awaited me once more.

But no; matters quickly took an unexpected turn. The hunter became the hunted; and instead of either making off or coming for the bait prepared for him, the lion began stealthily to stalk me! For about two hours he horrified me by slowly creeping round and round my crazy structure, gradually edging his way nearer and nearer. Every moment I expected him to rush it; and the staging had not been constructed with an eye to such a possibility. If one of the rather flimsy poles should break, or if the lion could spring the twelve feet which separated me from the ground . . . the thought was scarcely a pleasant one. I began to feel distinctly "creepy," and heartily repented my folly in having placed myself in such a dangerous position. I kept perfectly still, however, hardly daring even to blink my eyes: but the long-continued strain was telling on my nerves, and my feelings may be better imagined than described when about midnight suddenly something came flop and struck me on the back of the head. For a moment I was so terrified that I nearly fell off the plank, as I thought that the lion had sprung on me from behind. Regaining my senses in a second or two, I realised that I had been hit by nothing more formidable than an owl, which had doubtless mistaken me for the branch of a tree—not a very alarming thing to happen in ordinary circumstances, I admit, but coming at the time it did, it almost paralysed me. The involuntary start which I could not help giving was immediately answered by a sinister growl from below.

After this I again kept as still as I could, though absolutely trembling with excitement; and in a short while I heard the lion begin to creep stealthily towards me. I could barely make out his form as he crouched among the whitish undergrowth; but I saw enough for my purpose, and before he could come any nearer, I took careful aim and pulled the trigger. The sound of the shot was at once followed by a most terrific roar, and then I could hear him leaping about in all directions. I was no longer able to see him, however, as his first bound had taken him into the thick bush; but to make assurance doubly sure, I kept blazing away in the direction in which I heard him plunging about. At length came a series of mighty groans, gradually subsiding into deep sighs, and finally ceasing altogether; and I felt convinced that one of the "devils" who had so long harried us would trouble us no more.

As soon as I ceased firing, a tumult of inquiring voices was borne across the dark jungle from the men in camp about a quarter of a mile away. I shouted back that I was safe and sound, and that one of the lions was dead: whereupon such a mighty cheer went up from all the camps as must have astonished the denizens of the jungle for miles around. Shortly I saw scores of lights twinkling through the bushes: every man in camp turned out, and with tom-toms beating and horns blowing came running to the scene. They surrounded my eyrie, and to my amazement prostrated themselves on the ground before me, saluting me with cries of "Mabarak! Mabarak!" which I believe means "blessed one" or "saviour." All the same, I refused to allow any search to be made that night for the body of the lion, in case his companion might be close by; besides, it was possible that he might be still alive, and capable of making a last spring. Accordingly we all returned in triumph to the camp, where great rejoicings were kept up for the remainder of the night, the Swahili and other African natives celebrating the occasion by an especially wild and savage dance.

For my part, I anxiously awaited the dawn; and even before it was thoroughly light I was on my way to the eventful spot, as I could not completely persuade myself that even yet the "devil" might not have eluded me in some uncanny and mysterious way. Happily my fears proved groundless, and I was relieved to find that my luck—after playing me so many exasperating tricks—had really turned at last. I had scarcely traced the blood for more than a few paces when, on rounding a bush, I was startled to see a huge lion right in front of me, seemingly alive and crouching for a spring. On looking closer, however, I satisfied myself that he was really and truly stone-dead, whereupon my followers crowded round, laughed and danced and shouted with joy like children, and bore me in triumph shoulder-high round the dead body. These thanksgiving ceremonies being over, I examined the body and found that two bullets had taken effect—one close behind the left shoulder, evidently penetrating the heart, and the other in the off hind leg. The prize was indeed one to be proud of; his length from tip of nose to tip of tail was nine feet eight inches, he stood three feet nine inches high, and it took eight men to carry him back to camp. The only blemish was that the skin was much scored by the boma thorns through which he had so often forced his way in carrying off his victims.

The news of the death of one of the notorious man-eaters soon spread far and wide over the country: telegrams of congratulation came pouring in, and scores of people flocked from up and down the railway to see the skin for themselves

Death of the Second Man-Eater

It must not be imagined that with the death of this lion our troubles at Tsavo were at an end; his companion was still at large, and very soon began to make us unpleasantly aware of the fact. Only a few nights elapsed before he made an attempt to get at the Permanent Way Inspector, climbing up the steps of his bungalow and prowling round the verandah. The Inspector, hearing the noise and thinking it was a drunken coolie, shouted angrily "Go away!" but, fortunately for him, did not attempt to come out or to open the door. Thus disappointed in his attempt to obtain a meal of human flesh, the lion seized a couple of the Inspector's goats and devoured them there and then.

On hearing of this occurrence, I determined to sit up the next night near the Inspector's bungalow. Fortunately there was a vacant iron shanty close at hand, with a convenient loophole in it for firing from; and outside this I placed three full-grown goats as bait, tying them to a half-length of rail, weighing about 250 lbs. The night passed uneventfully until just before daybreak, when at last the lion turned up, pounced on one of the goats and made off with it, at the same time dragging away the others, rail and all. I fired several shots in his direction, but it was pitch dark and quite impossible to see anything, so I only succeeded in hitting one of the goats. I often longed for a flash-light on such occasions.

Next morning I started off in pursuit and was joined by some others from the camp. I found that the trail of the goats and rail was easily followed, and we soon came up, about a quarter of a mile away, to where the lion was still busy at his meal. He was concealed in some thick bush and growled angrily on hearing our approach; finally, as we got closer, he suddenly made a charge, rushing through the bushes at a great pace. In an instant, every man of the party scrambled hastily up the nearest tree, with the exception of one of my assistants, Mr. Winkler, who stood steadily by me throughout. The brute, however, did not press his charge home: and on throwing stones into the bushes where we had last seen him, we guessed by the silence that he had slunk off. We therefore advanced cautiously, and on getting up to the place discovered that he had indeed escaped us, leaving two of the goats scarcely touched.

Thinking that in all probability the lion would return as usual to finish his meal, I had a very strong scaffolding put up a few feet away from the dead goats, and took up my position on it before dark. On this occasion I brought my gun-bearer, Mahina, to take a turn at watching, as I was by this time worn out for want of sleep, having spent so many nights on the look-out. I was just dozing off comfortably when suddenly I felt my arm seized, and on looking up saw Mahina pointing in the direction of the goats. "Sher!" ("Lion!") was all he whispered. I grasped my double smooth-bore, which I had charged with slug, and waited patiently. In a few moments I was rewarded, for as I watched the spot where I expected the lion to appear, there was a rustling among the bushes and I saw him stealthily emerge into the open and pass almost directly beneath us. I fired both barrels practically together into his shoulder, and to my joy could see him go down under the force of the blow. Quickly I reached for the magazine rifle, but before I could use it, he was out of sight among the bushes, and I had to fire after him quite at random. Nevertheless I was confident of getting him in the morning, and accordingly set out as soon as it was light. For over a mile there was no difficulty in following the blood-trail, and as he had rested several times I felt sure that he had been badly wounded. In the end, however, my hunt proved fruitless, for after a time the traces of blood ceased and the surface of the ground became rocky, so that I was no longer able to follow the spoor.

About this time Sir Guilford Molesworth, K.C.I.E., late Consulting Engineer to the Government of India for State Railways, passed through Tsavo on a tour of inspection on behalf of the Foreign Office. After examining the bridge and other works and expressing his satisfaction, he took a number of photographs, one or two of which he has kindly allowed me to reproduce in this book. He thoroughly sympathised with us in all the trials we had endured from the man-eaters, and was delighted that one at least was dead. When he asked me if I expected to get the second lion soon, I well remember his half-doubting smile as I rather too confidently asserted that I hoped to bag him also in the course of a few days.

As it happened, there was no sign of our enemy for about ten days after this, and we began to hope that he had died of his wounds in the bush.

All the same we still took every precaution at night, and it was fortunate that we did so, as otherwise at least one more victim would have been added to the list. For on the night of December 27, I was suddenly aroused by terrified shouts from my trolley men, who slept in a tree close outside my boma, to the effect that a lion was trying to get at them. It would have been madness to have gone out, as the moon was hidden by dense clouds and it was absolutely impossible to see anything more than a yard in front of one; so all I could do was to fire off a few rounds just to frighten the brute away. This apparently had the desired effect, for the men were not further molested that night; but the man-eater had evidently prowled about for some time, for we found in the morning that he had gone right into every one of their tents, and round the tree was a regular ring of his footmarks.

The following evening I took up my position in this same tree, in the hope that he would make another attempt. The night began badly, as, while climbing up to my perch, I very nearly put my hand on a venomous snake which was lying coiled round one of the branches. As may be imagined, I came down again very quickly, but one of my men managed to despatch it with a long pole. Fortunately the night was clear and cloudless, and the moon made every thing almost as bright as day. I kept watch until about 2 a.m., when I roused Mahina to take his turn.

For about an hour I slept peacefully with my back to the tree, and then woke suddenly with an uncanny feeling that something was wrong. Mahina, however, was on the alert, and had seen nothing; and although I looked carefully round us on all sides, I too could discover nothing unusual.

Only half satisfied, I was about to lie back again, when I fancied I saw something move a little way off among the low bushes. On gazing intently at the spot for a few seconds, I found I was not mistaken. It was the man-eater, cautiously stalking us.

The ground was fairly open round our tree, with only a small bush every here and there; and from our position it was a most fascinating sight to watch this great brute stealing stealthily round us, taking advantage of every bit of cover as he came. His skill showed that he was an old hand at the terrible game of man-hunting: so I determined to run no undue risk of losing him this time. I accordingly waited until he got quite close—about twenty yards away—and then fired my .303 at his chest. I heard the bullet strike him, but unfortunately it had no knockdown effect, for with a fierce growl he turned and made off with great long bounds. Before he disappeared from sight, however, I managed to have three more shots at him from the magazine rifle, and another growl told me that the last of these had also taken effect.

We awaited daylight with impatience, and at the first glimmer of dawn we set out to hunt him down. I took a native tracker with me, so that I was free to keep a good look-out, while Mahina followed immediately behind with a Martini carbine. Splashes of blood being plentiful, we were able to get along quickly; and we had not proceeded more than a quarter of a mile through the jungle when suddenly a fierce warning growl was heard right in front of us. Looking cautiously through the bushes, I could see the man-eater glaring out in our direction, and showing his tusks in an angry snarl. I at once took careful aim and fired. Instantly he sprang out and made a most determined charge down on us. I fired again and knocked him over; but in a second he was up once more and coming for me as fast as he could in his crippled condition. A third shot had no apparent effect, so I put out my hand for the Martini, hoping to stop him with it. To my dismay, however, it was not there. The terror of the sudden charge had proved too much for Mahina, and both he and the carbine were by this time well on their way up a tree. In the circumstances there was nothing to do but follow suit, which I did without loss of time: and but for the fact that one of my shots had broken a hind leg, the brute would most certainly have had me. Even as it was, I had barely time to swing myself up out of his reach before he arrived at the foot of the tree.

When the lion found he was too late, he started to limp back to the thicket; but by this time I had seized the carbine from Mahina, and the first shot I fired from it seemed to give him his quietus, for he fell over and lay motionless. Rather foolishly, I at once scrambled down from the tree and walked up towards him. To my surprise and no little alarm he jumped up and attempted another charge. This time, however, a Martini bullet in the chest and another in the head finished him for good and all; he dropped in his tracks not five yards away from me, and died gamely, biting savagely at a branch which had fallen to the ground.

By this time all the workmen in camp, attracted by the sound of the firing, had arrived on the scene, and so great was their resentment against the brute who had killed such numbers of their comrades that it was only with the greatest difficulty that I could restrain them from tearing the dead body to pieces. Eventually, amid the wild rejoicings of the natives and coolies, I had the lion carried to my boma, which was close at hand. On examination we found no less than six bullet holes in the body, and embedded only a little way in the flesh of the back was the slug which I had fired into him from the scaffolding about ten days previously. He measured nine feet six inches from tip of nose to tip of tail, and stood three feet eleven and a half inches high; but, as in the case of his companion, the skin was disfigured by being deeply scored all over by the boma thorns.

The news of the death of the second "devil" soon spread far and wide over the country, and natives actually travelled from up and down the line to have a look at my trophies and at the "devil-killer," as they called me. Best of all, the coolies who had absconded came flocking back to Tsavo, and much to my relief work was resumed and we were never again troubled by man-eaters. It was amusing, indeed, to notice the change which took place in the attitude of the workmen towards me after I had killed the two lions. Instead of wishing to murder me, as they once did, they could not now do enough for me, and as a token of their gratitude they presented me with a beautiful silver bowl, as well as with a long poem written in Hindustani describing all our trials and my ultimate victory. As the poem relates our troubles in somewhat quaint and biblical language, I have given a translation of it in the appendix. The bowl I shall always consider my most highly prized and hardest won trophy. The inscription on it reads as follows:—

SIR,—We, your Overseer, Timekeepers, Mistaris and Workmen, present you with this bowl as a token of our gratitude to you for your bravery in killing two man-eating lions at great risk to your own life, thereby saving us from the fate of being devoured by these terrible monsters who nightly broke into our tents and took our fellow-workers from our side. In presenting you with this bowl, we all add our prayers for your long life, happiness and prosperity. We shall ever remain, Sir, Your grateful servants, Baboo PURSHOTAM HURJEE PURMAR, Overseer and Clerk of Works, on behalf of your Workmen.

Dated at Tsavo, January 30, 1899.

Before I leave the subject of "the man-eaters of Tsavo," it may be of interest to mention that these two lions possess the distinction, probably unique among wild animals, of having been specifically referred to in the House of Lords by the Prime Minister of the day.

Speaking of the difficulties which had been encountered in the construction of the Uganda Railway, the late Lord Salisbury said:—

"The whole of the works were put a stop to for three weeks because a party of man-eating lions appeared in the locality and conceived a most unfortunate taste for our porters. At last the labourers entirely declined to go on unless they were guarded by an iron entrenchment. Of course it is difficult to work a railway under these conditions, and until we found an enthusiastic sportsman to get rid of these lions, our enterprise was seriously hindered."

Also, *The Spectator* of March 3, 1900, had an article entitled "The Lions That Stopped the Railway," from which the following extracts are taken:—

"The parallel to the story of the lions which stopped the rebuilding of Samaria must occur to everyone, and if the Samaritans had quarter as good cause for their fears as had the railway coolies, their wish to propitiate the local deities is easily understood. If the whole body of lion anecdote, from the days of the Assyrian Kings till the last year of the nineteenth century, were collated and brought together, it would not equal in tragedy or atrocity, in savageness or in sheer insolent contempt for man, armed or unarmed, white or black, the story of these two beasts.

"To what a distance the whole story carries us back, and how impossible it becomes to account for the survival of primitive man against this kind of foe! For fire—which has hitherto been regarded as his main safeguard against the carnivora—these cared nothing. It is curious that the Tsavo lions were not killed by poison, for strychnine is easily used, and with effect. (I may mention that poison was tried, but without effect. The poisoned carcases of transport animals which had died from the bite of the tsetse fly were placed in likely spots, but the wily man-eaters would not touch them, and much preferred live men to dead donkeys.) Poison may have been used early in the history of man, for its powers are employed with strange skill by the men in the tropical forest, both in America and West Central Africa. But there is no evidence that the old inhabitants of Europe, or of Assyria or Asia Minor, ever killed lions or wolves by this means. They looked to the King or chief, or some champion, to kill these monsters for them. It was not the sport but the duty of Kings, and was in itself a title to be a ruler of men. Theseus, who cleared the roads of beasts and robbers; Hercules, the lion killer; St. George, the dragon-slayer, and all the rest of their class owed

to this their everlasting fame. From the story of the Tsavo River we can appreciate their services to man even at this distance of time. When the jungle twinkled with hundreds of lamps, as the shout went on from camp to camp that the first lion was dead, as the hurrying crowds fell prostrate in the midnight forest, laying their heads on his feet, and the Africans danced savage and ceremonial dances of thanksgiving, Mr. Patterson must have realised in no common way what it was to have been a hero and deliverer in the days when man was not yet undisputed lord of the creation, and might pass at any moment under the savage dominion of the beasts."

Well had the two man-eaters earned all this fame; they had devoured between them no less than twenty-eight Indian coolies, in addition to scores of unfortunate African natives of whom no official record was kept.

Chapter 8

An Adventure with a Dog and a Glacier

John Muir

Depending on good luck to make your escape from a deadly wilderness trap isn't a likely choice for survival. But that is exactly what happened to John Muir, one of America's most distinguished naturalist authors. Muir (1838–1914) wrote engaging accounts of his travels among the mountain peaks of the American West and Alaska. This tale is typical Muir and is from his 1915 Travels in Alaska.

In the summer of 1880 I set out from Fort Wrangel in a canoe, with the Rev. S. H. Young, my former companion, and a crew of Indians, to continue the exploration of the icy region of southeastern Alaska, begun in the fall of 1879. After the necessary provisions, blankets, etc., had been collected and stowed away, and the Indians were in their places ready to dip their paddles, while a crowd of their friends were looking down from the wharf to bid them good-by and good luck, Mr. Young, for whom we were waiting, at length came aboard, followed by a little black dog that immediately made himself at home by curling up in a hollow among the baggage. I like dogs, but this one seemed so small, dull, and worthless that I objected to his going, and asked the missionary why he was taking him. "Such a helpless wisp of hair will only be in the way," I said; "you had better pass him up to one of the Indian boys on the wharf, to be taken home to play with the children. This trip is not likely to be a good one for toy dogs. He will be rained on and snowed on for weeks, and will require care like a baby." But the missionary assured me that he would be no trouble at all; that he was a perfect wonder of a dog—could endure cold and hunger like a polar bear, could swim like a seal, and was wondrous wise, etc., making out a list of virtues likely to make him the most interesting of the company.

Nobody could hope to unravel the lines of his ancestry. He was short-legged, bunchy-bodied, and almost featureless—something like a muskrat. Though smooth, his hair was long and silky, so that when the wind was at his back it ruffled, making him look shaggy. At first sight his only noticeable feature was his showy tail, which was about as shady and airy as a squirrel's, and was carried curling forward nearly to his ears. On closer inspection you might see his thin, sensitive ears and his keen dark eye with cunning tan spots. Mr. Young told me that when the dog was about the size of a wood-rat he was presented to his wife by an Irish prospector at Sitka, and that when he arrived at Fort Wrangel he was adopted by the Stickeen Indians as a sort of new good-luck totem, and named "Stickeen" for the tribe, with whom he became a favorite. On our trip he soon proved himself a queer character—odd, concealed, independent, keeping invincibly quiet, and doing many inexplicable things that piqued my curiosity. Sailing week after week through the long, intricate channels and inlets among the innumerable islands and mountains of the coast, he spent the dull days in sluggish ease, motionless, and apparently as unobserving as a hibernating marmot. But I discovered that somehow he always knew what was going forward. When the Indians were about to shoot at ducks or seals, or when anything interesting was to be seen along the shore, he would rest his chin on the edge of the canoe and calmly look out. When he heard us talking about making a landing, he roused himself to see what sort of place we were coming to, and made ready to jump overboard and swim ashore as soon as the canoe neared the beach. Then, with a vigorous shake to get rid of the brine in his hair, he went into the woods to hunt small game. But though always the first out of the canoe, he was always the last to get into it. When we were ready to start he could never be found, and refused to come to our call. We soon found out, however, that though we could not see him at such times, he saw us, and from the cover of the briers and huckleberry-bushes in the fringe of the woods was watching the canoe with wary eye. For as soon as we were fairly off, he came trotting down the beach, plunged into the surf, and swam after us, knowing well that we would cease rowing and take him in. When the contrary little vagabond came alongside, he was lifted by the neck, held at arm's length a moment to drip, and dropped aboard. We tried to cure him of this trick by compelling him to swim farther before stopping for him; but this did no good: the longer the swim, the better he seemed to like it.

Though capable of most spacious idleness, he was always ready for excursions or adventures of any sort. When the Indians went into the woods for a deer, Stickeen was sure to be at their heels, provided I had not yet left camp. For though I never carried a gun, he always followed me, forsaking the hunting Indians, and even his master, to share my wanderings. The days that were too stormy for sailing I spent in the woods, or on the mountains or glaciers, wherever I chanced to be; and Stickeen always insisted on following me, gliding through the dripping huckleberry-bushes and prickly *Panax* and *Rubus* tangles like a fox, scarce stirring their close-set branches, wading and wallowing through snow, swimming ice-cold streams, jumping logs and rocks and the crusty hummocks and crevasses of glaciers with the patience and endurance of a determined mountaineer, never tiring or getting discouraged. Once he followed me over a glacier the surface of which was so rough that it cut his feet until every step was marked with blood; but he trotted on with Indian fortitude until I noticed his pain and, taking pity on him, made him a set of moccasins out of a handkerchief. But he never asked help or made any complaint, as if, like a philosopher, he had learned that without hard work and suffering there could be no pleasure worth having.

Yet nobody knew what Stickeen was good for. He seemed to meet danger and hardships without reason, insisted on having his own way, never obeyed an order, and the hunters could never set him on anything against his will, or make him fetch anything that was shot. I tried hard to make his acquaintance, guessing there must be something in him; but he was as cold as a glacier, and about as invulnerable to fun, though his master assured me that he played at home, and in some measure conformed to the usages of civilization. His equanimity was so immovable it seemed due to unfeeling ignorance. Let the weather blow and roar, he was as tranquil as a stone; and no matter what advances you made, scarce a glance or a tail-wag would you get for your pains. No superannuated mastiff or bulldog grown old in office surpassed this soft midget in stoic dignity. He sometimes reminded me of those plump, squat, unshakable cacti of the Arizona deserts that give no sign of feeling. A true child of the wilderness, holding the even tenor of his hidden life with the silence and serenity of nature, he never displayed a trace of the elfish vivacity and fun of the terriers and collies that we all know, nor of their touching affection and devotion. Like children, most small dogs beg to be loved and allowed to love, but Stickeen seemed a very Diogenes, asking only to be let alone. He seemed neither old nor young. His strength lay in his eyes. They looked as old as the hills, and as young and as wild. I never tired looking into them. It was like looking into a landscape; but they were small and rather deep-set, and had no explaining puckers around them to give out particulars. I was accustomed to look into the faces of plants and animals, and I watched the little sphinx more and more keenly as an interesting study. But there is no estimating the wit and wisdom concealed and latent in our lower fellow-mortals until made manifest by profound experiences; for it is by suffering that dogs as well as saints are developed and made perfect.

After we had explored the glaciers of the Sumdum and Tahkoo inlets, we sailed through Stephen's Passage into Lynn Canal, and thence through Icy Strait into Cross Sound, looking for unexplored inlets leading toward the ice-fountains of the Fairweather Range. While the tide was in our favor in Cross Sound we were accompanied by a fleet of icebergs drifting out to the ocean from Glacier Bay. Slowly we crawled around Vancouver's Point, Wimbleton, our frail canoe tossed like a feather on the massive swells coming in past Cape Spenser. For miles the Sound is bounded by precipitous cliffs which looked terribly stern in gloomy weather. Had our canoe been crushed or upset, we could have gained no landing here; for the cliffs, as high as those of Yosemite, sink perfectly sheer into deep water. Eagerly we scanned the immense wall on the north side for the first sign of an opening, all of us anxious except Stickeen, who dozed in peace or gazed dreamily at the tremendous precipices when he heard us talking about them. At length we discovered the entrance of what is now called Taylor Bay, and about five o'clock reached the head of it, and encamped near the front of a large glacier which extends as an abrupt barrier all the way across from wall to wall of the inlet, a distance of three or four miles.

On first observation the glacier presented some unusual features, and that night I planned a grand excursion for the morrow. I awoke early, called not only by the glacier, but also by a storm. Rain, mixed with trailing films of scud and the ragged, drawn-out nether surfaces of gray clouds, filled the inlet, and was sweeping forward in a thick, passionate, horizontal flood, as if it were all passing over the country instead of falling on it. Everything was streaming with life and motion—woods, rocks, waters, and the sky. The main perennial streams were booming, and hundreds of new ones, born of the rain, were descending in gray and white cascades on each side of the inlet, fairly streaking their rocky slopes, and roaring like the sea. I had intended making a cup of coffee before starting, but when I heard the storm I made haste to join it; for in storms nature has always something extra fine to show us, and if we have wit to keep in right relations with them the danger is no more than in home-keeping, and we can go with them rejoicing, sharing their enthusiasm, and chanting with the old Norsemen, "The blast of the tempest aids our oars; the hurricane is our servant, and drives us whither we wish to go." So I took my ice-ax, buttoned my coat, put a piece of bread in my pocket, and set out. Mr. Young and the Indians were asleep, and so, I hoped, was Stickeen; but I had not gone a dozen rods before he left his warm bed in the tent, and came boring through the blast after me. That a man should welcome storms for their exhilarating music and motion, and go forth to see God making landscapes, is reasonable enough; but what fascination could there be in dismal weather for this poor, feeble wisp of a dog, so pathetically small? Anyhow, on he came, breakfastless, through the choking blast. I stopped, turned my back to the wind, and gave him a good, dissuasive talk. "Now don't," I said, shouting to make myself heard in the storm—"now don't, Stickeen. What has got into your queer noddle now? You must be daft. This wild day has nothing for you. Go back to camp and keep warm. There is no game abroad—nothing but weather. Not a foot or wing is stirring. Wait and get a good breakfast with your master, and be sensible for once. I can't feed you or carry you, and this storm will kill you." But nature, it seems, was at the bottom of the affair; and she gains her ends with dogs as well as with men, making us do as she likes, driving us on her ways, however rough. So after ordering him back again and again to ease my conscience, I saw that he was not to be shaken off; as well might the earth try to shake off the moon. I had once led his master into trouble, when he fell on one of the topmost jags of a mountain, and dislocated his arms. Now the turn of his humble companion was coming. The dog just stood there in the wind, drenched and blinking, saying doggedly, "Where thou goest I will go." So I told him to come on, if he must, and gave him a piece of the bread I had put in my pocket for breakfast. Then we pushed on in company, and thus began the most memorable of all my wild days.

The level flood, driving straight in our faces, thrashed and washed us wildly until we got into the shelter of the trees and ice-cliffs on the east side of the glacier, where we rested and listened and looked on in comfort. The exploration of the glacier was my main object, but the wind was too high to allow excursions over its open surface, where one might be dangerously shoved while balancing for a jump on the brink of a crevasse. In the meantime the storm was a fine study. Here the end of the glacier, descending over an abrupt swell of resisting rock about five hundred feet high, leans forward and falls in majestic ice-cascades. And as the storm came down the glacier from the north, Stickeen and I were beneath the main current of the blast, while favorably located to see and hear it. A broad torrent, draining the side of the glacier, now swollen by scores of new streams from the mountains, was rolling boulders along its rocky channel between the glacier and the woods with thudding, bumping, muffled sounds, rushing toward the bay with tremendous energy, as if in haste to get out of the mountains, the waters above and beneath calling to each other, and all to the ocean, their home. Looking southward from our shelter, we had this great torrent on our left, with mossy woods on the mountain slope above it, the glacier on our right, the wild, cascading portion of it forming a multitude of towers, spires, and flat-topped battlements seen through the trees, and smooth gray gloom ahead. I tried to draw the marvelous scene in my note-book, but the rain fell on my page in spite of all that I could do to shelter it, and the sketch seemed miserably defective.

When the wind began to abate I traced the east side of the glacier. All the trees standing on the edge of the woods were barked and bruised, showing high ice-mark in a very telling way, while tens of thousands of those that had stood for centuries on the bank of the glacier farther out lay crushed and being crushed. In many places I could see, down fifty feet or so beneath, the margin of the glacier mill, where trunks from one to two feet in diameter were being ground to pulp against outstanding rock-ribs and bosses of the bank. About three miles above the front of the glacier, I climbed to the surface of it by means of ax-steps, made easy for Stickeen; and as far as the eye could reach, the level, or nearly level, glacier stretched away indefinitely beneath the gray sky, a seemingly boundless prairie of ice. The rain continued, which I did not mind; but a tendency to fogginess in the drooping clouds made me hesitate about venturing far from land. No trace of the west shore was visible, and in case the misty clouds should settle, or the wind again become violent, I feared getting caught in a tangle of crevasses. Lingering undecided, watching the weather, I sauntered about on the crystal sea. For a mile or two out I found the ice remarkably safe. The marginal crevasses were mostly narrow, while the few wider ones were easily avoided by passing around them, and the clouds began to open here and there. Thus encouraged, I at last pushed out for the other side; for nature can make us do anything she likes, luring us along appointed ways for the fulfillment of her plans. At first we made rapid progress, and the sky was not very threatening, while I took bearings occasionally with a pocket-compass, to enable me to retrace my way more surely in case the storm should become blinding; but the structure-lines of the ice were my main guide. Toward the west side we came to a closely crevassed section, in which we had to make long, narrow tacks and doublings, tracing the edges of tremendous longitudinal crevasses, many of which were from twenty to thirty feet wide, and perhaps a thousand feet deep, beautiful and awful. In working a way through them I was severely cautious, but Stickeen came on as unhesitatingly as the flying clouds. Any crevasse that I could jump he would leap without so much as halting to examine it. The weather was bright and dark, with quick flashes of summer and winter close together. When the clouds opened and the sun shone, the glacier was seen from shore to shore, with a bright array of encompassing mountains partly revealed, wearing the clouds as garments, black in the middle, burning on the edges, and the whole icy prairie seemed to burst into a bloom of iris colors from myriads of crystals. Then suddenly all the glorious show would be again smothered in gloom. But Stickeen seemed to care for none of these things, bright or dark, nor for the beautiful wells filled to the brim with water so pure that it was nearly invisible, the rumbling, grinding moulins, or the quick-flashing, glinting, swirling streams in frictionless channels of living ice. Nothing seemed novel to him. He showed neither caution nor curiosity. His courage was so unwavering that it seemed due to dullness of perception, as if he were only blindly bold; and I warned him that he might slip or fall short. His bunchy body seemed all one skipping muscle, and his peg legs appeared to be jointed only at the top.

We gained the west shore in about three hours, the width of the glacier here being about seven miles. Then I pushed northward, in order to see as far back as possible into the fountains of the Fairweather Mountains, in case the clouds should rise. The walking was easy along the margin of the forest, which, of course, like that on the other side, had been invaded and crushed by the swollen glacier. In an hour we rounded a massive headland and came suddenly on another outlet of the glacier, which, in the form of a wild ice-cascade, was pouring over the rim of the main basin toward the ocean with the volume of a thousand Niagaras. The surface was broken into a multitude of sharp blades and pinnacles leaning forward, something like the updashing waves of a flood of water descending a rugged channel. But these ice-waves were many times higher than those of river cataracts, and to all appearance motionless. It was a dazzling white torrent two miles wide, flowing between high banks black with trees. Tracing its left bank three or four miles, I found that it discharged into a fresh-water lake, filling it with icebergs.

I would gladly have followed the outlet, but the day was waning, and we had to make haste on the return trip to get off the ice before dark. When we were about two miles from the west shore the clouds dropped misty fringes, and snow soon began to fly. Then I began to feel anxiety as to finding a way in the storm through the intricate net-work of crevasses which we had entered. Stickeen showed no fear. He was still the same silent, sufficient, uncomplaining Indian philosopher. When the storm-darkness fell he kept close behind me. The snow warned us to make haste, but at the same time hid our way. At rare intervals the clouds thinned, and mountains, looming in the gloom, frowned and quickly vanished. I pushed on as best I could, jumping innumerable crevasses, and for every hundred rods or so of direct advance traveling a mile in doubling up and down in the turmoil of chasms and dislocated masses of ice. After an hour or two of this work we came to a series of longitudinal crevasses of appalling width, like immense furrows. These I traced with firm nerve, excited and strengthened by the danger, making wide jumps, poising cautiously on the dizzy edges after cutting hollows for my feet before making the spring, to avoid slipping or any uncertainty on the farther sides, where only one trial is granted—exercise at once frightful and inspiring. Stickeen flirted across every gap I jumped, seemingly without effort. Many a mile we thus traveled, mostly up and down, making but little real headway in crossing, most of the time running instead of walking, as the danger of spending the night on the glacier became threatening. No doubt we could have weathered the storm for one night, and I faced the chance of being compelled to do so; but we were hungry and wet, and the north wind was thick with snow and bitterly cold, and of course that night would have seemed a long one. Stickeen gave me no concern. He was still the wonderful, inscrutable philosopher, ready for anything. I could not see far enough to judge in which direction the best route lay, and had simply to grope my way in the snow-choked air and ice. Again and again I was put to my mettle, but Stickeen followed easily, his nerves growing more unflinching as the dangers thickened; so it always is with mountaineers.

At length our way was barred by a very wide and straight crevasse, which I traced rapidly northward a mile or so without finding a crossing or hope of one, then southward down the glacier about as far, to where it united with another crevasse. In all this distance of perhaps two miles there was only one place where I could possibly jump it; but the width of this jump was nearly the utmost I dared attempt, while the danger of slipping on the farther side was so great that I was loath to try it. Furthermore, the side I was on was about a foot higher than the other, and even with this advantage it seemed dangerously wide. One is liable to underestimate the width of crevasses where the magnitudes in general are great. I therefore measured this one again and again, until satisfied that I could jump it if necessary, but that in case I should be compelled to jump back to the higher side, I might fail. Now a cautious mountaineer seldom takes a step on unknown ground which seems at all dangerous, that he cannot retrace in case he should be stopped by unseen obstacles ahead. This is the rule of mountaineers who live long; and though in haste, I compelled myself to sit down and deliberate before I broke it. Retracing my devious path in imagination, as if it were drawn on a chart, I saw that I was recrossing the glacier a mile or two farther up-stream, and was entangled in a section I had not before seen. Should I risk this dangerous jump, or try to regain the woods on the west shore, make a fire, and have only hunger to endure while waiting for a new day? I had already crossed so broad a tangle of dangerous ice that I saw it would be difficult to get back to the woods through the storm; while the ice just beyond the present barrier seemed more promising, and the east shore was now perhaps about as near as the west. I was therefore eager to go on; but this wide jump was a tremendous obstacle. At length, because of the dangers already behind me, I determined to venture against those that might be ahead, jumped, and landed well, but with so little to spare that I more than ever dreaded being compelled to take that jump back from the lower side. Stickeen followed, making nothing of it. But within a distance of a few hundred yards we were stopped again by the widest crevasse yet encountered. Of course I made haste to explore it, hoping all might yet be well. About three fourths of a mile up-stream it united with the one we had just crossed, as I feared it would. Then, tracing it down, I found it joined the other great crevasse at the lower end, maintaining a width of forty to fifty feet. We were on an island about two miles long and from one hundred to three hundred yards wide, with two barely possible ways of escape—one by the way we came, the other by an almost inaccessible sliver-bridge that crossed the larger crevasse from near the middle of the island. After tracing the brink, I ran back to the sliver-bridge and cautiously studied it. Crevasses caused by strains from variations of the rate of motion of different parts of the glacier and by convexities in the channel are mere cracks when they first open,—so narrow as hardly to admit the blade of a pocket-knife,—and widen gradually, according to the extent of the strain. Now some of these cracks are interrupted like the cracks in wood, and, in opening, the strip of ice between overlapping ends is dragged out; and if the flow of the glacier there is such that no strain is made on the sliver, it maintains a continuous connection between the sides, just as the two sides of a slivered crack in wood that is being split are connected. Some crevasses remain open for years, and by the melting of their sides continue to increase in width long after the opening strain has ceased, while the sliver-bridges, level on top at first, and perfectly safe, are at length melted to thin, knife-edged blades, the upper portion being most exposed to the weather; and since the exposure is greatest in the middle, they at length curve downward like the cables of suspension-bridges. This one was evidently very old, for it had been wasted until it was the worst bridge I ever saw. The width of the crevasse was here about fifty feet, and the sliver, crossing diagonally, was about seventy feet long, was depressed twenty-five or thirty feet in the middle, and the up-curving ends were attached to the sides eight or ten feet below the surface of the glacier. Getting down the nearly vertical wall to the end of it and up the other side were the main difficulties, and they seemed all but insurmountable. Of the many perils encountered in my years of wandering in mountain altitudes, none seemed so plain and stern and merciless as this. And it was presented when we were wet to the skin and hungry, the sky was dark with snow, and the night near, and we had to fear the snow in our eyes and the disturbing action of the wind in any movement we might make. But we were forced to face it. It was a tremendous necessity.

Beginning not immediately above the sunken end of the bridge, but a little to one side, I cut nice hollows on the brink for my knees to rest in; then, leaning over, with my short-handled ax cut a step sixteen or eighteen inches below, which, on account of the sheerness of the wall, was shallow. That step, however, was well made; its floor sloped slightly inward, and formed a good hold for my heels. Then, slipping cautiously upon it, and crouching as low as possible, with my left side twisted toward the wall, I steadied myself with my left hand in a slight notch, while with the right I cut other steps and notches in succession, guarding against glinting of the ax, for life or death was in every stroke, and in the niceness of finish of every foothold. After the end of the bridge was reached, it was a delicate thing to poise on a little platform which I had chipped on its up-curving end, and, bending over the slippery surface, get astride of it. Crossing was easy, cutting off the sharp edge with careful strokes, and hitching forward a few inches at a time, keeping my balance with my knees pressed against its sides. The tremendous abyss on each side I studiously ignored. The surface of that blue sliver was then all the world. But the most trying part of the adventure was, after working my way across inch by inch, to rise from the safe position astride that slippery strip of ice, and to cut a ladder in the face of the wall—chipping, climbing, holding on with feet and fingers in mere notches. At such times one's whole body is eye, and common skill and fortitude are replaced by power beyond our call or knowledge. Never before had I been so long under deadly strain. How I got up the cliff at the end of the bridge I never could tell. The thing seemed to have been done by somebody else. I never have had contempt of death, though in the course of my explorations I oftentimes felt that to meet one's fate on a mountain, in a grand cañon, or in the heart of a crystal glacier would be blessed as compared with death from disease, a mean accident in a street, or from a sniff of sewer-gas. But the sweetest, cleanest death, set thus calmly and glaringly clear before us, is hard enough to face, even though we feel gratefully sure that we have already had happiness enough for a dozen lives.

But poor Stickeen, the wee, silky, sleekit beastie—think of him! When I had decided to try the bridge, and while I was on my knees cutting away the rounded brow, he came behind me, pushed his head past my shoulder, looked down and across, scanned the sliver and its approaches with his queer eyes, then looked me in the face with a startled air of surprise and concern, and began to mutter and whine, saying as plainly as if speaking with words, "Surely you are not going to try that awful place?" This was the first time I had seen him gaze deliberately into a crevasse or into my face with a speaking look. That he should have recognized and appreciated the danger at the first glance showed wonderful sagacity. Never before had the quick, daring midget seemed to know that ice was slippery, or that there was such a thing as danger anywhere. His looks and the tones of his voice when he began to complain and speak his fears were so human that I unconsciously talked to him as I would to a boy, and in trying to calm his fears perhaps in some measure moderated my own. "Hush your fears, my boy," I said; "we will get across safe, though it is not going to be easy. No right way is easy in this rough world. We must risk our lives to save them. At the worst we can only slip; and then how grand a grave we shall have! And by and by our nice bones will do good in the terminal moraine." But my sermon was far from reassuring him; he began to cry, and after taking another piercing look at the tremendous gulf, ran away in desperate excitement, seeking some other crossing. By the time he got back, baffled, of course, I had made a step or two. I dared not look back, but he made himself heard; and when he saw that I was certainly crossing, he cried aloud in despair. The danger was enough to daunt anybody, but it seems wonderful that he should have been able to weigh and appreciate it so justly. No mountaineer could have seen it more quickly or judged it more wisely, discriminating between real and apparent peril.

After I had gained the other side he howled louder than ever, and after running back and forth in vain search for a way of escape, he would return to the brink of the crevasse above the bridge, moaning and groaning as if in the bitterness of death. Could this be the silent, philosophic Stickeen? I shouted encouragement, telling him the bridge was not so bad as it looked, that I had left it flat for his feet, and he could walk it easily. But he was afraid to try it. Strange that so small an animal should be capable of such big, wise fears! I called again and again in a reassuring tone to come on and fear nothing; that he could come if he would only try. Then he would hush for a moment, look again at the bridge, and shout his unshakable conviction that he could never, never come that way; then lie back in despair, as if howling: "Oh-o-o, what a place! No-o-o; I can never go-o-o down there!" His natural composure and courage had vanished utterly in a tumultuous storm of fear.

Had the danger been less, his distress would have seemed ridiculous. But in this gulf—a huge, yawning sepulcher big enough to hold everybody in the territory—lay the shadow of death, and his heartrending cries might well have called Heaven to his help. Perhaps they did. So hidden before, he was transparent now, and one could see the workings of his mind like the movements of a clock out of its case. His voice and gestures were perfectly human, and his hopes and fears unmistakable, while he seemed to understand every word of mine. I was troubled at the thought of leaving him. It seemed impossible to get him to venture. To compel him to try by fear of being left, I started off as if leaving him to his fate, and disappeared back of a hummock; but this did no good, for he only lay down and cried. So after hiding a few minutes, I went back to the brink of the crevasse, and in a severe tone of voice shouted across to him that now I must certainly leave him—I could wait no longer; and that if he would not come, all I could promise was that I would return to seek him next day. I warned him that if he went back to the woods the wolves would kill him, and finished by urging him once more by words and gestures to come on. He knew very well what I meant, and at last, with the courage of despair, hushed and breathless, he lay down on the brink in the hollow I had made for my knees, pressed his body against the ice to get the advantage of the friction, gazed into the first step, put his little feet together, and slid them slowly down into it, bunching all four in it, and almost standing on his head. Then, without lifting them, as well as I could see through the snow, he slowly worked them over the edge of the step, and down into the next and the next in succession in the same way, and gained the bridge. Then lifting his feet with the regularity and slowness of the vibrations of a seconds' pendulum, as if counting and measuring one, two, three, holding himself in dainty poise, and giving separate attention to each little step, he gained the foot of the cliff, at the top of which I was kneeling to give him a lift should he get within reach. Here he halted in dead silence, and it was here I feared he might fail, for dogs are poor climbers. I had no cord. If I had had one, I would have dropped a noose over his head and hauled him up. But while I was thinking whether an available cord might be made out of clothing, he was looking keenly into the series of notched steps and finger-holds of the ice-ladder I had made, as if counting them and fixing the position of each one in his mind. Then suddenly up he came, with a nervy, springy rush, hooking his paws into the notches and steps so quickly that I could not see how it was done, and whizzed past my head, safe at last!

And now came a scene! "Well done, well done, little boy! Brave boy!" I cried, trying to catch and caress him; but he would not be caught. Never before or since have I seen anything like so passionate a revulsion from the depths of despair to uncontrollable, exultant, triumphant joy. He flashed and darted hither and thither as if fairly demented, screaming and shouting, swirling round and round in giddy loops and circles like a leaf in a whirlwind, lying down and rolling over and over, sidewise and heels over head, pouring forth a tumultuous flood of hysterical cries and sobs and gasping mutterings. And when I ran up to him to shake him, fearing he might die of joy, he flashed off two or three hundred yards, his feet in a mist of motion; then, turning suddenly, he came back in wild rushes, and launched himself at my face, almost knocking me down, all the time screeching and screaming and shouting as if saying, "Saved! saved! saved!" Then away again, dropping suddenly at times with his feet in the air, trembling, and fairly sobbing. Such passionate emotion was enough to kill him. Moses' stately song of triumph after escaping the Egyptians and the Red Sea was nothing to it. Who could have guessed the capacity of the dull, enduring little fellow for all that most stirs this mortal frame? Nobody could have helped crying with him.

But there is nothing like work for toning down either excessive fear or joy. So I ran ahead, calling him, in as gruff a voice as I could command, to come on and stop his nonsense, for we had far to go, and it would soon be dark. Neither of us feared another trial like this. Heaven would surely count one enough for a lifetime. The ice ahead was gashed by thousands of crevasses, but they were common ones. The joy of deliverance burned in us like fire, and we ran without fatigue, every muscle, with immense rebound, glorying in its strength. Stickeen flew across everything in his way, and not till dark did he settle into his normal fox-like, gliding trot. At last the mountains crowned with spruce came in sight, looming faintly in the gloaming, and we soon felt the solid rock beneath our feet, and were safe. Then came weariness. We stumbled down along the lateral moraine in the dark, over rocks and tree-trunks, through the bushes and devil-club thickets and mossy logs and boulders of the woods where we had sheltered ourselves in the morning. Then out on the level mud-slope of the terminal moraine. Danger had vanished, and so had our strength. We reached camp about ten o'clock, and found a big fire and a big supper. A party of Hoona Indians had visited Mr. Young, bringing a gift of porpoise-meat and wild strawberries, and hunter Joe had brought in a wild goat. But we lay down, too tired to eat much, and soon fell into a troubled sleep. The man who said, "The harder the toil the sweeter the rest," never was profoundly tired. Stickeen kept springing up and muttering in his sleep, no doubt dreaming that he was still on the brink of the crevasse; and so did I—that night and many others, long afterward, when I was nervous and overtired.

Thereafter Stickeen was a changed dog. During the rest of the trip, instead of holding aloof, he would come to me at night, when all was quiet about the camp-fire, and rest his head on my knee, with a look of devotion, as if I were his god. And often, as he caught my eye, he seemed to be trying to say, "Wasn't that an awful time we had together on the glacier?"

None of his old friends know what finally became of him. When my work for the season was done I departed for California, and never saw the dear little fellow again. Mr. Young wrote me that in the summer of 1883 he was stolen by a tourist at Fort Wrangel, and taken away on a steamer. His fate is wrapped in mystery. If alive he is very old. Most likely he has left this world—crossed the last crevasse—and gone to another. But he will not be forgotten. Come what may, to me Stickeen is immortal.

Chapter 9

Love of Life

Jack London

Like many Jack London tales, including the classic "To Build a Fire," this short story is set in the Yukon during the Gold Rush, which furnished a treasure trove of story material for London. Jack London (1876–1916) was an extraordinary man, whose life has always reminded me of a shooting star, brilliant, irresistible, suddenly gone. Not only did he write volumes of wonderful prose created from his seafaring and wilderness trail adventures, but he was a true champion of the weak and the poor, the abused people of his time. What a man he was. And what a writer!

When you're alone in the northern wilds—without food, guns and gear, even proper clothing—escape is a teasing thought. You might as well lie down and die. Right? Master storyteller of northern adventures Jack London shows the strength behind these famous words: Never give up! Never, ever give up!

This out of all will remain—
They have lived and have tossed;
So much of the game will be gain,
Though the gold of the dice has been lost.

They limped painfully down the bank, and once the foremost of the two men staggered among the rough-strewn rocks. They were tired and weak, and their faces had the drawn expression of patience which comes of hardship long endured. They were heavily burdened with blanket packs which were strapped to their shoulders. Head-straps, passing across the forehead, helped support these packs. Each man carried a rifle. They walked in a stooped posture, the shoulders well forward, the head still farther forward, the eyes bent upon the ground.

"I wish we had just about two of them cartridges that's layin' in that cache of ourn," said the second man.

His voice was utterly and drearily expressionless. He spoke without enthusiasm; and the first man, limping into the milky stream that foamed over the rocks, vouchsafed no reply.

The other man followed at his heels. They did not remove their footgear, though the water was icy cold—so cold that their ankles ached and their feet went numb. In places the water dashed against their knees, and both men staggered for footing.

The man who followed slipped on a smooth boulder, nearly fell, but recovered himself with a violent effort, at the same time uttering a sharp exclamation of pain. He seemed faint and dizzy and put out his free hand while he reeled, as though seeking support against the air. When he had steadied himself he stepped forward, but reeled again and nearly fell. Then he stood still and looked at the other man, who had never turned his head.

The man stood still for fully a minute, as though debating with himself. Then he called out: "I say, Bill, I've sprained my ankle."

Bill staggered on through the milky water. He did not look around. The man watched him go, and though his face was expressionless as ever, his eyes were like the eyes of a wounded deer.

The other man limped up the farther bank and continued straight on without looking back. The man in the stream watched him. His lips trembled a little, so that the rough thatch of brown hair which covered them was visibly agitated. His tongue even strayed out to moisten them.

"Bill!" he cried out.

It was the pleading cry of a strong man in distress, but Bill's head did not turn. The man watched him go, limping grotesquely and lurching forward with stammering gait up the slow slope toward the soft sky-line of the low-lying hill. He watched him go till he passed over the crest and disappeared. Then he turned his gaze and slowly took in the circle of the world that remained to him now that Bill was gone.

Near the horizon the sun was smoldering dimly, almost obscured by formless mists and vapors, which gave an impression of mass and density without outline or tangibility. The man pulled out his watch, the while resting his weight on one leg. It was four o'clock, and as the season was near the last of July or first of August,—he did not know the precise date within a week or two,—he knew that the sun roughly marked the northwest. He looked to the south and knew that somewhere beyond those bleak hills lay the Great Bear Lake; also, he knew that in that direction the Arctic Circle cut its forbidding way across the Canadian Barrens. This stream in which he stood was a feeder to the Coppermine River, which in turn flowed north and emptied into Coronation Gulf and the Arctic Ocean. He had never been there, but he had seen it, once, on a Hudson Bay Company chart.

Again his gaze completed the circle of the world about him. It was not a heartening spectacle. Everywhere was soft sky-line. The hills were all low-lying. There were no trees, no shrubs, no grasses—naught but a tremendous and terrible desolation that sent fear swiftly dawning into his eyes.

"Bill!" he whispered, once and twice; "Bill!"

He cowered in the midst of the milky water, as though the vastness were pressing in upon him with overwhelming force, brutally crushing him with its complacent awfulness. He began to shake as with an ague-fit, till the gun fell from his hand with a splash. This served to rouse him. He fought with his fear and pulled himself together, groping in the water and recovering the weapon. He hitched his pack farther over on his left shoulder, so as to take a portion of its weight from off the injured ankle. Then he proceeded, slowly and carefully, wincing with pain, to the bank.

He did not stop. With a desperation that was madness, unmindful of the pain, he hurried up the slope to the crest of the hill over which his comrade had disappeared—more grotesque and comical by far than that limping, jerking comrade. But at the crest he saw a shallow valley, empty of life. He fought with his fear again, overcame it, hitched the pack still farther over on his left shoulder, and lurched on down the slope.

The bottom of the valley was soggy with water, which the thick moss held, spongelike, close to the surface. This water squirted out from under his feet at every step, and each time he lifted a foot the action culminated in a sucking sound as the wet moss reluctantly released its grip. He picked his way from muskeg to muskeg, and followed the other man's footsteps along and across the rocky ledges which thrust like islets through the sea of moss.

Though alone, he was not lost. Farther on he knew he would come to where dead spruce and fir, very small and weazened, bordered the shore of a little lake, the *titchin-nichilie,* in the tongue of the country, the "land of little sticks." And into that lake flowed a small stream, the water of which was not milky. There was rush-grass on that stream—this he remembered well—but no timber, and he would follow it till its first trickle ceased at a divide. He would cross this divide to the first trickle of another stream, flowing to the west, which he would follow until it emptied into the river Dease, and here he would find a cache under an upturned canoe and piled over with many rocks. And in this cache would be ammunition for his empty gun, fish-hooks and lines, a small net—all the utilities for the killing and snaring of food. Also, he would find flour,—not much,—a piece of bacon, and some beans.

Bill would be waiting for him there, and they would paddle away south down the Dease to the Great Bear Lake. And south across the lake they would go, ever south, till they gained the Mackenzie. And south, still south, they would go, while the winter raced vainly after them, and the ice formed in the eddies, and the days grew chilly and crisp, south to some warm Hudson Bay Company post, where timber grew tall and generous and there was grub without end.

These were the thoughts of the man as he strove onward. But hard as he strove with his body, he strove equally hard with his mind, trying to think that Bill had not deserted him, that Bill would surely wait for him at the cache. He was compelled to think this thought, or else there would not be any use to strive, and he would have lain down and died. And as the dim ball of the sun sank slowly into the northwest he covered every inch—and many times—of his and Bill's flight south before the downcoming winter. And he conned the grub of the cache and the grub of the Hudson Bay Company post over and over again. He had not eaten for two days; for a far longer time he had not had all he wanted to eat. Often he stooped and picked pale muskeg berries, put them into his mouth, and chewed and swallowed them. A muskeg berry is a bit of seed enclosed in a bit of water. In the mouth the water melts away and the seed chews sharp and bitter. The man knew there was no nourishment in the berries, but he chewed them patiently with a hope greater than knowledge and defying experience.

At nine o'clock he stubbed his toe on a rocky ledge, and from sheer weariness and weakness staggered and fell. He lay for some time, without movement, on his side. Then he slipped out of the pack-straps and clumsily dragged himself into a sitting posture. It was not yet dark, and in the lingering twilight he groped about among the rocks for shreds of dry moss. When he had gathered a heap he built a fire,—a smouldering, smudgy fire,—and put a tin pot of water on to boil.

He unwrapped his pack and the first thing he did was to count his matches. There were sixty-seven. He counted them three times to make sure. He divided them into several portions, wrapping them in oil paper, disposing of one bunch in his empty tobacco pouch, of another bunch in the inside band of his battered hat, of a third bunch under his shirt on the chest. This accomplished, a panic came upon him, and he unwrapped them all and counted them again. There were still sixty-seven.

He dried his wet foot-gear by the fire. The moccasins were in soggy shreds. The blanket socks were worn through in places, and his feet were raw and bleeding. His ankle was throbbing, and he gave it an examination. It had swollen to the size of his knee. He tore a long strip from one of his two blankets and bound the ankle tightly. He tore other strips and bound them about his feet to serve for both moccasins and socks. Then he drank the pot of water, steaming hot, wound his watch, and crawled between his blankets.

He slept like a dead man. The brief darkness around midnight came and went. The sun arose in the northeast—at least the day dawned in that quarter, for the sun was hidden by gray clouds.

At six o'clock he awoke, quietly lying on his back. He gazed straight up into the gray sky and knew that he was hungry. As he rolled over on his elbow he was startled by a loud snort, and saw a bull caribou regarding him with alert curiosity. The animal was not more than fifty feet away, and instantly into the man's mind leaped the vision and the savor of a caribou steak sizzling and frying over a fire. Mechanically he reached for the empty gun, drew a bead, and pulled the trigger. The bull snorted and leaped away, his hoofs rattling and clattering as he fled across the ledges.

The man cursed and flung the empty gun from him. He groaned aloud as he started to drag himself to his feet. It was a slow and arduous task. His joints were like rusty hinges. They worked harshly in their sockets, with much friction, and each bending or unbending was accomplished only through a sheer exertion of will. When he finally gained his feet, another minute or so was consumed in straightening up, so that he could stand erect as a man should stand.

He crawled up a small knoll and surveyed the prospect. There were no trees, no bushes, nothing but a gray sea of moss scarcely diversified by gray rocks, gray lakelets, and gray streamlets. The sky was gray. There was no sun nor hint of sun. He had no idea of north, and he had forgotten the way he had come to this spot the night before. But he was not lost. He knew that. Soon he would come to the land of the little sticks. He felt that it lay off to the left somewhere, not far—possibly just over the next low hill.

He went back to put his pack into shape for traveling. He assured himself of the existence of his three separate parcels of matches, though he did not stop to count them. But he did linger, debating, over a squat moose-hide sack. It was not large. He could hide it under his two hands. He knew that it weighed fifteen pounds,—as much as all the rest of the pack,—and it worried him. He finally set it to one side and proceeded to roll the pack. He paused to gaze at the squat moose-hide sack. He picked it up hastily with a defiant glance about him, as though the desolation were trying to rob him of it; and when he rose to his feet to stagger on into the day, it was included in the pack on his back.

He bore away to the left, stopping now and again to eat muskeg berries. His ankle had stiffened, his limp was more pronounced, but the pain of it was as nothing compared with the pain of his stomach. The hunger pangs were sharp. They gnawed and gnawed until he could not keep his mind steady on the course he must pursue to gain the land of little sticks. The muskeg berries did not allay this gnawing, while they made his tongue and the roof of his mouth sore with their irritating bite.

He came upon a valley where rock ptarmigan rose on whirring wings from the ledges and muskegs. Ker—ker—ker was the cry they made. He threw stones at them, but could not hit them. He placed his pack on the ground and stalked them as a cat stalks a sparrow. The sharp rocks cut through his pants' legs till his knees left a trail of blood; but the hurt was lost in the hurt of his hunger.

He squirmed over the wet moss, saturating his clothes and chilling his body; but he was not aware of it, so great was his fever for food. And always the ptarmigan rose, whirring, before him, till their ker—ker—ker became a mock to him, and he cursed them and cried aloud at them with their own cry.

Once he crawled upon one that must have been asleep. He did not see it till it shot up in his face from its rocky nook. He made a clutch as startled as was the rise of the ptarmigan, and there remained in his hand three tail-feathers. As he watched its flight he hated it, as though it had done him some terrible wrong. Then he returned and shouldered his pack.

As the day wore along he came into valleys or swales where game was more plentiful. A band of caribou passed by, twenty and odd animals, tantalizingly within rifle range. He felt a wild desire to run after them, a certitude that he could run them down. A black fox came toward him, carrying a ptarmigan in his mouth. The man shouted. It was a fearful cry, but the fox, leaping away in fright, did not drop the ptarmigan.

Late in the afternoon he followed a stream, milky with lime, which ran through sparse patches of rush-grass. Grasping these rushes firmly near the root, he pulled up what resembled a young onion-sprout no larger than a shingle-nail. It was tender, and his teeth sank into it with a crunch that promised deliciously of food. But its fibers were tough. It was composed of stringy filaments saturated with water, like the berries, and devoid of nourishment. He threw off his pack and went into the rush-grass on hands and knees, crunching and munching, like some bovine creature.

He was very weary and often wished to rest—to lie down and sleep; but he was continually driven on—not so much by his desire to gain the land of little sticks as by his hunger. He searched little ponds for frogs and dug up the earth with his nails for worms, though he knew in spite that neither frogs nor worms existed so far north.

He looked into every pool of water vainly, until, as the long twilight came on, he discovered a solitary fish, the size of a minnow, in such a pool. He plunged his arm in up to the shoulder, but it eluded him. He reached for it with both hands and stirred up the milky mud at the bottom. In his excitement he fell in, wetting himself to the waist. Then the water was too muddy to admit of his seeing the fish, and he was compelled to wait until the sediment had settled.

The pursuit was renewed, till the water was again muddied. But he could not wait. He unstrapped the tin bucket and began to bale the pool. He baled wildly at first, splashing himself and flinging the water so short a distance that it ran back into the pool. He worked more carefully, striving to be cool, though his heart was pounding against his chest and his hands were trembling. At the end of half an hour the pool was nearly dry. Not a cupful of water remained. And there was no fish. He found a hidden crevice among the stones through which it had escaped to the adjoining and larger pool—a pool which he could not empty in a night and a day. Had he known of the crevice, he could have closed it with a rock at the beginning and the fish would have been his.

Thus he thought, and crumpled up and sank down upon the wet earth. At first he cried softly to himself, then he cried loudly to the pitiless desolation that ringed him around; and for a long time after he was shaken by great dry sobs.

He built a fire and warmed himself by drinking quarts of hot water, and made camp on a rocky ledge in the same fashion he had the night before. The last thing he did was to see that his matches were dry and to wind his watch. The blankets were wet and clammy. His ankle pulsed with pain. But he knew only that he was hungry, and through his restless sleep he dreamed of feasts and banquets and of food served and spread in all imaginable ways.

He awoke chilled and sick. There was no sun. The gray of earth and sky had become deeper, more profound. A raw wind was blowing, and the first flurries of snow were whitening the hilltops. The air about him thickened and grew white while he made a fire and boiled more water. It was wet snow, half rain, and the flakes were large and soggy. At first they melted as soon as they came in contact with the earth, but ever more fell, covering the ground, putting out the fire, spoiling his supply of moss-fuel.

This was a signal for him to strap on his pack and stumble onward, he knew not where. He was not concerned with the land of little sticks, nor with Bill and the cache under the upturned canoe by the river Dease. He was mastered by the verb "to eat." He was hunger-mad. He took no heed of the course he pursued, so long as that course led him through the swale bottoms. He felt his way through the wet snow to the watery muskeg berries, and went by feel as he pulled up the rush-grass by the roots. But it was tasteless stuff and did not satisfy. He found a weed that tasted sour and he ate all he could find of it, which was not much, for it was a creeping growth, easily hidden under the several inches of snow.

He had no fire that night, nor hot water, and crawled under his blanket to sleep the broken hunger-sleep. The snow turned into a cold rain. He awakened many times to feel it falling on his upturned face. Day came—a gray day and no sun. It had ceased raining. The keenness of his hunger had departed. Sensibility, as far as concerned the yearning for food, had been exhausted. There was a dull, heavy ache in his stomach, but it did not bother him so much. He was more rational, and once more he was chiefly interested in the land of little sticks and the cache by the river Dease.

He ripped the remnant of one of his blankets into strips and bound his bleeding feet. Also, he recinched the injured ankle and prepared himself for a day of travel. When he came to his pack, he paused long over the squat moose-hide sack, but in the end it went with him.

The snow had melted under the rain, and only the hilltops showed white. The sun came out, and he succeeded in locating the points of the compass, though he knew now that he was lost. Perhaps, in his previous days' wanderings, he had edged away too far to the left. He now bore off to the right to counteract the possible deviation from his true course.

Though the hunger pangs were no longer so exquisite, he realized that he was weak. He was compelled to pause for frequent rests, when he attacked the muskeg berries and rush-grass patches. His tongue felt dry and large, as though covered with a fine hairy growth, and it tasted bitter in his mouth. His heart gave him a great deal of trouble. When he had travelled a few minutes it would begin a remorseless thump, thump, thump, and then leap up and away in a painful flutter of beats that choked him and made him go faint and dizzy.

In the middle of the day he found two minnows in a large pool. It was impossible to bale it, but he was calmer now and managed to catch them in his tin bucket. They were no longer than his little finger, but he was not particularly hungry. The dull ache in his stomach had been growing duller and fainter. It seemed almost that his stomach was dozing. He ate the fish raw, masticating with painstaking care, for the eating was an act of pure reason. While he had no desire to eat, he knew that he must eat to live.

In the evening he caught three more minnows, eating two and saving the third for breakfast. The sun had dried stray shreds of moss, and he was able to warm himself with hot water. He had not covered more than ten miles that day; and the next day, travelling whenever his heart permitted him, he covered no more than five miles. But his stomach did not give him the slightest uneasiness. It had gone to sleep. He was in a strange country, too, and the caribou were growing more plentiful, also the wolves. Often their yelps drifted across the desolation, and once he saw three of them slinking away before his path.

Another night; and in the morning, being more rational, he untied the leather string that fastened the squat moose-hide sack. From its open mouth poured a yellow stream of coarse gold-dust and nuggets. He roughly divided the gold in halves, caching one half on a prominent ledge, wrapped in a piece of blanket, and returning the other half to the sack. He also began to use strips of the one remaining blanket for his feet. He still clung to his gun, for there were cartridges in that cache by the river Dease.

This was a day of fog, and this day hunger awoke in him again. He was very weak and was afflicted with a giddiness which at times blinded him. It was no uncommon thing now for him to stumble and fall; and stumbling once, he fell squarely into a ptarmigan nest. There were four newly hatched chicks, a day old—little specks of pulsating life no more than a mouthful; and he ate them ravenously, thrusting them alive into his mouth and crunching them like eggshells between his teeth. The mother ptarmigan beat about him with great outcry. He used his gun as a club with which to knock her over, but she dodged out of reach. He threw stones at her and with one chance shot broke a wing. Then she fluttered away, running, trailing the broken wing, with him in pursuit.

The little chicks had no more than whetted his appetite. He hopped and bobbed clumsily along on his injured ankle, throwing stones and screaming hoarsely at times; at other times hopping and bobbing silently along, picking himself up grimly and patiently when he fell, or rubbing his eyes with his hand when the giddiness threatened to overpower him.

The chase led him across swampy ground in the bottom of the valley, and he came upon footprints in the soggy moss. They were not his own—he could see that. They must be Bill's. But he could not stop, for the mother ptarmigan was running on. He would catch her first, then he would return and investigate.

He exhausted the mother ptarmigan; but he exhausted himself. She lay panting on her side. He lay panting on his side, a dozen feet away, unable to crawl to her. And as he recovered she recovered, fluttering out of reach as his hungry hand went out to her. The chase was resumed. Night settled down and she escaped. He stumbled from weakness and pitched head foremost on his face, cutting his cheek, his pack upon his back. He did not move for a long while; then he rolled over on his side, wound his watch, and lay there until morning.

Another day of fog. Half of his last blanket had gone into foot-wrappings. He failed to pick up Bill's trail. It did not matter. His hunger was driving him too compellingly—only—only he wondered if Bill, too, were lost. By midday the irk of his pack became too oppressive. Again he divided the gold, this time merely spilling half of it on the ground. In the afternoon he threw the rest of it away, there remaining to him only the half-blanket, the tin bucket, and the rifle.

An hallucination began to trouble him. He felt confident that one cartridge remained to him. It was in the chamber of the rifle and he had overlooked it. On the other hand, he knew all the time that the chamber was empty. But the hallucination persisted. He fought it off for hours, then threw his rifle open and was confronted with emptiness. The disappointment was as bitter as though he had really expected to find the cartridge.

He plodded on for half an hour, when the hallucination arose again. Again he fought it, and still it persisted, till for very relief he opened his rifle to unconvince himself. At times his mind wandered farther afield, and he plodded on, a mere automaton, strange conceits and whimsicalities gnawing at his brain like worms. But these excursions out of the real were of brief duration, for ever the pangs of the hunger-bite called him back. He was jerked back abruptly once from such an excursion by a sight that caused him nearly to faint. He reeled and swayed, doddering like a drunken man to keep from falling. Before him stood a horse. A horse! He could not believe his eyes. A thick mist was in them, intershot with sparkling points of light. He rubbed his eyes savagely to clear his vision, and beheld, not a horse, but a great brown bear. The animal was studying him with bellicose curiosity.

The man had brought his gun halfway to his shoulder before he realized. He lowered it and drew his hunting-knife from its beaded sheath at his hip. Before him was meat and life. He ran his thumb along the edge of his knife. It was sharp. The point was sharp. He would fling himself upon the bear and kill it. But his heart began its warning thump, thump, thump. Then followed the wild upward leap and tattoo of flutters, the pressing as of an iron band about his forehead, the creeping of the dizziness into his brain.

His desperate courage was evicted by a great surge of fear. In his weakness, what if the animal attacked him? He drew himself up to his most imposing stature, gripping the knife and staring hard at the bear. The bear advanced clumsily a couple of steps, reared up, and gave vent to a tentative growl. If the man ran, he would run after him; but the man did not run. He was animated now with the courage of fear. He, too, growled, savagely, terribly, voicing the fear that is to life germane and that lies twisted about life's deepest roots.

The bear edged away to one side, growling menacingly, himself appalled by this mysterious creature that appeared upright and unafraid. But the man did not move. He stood like a statue till the danger was past, when he yielded to a fit of trembling and sank down into the wet moss.

He pulled himself together and went on, afraid now in a new way. It was not the fear that he should die passively from lack of food, but that he should be destroyed violently before starvation had exhausted the last particle of the endeavor in him that made toward surviving. There were the wolves. Back and forth across the desolation drifted their howls, weaving the very air into a fabric of menace that was so tangible that he found himself, arms in the air, pressing it back from him as it might be the walls of a wind-blown tent.

Now and again the wolves, in packs of two and three, crossed his path. But they steered clear of him. They were not in sufficient numbers, and besides they were hunting the caribou, which did not battle, while this strange creature that walked erect might scratch and bite.

In the late afternoon he came upon scattered bones where the wolves had made a kill. The débris had been a caribou calf an hour before, squawking and running and very much alive. He contemplated the bones, clean-picked and polished, pink with the cell-life in them which had not yet died. Could it possibly be that he might be that ere the day was done! Such was life, eh? A vain and fleeting thing. It was only life that pained. There was no hurt in death. To die was to sleep. It meant cessation, rest. Then why was he not content to die?

But he did not moralize long. He was squatting in the moss, a bone in his mouth, sucking at the shreds of life that still dyed it faintly pink. The sweet meaty taste, thin and elusive almost as a memory, maddened him. He closed his jaws on the bones and crunched. Sometimes it was the bone that broke, sometimes his teeth. Then he crushed the bones between rocks, pounded them to a pulp, and swallowed them. He pounded his fingers, too, in his haste, and yet found a moment in which to feel surprise at the fact that his fingers did not hurt much when caught under the descending rock.

Came frightful days of snow and rain. He did not know when he made camp, when he broke camp. He travelled in the night as much as in the day. He rested wherever he fell, crawled on whenever the dying life in him flickered up and burned less dimly. He, as a man, no longer strove. It was the life in him, unwilling to die, that drove him on. He did not suffer. His nerves had become blunted, numb, while his mind was filled with weird visions and delicious dreams.

But ever he sucked and chewed on the crushed bones of the caribou calf, the least remnants of which he had gathered up and carried with him. He crossed no more hills or divides, but automatically followed a large stream which flowed through a wide and shallow valley. He did not see this stream nor this valley. He saw nothing save visions. Soul and body walked or crawled side by side, yet apart, so slender was the thread that bound them.

He awoke in his right mind, lying on his back on a rocky ledge. The sun was shining bright and warm. Afar off he heard the squawking of caribou calves. He was aware of vague memories of rain and wind and snow, but whether he had been beaten by the storm for two days or two weeks he did not know.

For some time he lay without movement, the genial sunshine pouring upon him and saturating his miserable body with its warmth. A fine day, he thought. Perhaps he could manage to locate himself. By a painful effort he rolled over on his side. Below him flowed a wide and sluggish river. Its unfamiliarity puzzled him. Slowly he followed it with his eyes, winding in wide sweeps among the bleak, bare hills, bleaker and barer and lower-lying than any hills he had yet encountered. Slowly, deliberately, without excitement or more than the most casual interest, he followed the course of the strange stream toward the sky-line and saw it emptying into a bright and shining sea. He was still unexcited. Most unusual, he thought, a vision or a mirage—more likely a vision, a trick of his disordered mind. He was confirmed in this by sight of a ship lying at anchor in the midst of the shining sea. He closed his eyes for a while, then opened them. Strange how the vision persisted! Yet not strange. He knew there were no seas or ships in the heart of the barren lands, just as he had known there was no cartridge in the empty rifle.

He heard a snuffle behind him—a half-choking gasp or cough. Very slowly, because of his exceeding weakness and stiffness, he rolled over on his other side. He could see nothing near at hand, but he waited patiently. Again came the snuffle and cough, and outlined between two jagged rocks not a score of feet away he made out the gray head of a wolf. The sharp ears were not pricked so sharply as he had seen them on other wolves; the eyes were bleared and bloodshot, the head seemed to droop limply and forlornly. The animal blinked continually in the sunshine. It seemed sick. As he looked it snuffled and coughed again.

This, at least, was real, he thought, and turned on the other side so that he might see the reality of the world which had been veiled from him before by the vision. But the sea still shone in the distance and the ship was plainly discernible. Was it reality, after all? He closed his eyes for a long while and thought, and then it came to him. He had been making north by east, away from the Dease Divide and into the Coppermine Valley. This wide and sluggish river was the Coppermine. That shining sea was the Arctic Ocean. That ship was a whaler, strayed east, far east, from the mouth of the Mackenzie, and it was lying at anchor in Coronation Gulf. He remembered the Hudson Bay Company chart he had seen long ago, and it was all clear and reasonable to him.

He sat up and turned his attention to immediate affairs. He had worn through the blanket-wrappings, and his feet were shapeless lumps of raw meat. His last blanket was gone. Rifle and knife were both missing. He had lost his hat somewhere, with the bunch of matches in the band, but the matches against his chest were safe and dry inside the tobacco pouch and oil paper. He looked at his watch. It marked eleven o'clock and was still running. Evidently he had kept it wound.

He was calm and collected. Though extremely weak, he had no sensation of pain. He was not hungry. The thought of food was not even pleasant to him, and whatever he did was done by reason alone. He ripped off his pants' legs to the knees and bound them about his feet. Somehow he had succeeded in retaining the tin bucket. He would have some hot water before he began what he foresaw was to be a terrible journey to the ship.

His movements were slow. He shook as with a palsy. When he started to collect dry moss, he found he could not rise to his feet. He tried again and again, then contented himself with crawling about on hands and knees. Once he crawled near to the sick wolf. The animal dragged itself reluctantly out of his way, licking its chops with a tongue which seemed hardly to have the strength to curl. The man noticed that tongue was not the customary healthy red. It was a yellowish brown and seemed coated with a rough and half-dry mucus.

After he had drunk a quart of hot water the man found he was able to stand, and even to walk as well as a dying man might be supposed to walk. Every minute or so he was compelled to rest. His steps were feeble and uncertain, just as the wolf's that trailed him were feeble and uncertain; and that night, when the shining sea was blotted out by blackness, he knew he was nearer to it by no more than four miles.

Throughout the night he heard the cough of the sick wolf, and now and then the squawking of the caribou calves. There was life all around him, but it was strong life, very much alive and well, and he knew the sick wolf clung to the sick man's trail in the hope that the man would die first. In the morning, on opening his eyes, he beheld it regarding him with a wistful and hungry stare. It stood crouched, with tail between its legs, like a miserable and woebegone dog. It shivered in the chill morning wind, and grinned dispiritedly when the man spoke to it in a voice that achieved no more than a hoarse whisper.

The sun rose brightly, and all morning the man tottered and fell toward the ship on the shining sea. The weather was perfect. It was the brief Indian Summer of the high latitudes. It might last a week. To-morrow or next day it might be gone.

In the afternoon the man came upon a trail. It was of another man, who did not walk, but who dragged himself on all fours. The man thought it might be Bill, but he thought in a dull, uninterested way. He had no curiosity. In fact, sensation and emotion had left him. He was no longer susceptible to pain. Stomach and nerves had gone to sleep. Yet the life that was in him drove him on. He was very weary, but it refused to die. It was because it refused to die that he still ate muskeg berries and minnows, drank his hot water, and kept a wary eye on the sick wolf.

He followed the trail of the other man who dragged himself along, and soon came to the end of it—a few fresh-picked bones where the soggy moss was marked by the foot-pads of many wolves. He saw a squat moose-hide sack, mate to his own, which had been torn by sharp teeth. He picked it up, though its weight was almost too much for his feeble fingers. Bill had carried it to the last. Ha! ha! He would have the laugh on Bill. He would survive and carry it to the ship in the shining sea. His mirth was hoarse and ghastly, like a raven's croak, and the sick wolf joined him, howling lugubriously. The man ceased suddenly. How could he have the laugh on Bill if that were Bill; if those bones, so pinky-white and clean, were Bill?

He turned away. Well, Bill had deserted him; but he would not take the gold, nor would he suck Bill's bones. Bill would have, though, had it been the other way around, he mused as he staggered on.

He came to a pool of water. Stooping over in quest of minnows, he jerked his head back as though he had been stung. He had caught sight of his reflected face. So horrible was it that sensibility awoke long enough to be shocked. There were three minnows in the pool, which was too large to drain; and after several ineffectual attempts to catch them in the tin bucket he forbore. He was afraid, because of his great weakness, that he might fall in and drown. It was for this reason that he did not trust himself to the river astride one of the many drift-logs which lined its sand-spits.

That day he decreased the distance between him and the ship by three miles; the next day by two—for he was crawling now as Bill had crawled; and the end of the fifth day found the ship still seven miles away and him unable to make even a mile a day. Still the Indian Summer held on, and he continued to crawl and faint, turn and turn about; and ever the sick wolf coughed and wheezed at his heels. His knees had become raw meat like his feet, and though he padded them with the shirt from his back it was a red track he left behind him on the moss and stones. Once, glancing back, he saw the wolf licking hungrily his bleeding trail, and he saw sharply what his own end might be—unless—unless he could get the wolf. Then began as grim a tragedy of existence as was ever played—a sick man that crawled, a sick wolf that limped, two creatures dragging their dying carcasses across the desolation and hunting each other's lives.

Had it been a well wolf, it would not have mattered so much to the man; but the thought of going to feed the maw of that loathsome and all but dead thing was repugnant to him. He was finicky. His mind had begun to wander again, and to be perplexed by hallucinations, while his lucid intervals grew rarer and shorter.

He was awakened once from a faint by a wheeze close in his ear. The wolf leaped lamely back, losing its footing and falling in its weakness. It was ludicrous, but he was not amused. Nor was he even afraid. He was too far gone for that. But his mind was for the moment clear, and he lay and considered. The ship was no more than four miles away. He could see it quite distinctly when he rubbed the mists out of his eyes, and he could see the white sail of a small boat cutting the water of the shining sea. But he could never crawl those four miles. He knew that, and was very calm in the knowledge. He knew that he could not crawl half a mile. And yet he wanted to live. It was unreasonable that he should die after all he had undergone. Fate asked too much of him. And, dying, he declined to die. It was stark madness, perhaps, but in the very grip of Death he defied Death and refused to die.

He closed his eyes and composed himself with infinite precaution. He steeled himself to keep above the suffocating languor that lapped like a rising tide through all the wells of his being. It was very like a sea, this deadly languor, that rose and rose and drowned his consciousness bit by bit. Sometimes he was all but submerged, swimming through oblivion with a faltering stroke; and again, by some strange alchemy of soul, he would find another shred of will and strike out more strongly.

Without movement he lay on his back, and he could hear, slowly drawing near and nearer, the wheezing intake and output of the sick wolf's breath. It drew closer, ever closer, through an infinitude of time, and he did not move. It was at his ear. The harsh dry tongue grated like sandpaper against his cheek. His hands shot out—or at least he willed them to shoot out. The fingers were curved like talons, but they closed on empty air. Swiftness and certitude require strength, and the man had not this strength.

The patience of the wolf was terrible. The man's patience was no less terrible. For half a day he lay motionless, fighting off unconsciousness and waiting for the thing that was to feed upon him and upon which he wished to feed. Sometimes the languid sea rose over him and he dreamed long dreams; but ever through it all, waking and dreaming, he waited for the wheezing breath and the harsh caress of the tongue.

He did not hear the breath, and he slipped slowly from some dream to the feel of the tongue along his hand. He waited. The fangs pressed softly; the pressure increased; the wolf was exerting its last strength in an effort to sink teeth in the food for which it had waited so long. But the man had waited long, and the lacerated hand closed on the jaw. Slowly, while the wolf struggled feebly and the hand clutched feebly, the other hand crept across to a grip. Five minutes later the whole weight of the man's body was on top of the wolf. The hands had not sufficient strength to choke the wolf, but the face of the man was pressed close to the throat of the wolf and the mouth of the man was full of hair. At the end of half an hour the man was aware of a warm trickle in his throat. It was not pleasant. It was like molten lead being forced into his stomach, and it was forced by his will alone. Later the man rolled over on his back and slept.

There were some members of a scientific expedition on the whale-ship *Bedford.* From the deck they remarked a strange object on the shore. It was moving down the beach toward the water. They were unable to classify it, and, being scientific men, they climbed into the whale-boat alongside and went ashore to see. And they saw something that was alive but which could hardly be called a man. It was blind, unconscious. It squirmed along the ground like some monstrous worm. Most of its efforts were ineffectual, but it was persistent, and it writhed and twisted and went ahead perhaps a score of feet an hour.

Three weeks afterward the man lay in a bunk on the whale-ship *Bedford,* and with tears streaming down his wasted cheeks told who he was and what he had undergone. He also babbled incoherently of his mother, of sunny Southern California, and a home among the orange groves and flowers.

The days were not many after that when he sat at table with the scientific men and ship's officers. He gloated over the spectacle of so much food, watching it anxiously as it went into the mouths of others. With the disappearance of each mouthful an expression of deep regret came into his eyes. He was quite sane, yet he hated those men at meal-time. He was haunted by a fear that the food would not last. He inquired of the cook, the cabin-boy, the captain, concerning the food stores. They reassured him countless times; but he could not believe them, and pried cunningly about the lazarette to see with his own eyes.

It was noticed that the man was getting fat. He grew stouter with each day. The scientific men shook their heads and theorized.

They limited the man at his meals, but still his girth increased and he swelled prodigiously under his shirt.

The sailors grinned. They knew. And when the scientific men set a watch on the man, they knew too. They saw him slouch for'ard after breakfast, and, like a mendicant, with outstretched palm, accost a sailor. The sailor grinned and passed him a fragment of sea biscuit. He clutched it avariciously, looked at it as a miser looks at gold, and thrust it into his shirt bosom. Similar were the donations from other grinning sailors.

The scientific men were discreet. They let him alone. But they privily examined his bunk. It was lined with hardtack; the mattress was stuffed with hardtack; every nook and cranny was filled with hardtack. Yet he was sane. He was taking precautions against another possible famine—that was all. He would recover from it, the scientific men said, and he did, ere the *Bedford*'s anchor rumbled down in San Francisco Bay.

Chapter 10

The Midwinter Beach

Henry Beston

Some experiences that might be called "adventures" do not fit the usual format: they are quiet, even contemplative. While elements of dangerous and powerful forces of nature may be present, the "adventure" is an event of multifaceted experience, including observing the environment in its most interesting and dramatic phases and working one's way through hardships that, while not life threatening, are not the comfortable norm of modern living.

Such an adventure is the force behind The Outermost House *by Henry Beston (1888–1968), one of the greatest books ever written about life in the great outdoors. Set on the outer dunes of Cape Cod near Eastham and the Nauset Coast Guard Station,* The Outermost House *is the story of Beston's year living in a small beach cabin on land he had purchased at the end of World War I.*

In this excerpt from The Outermost House, *Beston's account begins in September and continues through a winter of devasting shipwrecks, with the remains of ships and crews washed onto Beston's beaches.*

Beston's home site was made into a National Literary Landmark, marked by a plaque, in a ceremony in 1964.

I

A year indoors is a journey along a paper calendar; a year in outer nature is the accomplishment of a tremendous ritual. To share in it, one must have a knowledge of the pilgrimages of the sun, and something of that natural sense of him and feeling for him which made even the most primitive people mark the summer limits of his advance and the last December ebb of his decline. All these autumn weeks I have watched the great disk going south along the horizon of moorlands beyond the marsh, now sinking behind this field, now behind this leafless tree, now behind this sedgy hillock dappled with thin snow. We lose a great deal, I think, when we lose this sense and feeling for the sun. When all has been said, the adventure of the sun is the great natural drama by which we live, and not to have joy in it and awe of it, not to share in it, is to close a dull door on nature's sustaining and poetic spirit.

The splendour of colour in this world of sea and dune ebbed from it like a tide; it shallowed first without seeming to lose ground, and presently vanished all at once, almost, so it seemed, in one grey week. Warmth left the sea, and winter came down with storms of rushing wind and icy, pelting rain. The first snow fell early in November, just before the dawn of a grey and bitter day. I had written a letter the night before, intending to give it to the coast guardsman who came south at seven o'clock, but somehow or other I missed him; and no welcome light flashed an answer to mine as I stood on the crest of my dune looking into the darkness of the beach and listening to the sombre thunder of a rising sea. Unwilling to stay up till after midnight for the next patrol, I went out and put a note on the coast guard key post just south of me asking the last man south in the morning to wake me up and come in and get the letter. At about half-past five I woke to a stamping of feet and a knock on the door, and in came John Blood, the tall, light-haired New Yorker, very much buttoned up into his blue pea jacket, and with his watch cap well pulled down upon his ears.

"Ahoy, John—thanks for coming in. What's it like outside?"

"It's snowing. Winter's come, I guess," he said, with a meditative grin.

We talked, I gave him the letter, and he went out into the dark break of dawn, the wind, and the snow.

My fire had gone out, the Fo'castle was raw and cold, but my wood was ready, and I soon had a fire crackling. All winter long, I kept a basket of little sticks and fragments of driftwood ready for the morning, and began the day with a bonfire in the fireplace. A hearthful of high, leaping flame sends out a quick and plentiful heat. Light came slowly into the world, coming not so much from the east as from some vague, general nowhere—a light that did not grow brighter but only increased in quantity. A northwest snow squall was blowing across the sedgy marshes and the dunes, "seeming nowhere to alight" in the enormous landscape, and whirling off to the sullen, iron-green, and icy sea. As I watched, half-a-dozen gulls came sailing over from the marsh. These birds like foul weather and have a way of flying out over along the breakers a few minutes after the edge of a cloud has hidden the sun, and there is a strange, ominous sense of storm in this great natural scene.

The snow skirted along the beach, the wind suffering it no rest; I saw little whirlpools of it driving down the sand into the onrush of the breakers, it gathered in the footprints of the coast guard patrols, building up on their leeward side and patterning them in white on the empty beach. The very snow in the air had a character of its own, for it was the snow of the outer Cape and the North Atlantic, snow icy and crystalline, and sweeping across the dunes and moors rather than down upon them. Chancing to look to the north, I saw Nauset Light still turning and gleaming, and as I watched, it suddenly sank to a storm-smothered and distant glow and stopped. By the almanac, the sun had risen. So began the worst winter on the Cape for close upon fifty years, a winter marked by great storms and tides, six wrecks, and the loss of many lives.

The sun, this December morning, has come to the end of his southern journey, he climbs the whitish sky to the south over the white fury of the Orleans shoals, and takes on a silvery quality from the pallor of the sky. On such a morning went ancient peoples to their hills, and cried to the pale god to return to their woods and fields; perhaps the vanished Nausets danced a ceremonial dance on those inland moors, and the same northwest wind carried the measured drumming to these dunes. A morning to go out upon the dunes and study the work of winter. Between the cold blue of the sea and the levels of the marshes, the long wall of the dunes lies blanched to a whiter pallor than the surrounding landscape, for there is no russet and but little gold in dune grass when it dies. That intricacy of green, full-fleshed life, which billowed like wild wheat in the summer's southwest wind, has thinned away now to a sparse world of separate heads, each one holding, as in a fist, a clump of whitish and mildewed wires.

The sand moves beneath. This shrinking of summer's vegetation, this uncovering of the body of the dune, has permitted the winter gales to reach the sand, and all up and down the great wall, on the tops of the dunes, the surface sand is moving. The direction of this movement varies, of course, with the direction of the wind, but in general the movement is toward the sea, for the prevailing winter winds are northwesterly. In some places the blown and creeping sand has covered the grass so deeply that only the very tips of the withered spikes rise out of it; in other places, on the landward rims of the dunes, the wind has blown the sand entirely away from the plant and left a withered tangle of roots and stalks sprawling in the wind. Here and there, in the dead, whitish grass, one encounters a stray tiny spotlet of snow, relic of a storm a fortnight past. Such spots linger here for inexplicable weeks and have an air of things disregarded and forgotten.

I have written of the movement of sand on the surface of the dune, yet the very essence of the work of winter here is the quieting, the enchainment of the mass of the sand. The sun no longer being hot enough to dry it, moisture lies on it and within it, it loses its fluidity, it takes on weight and definition. Footprints which the summer would erase in a quarter of an hour remain in well-sheltered places for days and even weeks. There is a winter change of colour, as well. The warm golden quality vanishes and is replaced by a tone of cold silver-grey, which makes no flashing answer to the sun.

Animal life has disappeared into the chill air, the heavy, lifeless sand. On the surface, nothing remains of the insect world. That multiplicity of insect tracks, those fantastic ribbons which grasshoppers, promenading flies, spiders, and beetles printed on the dunes as they went about their hungry and mysterious purposes, have come to an end in this world and left it all the poorer. Those trillions of unaccountable lives, those crawling, buzzing, intense presences which nature created to fulfil some unknown purpose or perhaps simply to satisfy a whim for a certain sound or a moment of exquisite colour, where are they now, in this vast world, silent save for the sombre thunder of the surf and the rumble of wind in the porches of the ears? As I muse here, it occurs to me that we are not sufficiently grateful for the great symphony of natural sound which insects add to the natural scene; indeed, we take it so much as a matter of course that it does not stir our fully conscious attention.

But all those little fiddles in the grass, all those cricket pipes, those delicate flutes, are they not lovely beyond words when heard in midsummer on a moonlight night? I like, too, the movement they give to a landscape with their rushes, their strange comings and goings, and their hoverings with the sun's brilliance reflected in their wings.

Here, and at this especial moment, there is no trace or vestige of the summer's insect world, yet one feels them here, the trillion, trillion tiny eggs in grass and marsh and sand, all faithfully spun from the vibrant flesh of innumerable mothers, all faithfully sealed and hidden away, all waiting for the rush of this earth through space and the resurgence of the sun.

I find no more paths of little paws and claw-tipped feet, each one with its own rhythm, its own mechanics of walking and running. The skunks, who linger till the last chilled grasshopper has been pounced on and eaten, are now lying torpid in their dark snuggles underground, their heartbeat stilled to a ghost of its summer self. They do not, apparently, make themselves burrows on the dunes, perhaps because a wise instinct warns them that a burrow in these open sands might collapse about them as they slept. November finds them travelling up the dunes to the firm soil of the mainland moors. The hill nearest the dunes is full of their winter parlours. Twice during the winter I saw a wildcat of domestic stock hunting along the edge of the marsh, and marked how savagery had completely altered the creature's gait, for it slunk along, belly close to the grass, like a panther. A large brown cat with long fur and a wild and extraordinarily foolish face.

I imagined it was out hunting the marsh larks who feed in the stubble of the salt-hay fields. Another time, I saw the hoofs of a deer in the sand, but of this deer and its adventures in the frozen marsh I shall speak later.

At Orleans, an otter, a rare animal here, has been seen, the man who saw it taking it for a seal until it came out of the breakers and ran along the sand. Every now and then, from the windows of the Fo'castle, I catch sight of a seal's black head swimming about close inshore.

In summer, seals are rarely seen on this part of the great outer beach—I myself have never seen one—but in winter they come along the breakers reconnoitring in search of food. They have a trick of swimming unperceived under a flock of sea ducks, seizing one of the unwary birds from underneath, and then disappearing with their mouths full of flesh and frantic feathers. A confusion follows; the survivors leap from the water with wildly beating wings, they scatter, wheel, and gather again, and presently nature has erased every sign of the struggle, and the sea rolls on as before.

There has been a strange tragedy to the north; one of those dread elemental things that happen in an elemental world. The other evening my friend Bill Eldredge, of Nauset, told me that there had been a disaster that same morning off the Race. Two fishermen who had left Provincetown in a big, thirty-foot motor dory were seen from the beach to be having trouble of some kind; the dory had then drifted into a tide rip churned up with surf, and capsized and drowned her crew. A few nights later, Bill came south again, and I stood for a moment talking to him on the beach at the foot of the Fo'castle dune. A lovely night of great winter stars and a quiet sea. "You remember those two fishermen I was telling you about?" said Bill. "They've found them both now. One of them had a son at Wood End Station, and when he was coming back from his patrol last night he saw his father's body on the beach."

II

On the night of Saturday, January 1st, it was almost pitch dark along the coast. In the murk, the eye of Nauset Light had a reddish tinge, and, turning, revealed a world shaped like a disk and pressed between a great darkness of earth and a low, black floor of cloud. The wind was on shore and blowing strong. Some time after midnight, a surfman from Cahoons Hollow Coast Guard Station, patrolling south, discovered a schooner in the surf, with the seas breaking over her, and the crew hollering in the rigging. I write "hollering" here without shame, for "hallooing," or whatever the proper spelling of the verb may be, simply would not tell the story, or convey the sound heard in the night. After holding up a red signal flare to tell the men on the wreck that they had been seen, the surfman hurried on to Cahoons and gave the alarm.

The crew of the station, under command of Captain Henry Daniels, then dragged their cart of life-saving apparatus down the beach through a surf running to the bank, and took off every single man safely in the breeches buoy. The prompt and gallant rescue had been no easy task, with the tide thus running high and the seas breaking over the schooner.

I had my first view of her the next afternoon. She turned out to be the two-masted, motor-auxiliary fishing schooner *A. Roger Hickey*, Boston-bound from the fishing grounds. Her compass had been at fault, they said. When I caught sight of her from the top of a path descending the great earth cliff of the Cape, the vessel lay on the open sand a mile up the beach to the north, a typical Boston fisherman with a red bottom and a black hull. A vessel, I judged, something over a hundred feet long. The whole vast view was really a picture of singular and moving beauty; it would be hard to forget, I think, that immense and jade-green ocean under a fine sky, the great, sepia-brown beach with its overhanging haze of faintest violet, the bright ship so forlorn, and the tiny black figures moving round and about it. The beach had already begun to break up its prize. Along it, on my way to the ship, I saw splintered wood, an undamaged hatch cover painted white, and several bunches of water-logged manila tags with a fish merchant's name printed on them in large black letters.

Presently there came walking toward me three ladies of Wellfleet, good, pleasant New England housewives, each one with a large haddock under her arm rolled up in a sheet of newspaper, the three dead-eyed haddock heads protruding as from paper collars, the three fish tails visible behind. Apparently the fish which the *Hickey* had on board when she struck were being given away.

Arriving at the wreck, I found that her rudder had already carried away, and that her timbers were badly wrenched, and her seams opened. The ship's dog, who had been thrillingly rescued in his master's arms, sat shivering on the beach, a most inoffensive and unromantic brown dog with what looked like an appalling case of mange. A handful of visitors, men and boys in workaday clothes and rubber boots, were wandering round the vessel, their boot prints making a chain about her on the beach, and other men were busy puttering round the steeply tilted deck. Finding Captain Henry Daniels of Cahoons aboard, an old friend of years' standing, I heard that the crew of the *Hickey*, two or three excepted, had already returned to Boston by train, and that the vessel was so badly damaged that she was to be stripped as soon as possible of all gear worth saving, and abandoned.

Midships, a discussion was going on round the open mouth of one of the fish holds. The *Hickey*'s catch was still there, a mass of big greyish fish bodies, haddocks with staring eyes, cod with chin whiskers, flounders, and huge lemon soles. The discussion concerned the possibility of the fish having had a bath in fuel oil when the seas washed into the *Hickey* at high tide. No one took serious alarm, and the fish, handed out to all comers by a member of the crew, proved excellent eating.

So they stripped the *A. Roger Hickey*, took out her engine and such gear as they could, and then someone set fire to the hulk. By the end of the winter, there was not even a splinter of this vessel on the beach. She was the third wreck, and there were others to come.

As the winter closed in upon the beach, I began to look forward to days when I might see what took place there during icy weather, but such opportunities proved even rarer than I had expected. Thrust forth as it is into the outer Atlantic, the Cape has a climate of island quality and island moderation. Low temperatures may occur, but the thermometer almost never falls as low as it does on the inner Massachusetts coast, nor do "spells" of cold weather "hang on" for any length of time. Storms which are snowstorms on the continental mainland turn to rainstorms on the Cape, and such snowstorms as do arrive form but a crust upon these Eastham moors. Two days after the storm the snow has thinned to great decorative patches on the slopes of sedgy hills; in another day only fragments, drifts, and stray islets remain. There is even a difference of temperature between the mainland moors of Eastham and the dunes. It is warmer on the bar. On a casual winter day I have noted a difference of eight degrees.

The work of cold weather—I mean weather when the temperature sinks toward zero—is thus to be observed only on occasion along this beach. When it comes, it comes all at once, creates a new world overnight, and vanishes overnight. The agency that brings it is the northwest wind sweeping down on us across Massachusetts Bay from the forests and frozen lakes of northern Canada. I remember one of the nights of its coming, a Thursday night early in January with great winter clouds moving out to sea, opening and closing over the cold stars, the wind on the beach so icy that I found myself, when I first went out into it, breathing it in little reluctant breaths. The next day was as cold and desolate a day as I have ever seen upon the beach. The ocean was purple-black, rough, and covered with sombre whitecaps; the morning light was pewter dull, and over earth and sea and the lonely sands hung a pall of purple-leaden cloud full of vast, tormented motion as it crossed the Cape on its way to the Atlantic. Looking off to sea, as I walked down my dune to go exploring, I saw a solitary freighter hugging the coast for shelter from the northwest wind; she was plunging heavily in the great seas and flinging up tons of spray with each plunge, and her bow and her forward deck were already thick with ice. Gulls flew along the iron-black and sombre breakers of the ebb, their white plumage chalky in that impure and arctic light. The wind was a thing to search the marrow of one's bones.

Two beaches had formed in the icy night, best seen and studied at low tide. The upper beach occupied the width between the dunes and the line of the night's high tide; the lower beach sloped from this high-tide mark to the open sea. The upper beach and the dunes were frozen hard.

The frozen sand was delightful to walk upon, for the tiny congealed grains afforded a safe, sustaining footing, and the surface, though solid, had the resiliency of thick, unvarnished linoleum on a good floor. It was an odd, an unnatural experience, to hit one's foot on a ridge of frozen sand. Fragments of wreckage imbedded in the sand, wreaths of imbedded seaweed—all these were as immovable as so many rocks. At the very foot of the largest of the dunes, I found a male surf scoter or skunk coot frozen stiff. A few solid kicks dislodged it, and I picked it up, but could find no wound. The lower beach, that is to say the width that had been covered by the tide during the night, was frozen solid at its junction with the upper beach, but the fine slope down to the breakers, though frozen firm, was not frozen through and through. Along the edge of the breakers, it was not frozen at all.

Between these two beaches, one above, one below, one frozen solid, the other crusted over, there ran a kind of frontier some eight or ten feet wide, a no-man's-land of conflicting natural forces. At the height of the night tide, the seething foam rims of the sliding surf, flung by the ocean into the face of the night cold, had frozen on the sloping beach in layers of salt ice which preserved all the curves and foamy ridges of the captured edge of the sea. The brim of a high tide, that very spirit of energy and motion, lay there motionless on a beach itself deprived of motion; the scalloped edges, the little curls of foam, the long, reaching, rushing tongues, all these were to be seen enchanted into that ocean ice which is so much like a kind of snow. At its upper edge this image of the surf brim was but a glaze of ice on the beach; at its lower edge it was twelve to fifteen inches in height and fell off sheer, like an ice cake, to the beach below. And north and south it ran, mile upon icy mile, as far as the eye could see.

The subsequent history of this ice is not without interest. After two days of bitter cold the wind changed in the night, and that night's tide quietly removed every vestige of the ice cakes from the beach. The swathe on which the ice had lain, however, remained half visible, for there water and sand had mingled and frozen deep. Presently the upper beach thawed, the cold crumbling drily out of the sand, and the lower beach, which had yielded its frozen surface to each succeeding tide and frozen again during the ebb, remained as the last tide left it. Between the two beaches, the width of buried ice lingered for a fortnight, resisting sun and whole days of winter rain. It had a way of coming suddenly to an end, and of beginning as suddenly again; sand drifted over it, the tide edge seeped through to it, the moving beach, forever adjusting itself to complex forces, burst it open, yet it lingered on. For all of us who used the beach, this buried width of ice became a secret road. The coast guards knew it well and followed along it in the night. As I set down these words, I think of the times I have come to a blind end and prodded the sand with my beach staff in search of that secret footing. Little by little the sun and the tides wore down its resistance, and so it disappeared, and our searching feet knew it no more.

The great marsh was another desolation on that same overcast and icy day. Salt ice had formed in wide rims along the edges of the great level islands, the shallower channels had frozen over, and the deeper ones were strewn with ice cakes sailing and turning about in the currents of the tides. The scene had taken on a certain winter unity, for the ice had bound the channels and the islands together into one wide and wintry plain.

On the next morning—it was sunny then, but still freezing cold—I chanced to go out for a moment to look at the marsh. About a mile and a half away, in one of the open channels, was a dark something which looked like a large, unfamiliar bird. A stray goose, perhaps? Taking my glass, I found the dark object to be the head of a deer swimming down the channel, and, even as I looked, there came to my ears the distant barking of dogs. A pair of marauding curs, out hunting on their own, had found a deer somewhere and driven the creature down the dunes and into the icy creeks. Down the channel it swam, and presently turned aside and climbed out on the marsh island just behind the Fo'castle.

The animal was a young doe. I thought then, and I still believe, that this doe and the unseen creature whose delicate hoofprints I often found near the Fo'castle were one and the same. It lived, I believe, in the pines on the northern shore of the marsh and came down to the dunes at earliest dawn. But to return to its adventures: All afternoon I watched it standing on the island far out in the marsh, the tall, dead sea grass rising about its russet body; when night came, it was still there, a tiny spot of forlorn mammalian life in that frozen scene. Was it too terrified to return? That night a tide of unusual height was due which would submerge the islands under at least two feet of water and floating ice. Would the doe swim ashore under cover of darkness?

I went out at midnight into my solitary world and saw the ice-covered marsh gleaming palely under a sky of brilliant stars, but could see nothing of the island of the doe save a ghostliness of salt ice along the nearer rim.

The first thing I did, on waking the next morning, was to search the island with my glass. The doe was still there.

I have often paused to wonder how that delicate and lovely creature endured so cruel a night, how she survived the slow rise of the icy tide about her poor legs, and the northwest gale that blustered about her all night long in that starlit loneliness of crunchy marsh mud and the murmur of the tides. The morning lengthened, the sun rose higher on the marsh, and presently the tide began to rise again. I watched it rising toward the refugee, and wondered if she could survive a second immersion. Just a little before noon, perhaps as the water was flooding round her feet, she came down to the edge of her island, and plunged into the channel. The creek was full of ice mush and of ice floes moving at a good speed; the doe was weak, the ice cakes bore down upon her, striking her heavily; she seemed confused, hesitated, swam here, swam there, stood still, and was struck cruelly by a floe which seemed to pass over her, yet on she swam, bewildered, but resolute for life.

I had almost given up hope for her, when rescue came unexpectedly. My friend Bill Eldredge, it appeared, while on watch in the station tower the day before had chanced to see the beginning of the story, and on the second morning had noticed the doe still standing in the marshes.

All the Nauset crew had taken an interest. Catching sight of the poor creature fighting for life in the drift, three of the men put off in a skiff, poled the ice away with their oars, and shepherded the doe ashore. "When she reached dry land, she couldn't rise, she was so weak, and fell down again and again. But finally she stood up and stayed up, and walked off into the pines."

III

I have now to tell of the great northeast storm of February 19th and 20th. They say here that it was the worst gale known on the outer Cape since the *Portland* went down with all hands on that terrible November night in '98.

It began after midnight on a Friday night, and the barometer gave but little warning of its coming. That Friday afternoon I had walked up the beach to Nauset Station, found Bill Eldredge on watch in the tower, and asked him to wake me up when he went by at midnight. "Never mind if you don't see a light," I said. "Come in anyway and wake me up. I may go down the beach with you." I often made the patrols with the men at the station, for I liked to walk the beach by night.

Shortly after midnight, Bill came to the door, but I did not get up and dress to go down the beach with him, for I was rather tired from piling up a mass of driftwood, so I sat up in bed and talked to him by the dying light of my fire. On bitter nights, I used to put a big log on in the hope that it might flicker and smoulder till morning, but on average nights, I let the fire die down to a bed of ashes, for I am a light sleeper, and the little play of flames on the hearth kept me awake. Living in outer nature keeps the senses keen, and living alone stirs in them a certain watchfulness.

The coast guardsman stood against the brick fireplace, his elbow propped for a moment on the shelf; I scarce could see his blue-clad figure in the gloom. "It's blowing up," he said. "I think we are going to have a northeaster." I apologized for not getting up, pleaded weariness, and, after a little talk, Bill said that he must be going, and returned to the beach. I saw him use his flashlight a moment as he plunged down the dune.

I woke in the morning to the dry rattle of sleet on my eastern windows and the howling of wind. A northeaster laden with sleet was bearing down on the Cape from off a furious ocean, an ebbing sea fought with a gale blowing directly on the coast; the lonely desolation of the beach was a thousand times more desolate in that white storm pouring down from a dark sky. The sleet fell as a heavy rain falls when it is blown about by the wind. I built up my fire, dressed, and went out, shielding my face from the sleet by pulling my head down into the collar of my coat. I brought in basket after basket of firewood, till the corner of the room resembled a woodshed. Then I folded up the bedclothes, threw my New Mexican blanket over the couch, lighted the oil stove, and prepared breakfast. An apple, oatmeal porridge, toast made at the fireplace, a boiled egg, and coffee.

Sleet and more of it, rushes of it, attacks of it, screaming descents of it; I heard it on the roof, on the sides of the house, on the windowpanes. Within, my fire fought against the cold, tormented light. I wondered about a small fishing boat, a thirty-foot "flounder dragger" that had anchored two miles or so off the Fo'castle the evening before. I looked for her with my glass, but could not see into the storm.

Streaming over the dunes, the storm howled on west over the moors. The islands of the marsh were brownish black, the channels leaden and whipped up by the wind; and along the shores of the desolate islands, channel waves broke angrily, chidingly, tossing up heavy ringlets of lifeless white. A scene of incredible desolation and cold. All day long I kept to my house, building up the fire and keeping watch from the windows; now and then I went out to see that all was well with the Fo'castle and its foundations, and to glimpse what I could, through the sleet, of the storm on the sea. For a mile or so offshore the North Atlantic was a convulsion of elemental fury whipped by the sleety wind, the great parallels of the breakers tumbling all together and mingling in one seething and immense confusion, the sound of this mile of surf being an endless booming roar, a seethe, and a dread grinding, all intertwined with the high scream of the wind. The rush of the inmost breakers up the beach was a thing of violence and blind will. Darkness coming early, I closed my shutters on the uproar of the outer world, all save one shutter on the landward side.

With the coming of night the storm increased; the wind reaching a velocity of seventy to eighty miles an hour. It was at this time, I am told, that friends on the mainland began to be worried about me, many of them looking for my light. My lamp, a simple kerosene affair with a white china shade, stood on a table before the unshuttered window facing the land. An old friend said he would see it or think that he saw it for a half minute or so, and then it would vanish for hours into the darkness of the gale. It was singularly peaceful in the little house. Presently, the tide, which had ebbed a little during the afternoon, turned and began to come in. All afternoon long the surf had thundered high upon the beach, the ebb tide backed up against the wind. With the turn of the tide came fury unbelievable. The great rhythm of its waters now at one with the rhythm of the wind, the ocean rose out of the night to attack the ancient rivalry of earth, hurling breaker after thundering breaker against the long bulwark of the sands. The Fo'castle, being low and strongly built, stood solid as a rock, but its walls thrummed in the gale. I could feel the vibration in the bricks of the chimney, and the dune beneath the house trembled incessantly with the onslaught of the surf.

Where were my friends at Nauset Station, thought I, in this furious night. Who was on his way north, with seven miles of night and sleet to battle through before he returned to the shelter of the station and the warmth of that kitchen stove which is kept polished to a brilliance beyond all stoves? It was Bill, as a matter of fact, and because of the surf on the beach he was using the path which runs along the top of the cliff close by its brim, a path exposed to the full violence of the gale. As I mused thus, troubled about my friends, there came a knock at my open window, and then steps outside and a knock at the door. Letting my visitor in was easy enough, but to close the door after him was another matter. Closing the door against the force of the gale was like trying to close it upon something material; it was exactly as if I were pressing the door against a bulging mass of felt. My visitor was Albert Robbins, first man south from Nauset, a big powerful youngster and a fine lad; he was covered with sleet and sand, sand and sleet in his hair, in his eyebrows, in the corners of his eyes, in his ears, behind his ears, in the corners of his mouth, in his nostrils even. And a cheerful, determined grin!

"Wanted to see if you were still here," he said humorously, rooting sand out of his eyes with a knuckle. I busied myself getting him a cup of steaming coffee.

"Any news? Anyone in trouble?" I asked.

"Yes, there's a coast guard patrol boat off the Highland; something's the matter with her engine. She's anchored off there, and they've sent two destroyers out from Boston to get her."

"When did you hear that?"

"This afternoon."

"Didn't hear anything else?"

"No, the wires blew down, and we can't get beyond Cahoons."

"Think they've got any chance if the destroyers haven't got to them?"

"Gosh, I hope so," he said; and then, after a pause, "but it don't look like it." And then, "So long," and into the storm again.

I did not go to bed, for I wanted to be ready for any eventuality. As the hour of flood tide neared, I dressed as warmly as I could, turned down my lamp, and went out upon the dunes.

An invisible moon, two days past the full, had risen behind the rushing floor of cloud, and some of its wan light fell on the tortured earth and the torment of the sea. The air was full of sleet, hissing with a strange, terrible, insistent sound on the dead grass, and sand was being whirled up into the air. Being struck on the face by this sand and sleet was like being lashed by a tiny, pin-point whip. I have never looked on such a tide. It had crossed the beach, climbed the five-foot wall of the dune levels that run between the great mounds, and was hurling wreckage fifty and sixty feet into the starved white beach grass; the marsh was an immense flooded bay, and the "cuts" between the dunes and the marsh rivers of breakers. A hundred yards to the north of me was such a river; to the south, the surf was attempting to flank the dune, an attempt which did not succeed. Between these two onslaughts, no longer looking *down* upon the sea, but directly into it and just over it, the Fo'castle stood like a house built out into the surf on a mound of sand. A third of a mile or so to the north I chanced to see rather a strange thing. The dune bank there was washing away and caving in under the onslaught of the seas, and presently there crumbled out the blackened skeleton of an ancient wreck which the dunes had buried long ago. As the tide rose this ghost floated and lifted itself free, and then washed south close along the dunes. There was something inconceivably spectral in the sight of this dead hulk thus stirring from its grave and yielding its bones again to the fury of the gale.

As I walked in the night I wondered about the birds who live here in the marsh. That great population of gulls, ducks, and geese and their rivals and allies—where were they all crouching, where were they hidden in that wild hour?

All Sunday morning there was sleet—more sleet fell in this storm than the Cape had seen in a generation—and then, about the middle of the afternoon, the wind died down, leaving a wild sea behind. Going to Nauset Station, I had news of the disaster at the Highland. The destroyers, in spite of a splendid battle, had been unable to reach the disabled patrol boat, and the luckless ship had gone to pieces. It is thought that she dragged onto the outer bar. Nine men had perished. Two bodies came ashore next day; their watches had stopped at five o'clock, so we knew that the vessel had weathered the night and gone to pieces in the morning. What a night they must have had, poor souls!

There was wreckage everywhere, great logs, tree stumps, fragments of ships, planking, splintered beams, boards, rough timber, and, by itself in the surf, the enormous rudder of the *Hickey*, splintered sternpost and all. The day after the storm, people came down from Eastham in farm wagons and Fords, looked at the sea for a while, talked over the storm with whoever happened to be standing by, paid a call on the coast guards, and then went casually to work piling up the best of the timber. I saw Bill Eldredge in one of the cuts sorting out planks to be used in building a henhouse. Gulls were milling over the surf and spume—the greatest numbers gathering where the surf was most discoloured—and gulls were flying back and forth between the breakers and the marsh. From their point of view, perhaps, nothing had happened.

Chapter 11

The Tragedies of the Nests

John Burroughs

This chapter marks a change of pace for this story collection, from tales of humans battling for their lives to small creatures of nature doing the same thing. For prose focused on the lives of birds, one of the finest writers—if not the finest—is John Burroughs (1837–1921). Burroughs lived in and wrote about nature in New York's upper Hudson River Valley. His many books, now classics, describe scenes from snowstorms and animal travels in winter to walks and trout fishing in summer. If there is a better writer about nature than John Burroughs, please point him or her out to me. I will be most anxious to read that writer.

The life of the birds, especially of our migratory song-birds, is a series of adventures and of hair-breadth escapes by flood and field. Very few of them probably die a natural death, or even live out half their appointed days. The home instinct is strong in birds as it is in most creatures; and I am convinced that every spring a large number of those which have survived the Southern campaign return to their old haunts to breed. A Connecticut farmer took me out under his porch, one April day, and showed me a phoebe-bird's nest six stories high. The same bird had no doubt returned year after year; and as there was room for only one nest upon her favorite shelf, she had each season reared a new superstructure upon the old as a foundation. I have heard of a white robin—an albino—that nested several years in succession in the suburbs of a Maryland city. A sparrow with a very marked peculiarity of song I have heard several seasons in my own locality. But the birds do not all live to return to their old haunts: the bobolinks and starlings run a gauntlet of fire from the Hudson to the Savannah, and the robins and meadow-larks and other song-birds are shot by boys and pot-hunters in great numbers,—to say nothing of their danger from hawks and owls. But of those that do return, what perils beset their nests, even in the most favored localities! The cabins of the early settlers, when the country was swarming with hostile Indians, were not surrounded by such dangers. The tender households of the birds are not only exposed to hostile Indians in the shape of cats and collectors, but to numerous murderous and bloodthirsty animals, against whom they have no defense but concealment. They lead the darkest kind of pioneer life, even in our gardens and orchards, and under the walls of our houses. Not a day or a night passes, from the time the eggs are laid till the young are flown, when the chances are not greatly in favor of the nest being rifled and its contents devoured,—by owls, skunks, minks, and coons at night, and by crows, jays, squirrels, weasels, snakes, and rats during the day. Infancy, we say, is hedged about by many perils; but the infancy of birds is cradled and pillowed in peril. An old Michigan settler told me that the first six children that were born to him died; malaria and teething invariably carried them off when they had reached a certain age; but other children were born, the country improved, and by and by the babies weathered the critical period and the next six lived and grew up. The birds, too, would no doubt persevere six times and twice six times, if the season were long enough, and finally rear their family, but the waning summer cuts them short, and but a few species have the heart and strength to make even the third trial.

The first nest-builders in spring, like the first settlers near hostile tribes, suffer the most casualties. A large portion of the nests of April and May are destroyed; their enemies have been many months without eggs and their appetites are keen for them. It is a time, too, when other food is scarce, and the crows and squirrels are hard put. But the second nests of June, and still more the nests of July and August, are seldom molested. It is rarely that the nest of the goldfinch or the cedar-bird is harried.

My neighborhood on the Hudson is perhaps exceptionally unfavorable as a breeding haunt for birds, owing to the abundance of fish-crows and of red squirrels; and the season of which this chapter is mainly a chronicle, the season of 1881, seems to have been a black-letter one even for this place, for at least nine nests out of every ten that I observed during that spring and summer failed of their proper issue. From the first nest I noted, which was that of a bluebird,—built (very imprudently I thought at the time) in a squirrel-hole in a decayed apple-tree, about the last of April, and which came to naught, even the mother-bird, I suspect, perishing by a violent death,—to the last, which was that of a snowbird, observed in August, among the Catskills, deftly concealed in a mossy bank by the side of a road that skirted a wood, where the tall thimble blackberries grew in abundance, from which the last young one was taken, when it was about half grown, by some nocturnal walker or daylight prowler, some untoward fate seemed hovering about them. It was a season of calamities, of violent deaths, of pillage and massacre, among our feathered neighbors. For the first time I noticed that the orioles were not safe in their strong, pendent nests. Three broods were started in the apple-trees, only a few yards from the house, where, for previous seasons, the birds had nested without molestation; but this time the young were all destroyed when about half grown. Their chirping and chattering, which was so noticeable one day, suddenly ceased the next. The nests were probably plundered at night, and doubtless by the little red screech-owl, which I know is a denizen of these old orchards, living in the deeper cavities of the trees. The owl could alight on the top of the nest, and easily thrust his murderous claw down into its long pocket and seize the young and draw them forth. The tragedy of one of the nests was heightened, or at least made more palpable, by one of the half-fledged birds, either in its attempt to escape or while in the clutches of the enemy, being caught and entangled in one of the horse-hairs by which the nest was stayed and held to the limb above. There it hung bruised and dead, gibbeted to its own cradle. This nest was the theatre of another little tragedy later in the season. Some time in August a bluebird, indulging its propensity to peep and pry into holes and crevices, alighted upon it and probably inspected the interior; but by some unlucky move it got its wings entangled in this same fatal horse-hair. Its efforts to free itself appeared only to result in its being more securely and hopelessly bound; and there it perished; and there its form, dried and embalmed by the summer heats, was yet hanging in September, the outspread wings and plumage showing nearly as bright as in life.

A correspondent writes me that one of his orioles got entangled in a cord while building her nest, and that though by the aid of a ladder he reached and liberated her, she died soon afterward. He also found a "chippie" (called also "hair bird") suspended from a branch by a horse-hair, beneath a partly constructed nest. I heard of a cedar-bird caught and destroyed in the same way, and of two young bluebirds, around whose legs a horse-hair had become so tightly wound that the legs withered up and dropped off. The birds became fledged, and left the nest with the others. Such tragedies are probably quite common.

Before the advent of civilization in this country, the oriole probably built a much deeper nest than it usually does at present. When now it builds in remote trees and along the borders of the woods, its nest, I have noticed, is long and gourd-shaped; but in orchards and near dwellings it is only a deep cup or pouch. It shortens it up in proportion as the danger lessens. Probably a succession of disastrous years, like the one under review, would cause it to lengthen it again beyond the reach of owl's talons or jay-bird's beak.

The first song-sparrow's nest I observed in the spring of 1881 was in the field under a fragment of a board, the board being raised from the ground a couple of inches by two poles. It had its full complement of eggs, and probably sent forth a brood of young birds, though as to this I cannot speak positively, as I neglected to observe it further. It was well sheltered and concealed, and was not easily come at by any of its natural enemies, save snakes and weasels. But concealment often avails little. In May, a song-sparrow, that had evidently met with disaster earlier in the season, built its nest in a thick mass of woodbine against the side of my house, about fifteen feet from the ground. Perhaps it took the hint from its cousin, the English sparrow. The nest was admirably placed, protected from the storms by the overhanging eaves and from all eyes by the thick screen of leaves. Only by patiently watching the suspicious bird, as she lingered near with food in her beak, did I discover its whereabouts. That brood is safe, I thought, beyond doubt. But it was not; the nest was pillaged one night, either by an owl, or else by a rat that had climbed into the vine, seeking an entrance to the house. The mother-bird, after reflecting upon her ill-luck about a week, seemed to resolve to try a different system of tactics and to throw all appearances of concealment aside. She built a nest few yards from the house beside the drive, upon a smooth piece of greensward. There was not a weed or a shrub or anything whatever to conceal it or mark its site. The structure was completed and incubation had begun before I discovered what was going on. "Well, well," I said, looking down upon the bird almost at my feet, "this is going to the other extreme indeed; now, the cats will have you." The desperate little bird sat there day after day, looking like a brown leaf pressed down in the short green grass. As the weather grew hot, her position became very trying. It was no longer a question of keeping the eggs warm, but of keeping them from roasting. The sun had no mercy on her, and she fairly panted in the middle of the day. In such an emergency the male robin has been known to perch above the sitting female and shade her with his outstretched wings. But in this case there was no perch for the male bird, had he been disposed to make a sunshade of himself. I thought to lend a hand in this direction myself, and so stuck a leafy twig beside the nest. This was probably an unwise interference; it guided disaster to the spot; the nest was broken up, and the mother-bird was probably caught, as I never saw her afterward.

For several previous summers a pair of kingbirds had reared, unmolested, a brood of young in an apple-tree, only a few yards from the house; but during this season disaster overtook them also. The nest was completed, the eggs laid, and incubation had begun, when, one morning about sunrise, I heard cries of distress and alarm proceed from the old apple-tree. Looking out of the window I saw a crow, which I knew to be a fish-crow, perched upon the edge of the nest, hastily bolting the eggs. The parent birds, usually so ready for the attack, seemed over-come with grief and alarm. They fluttered about in the most helpless and bewildered manner, and it was not till the robber fled on my approach that they recovered themselves and charged upon him. The crow scurried away with upturned, threatening head, the furious kingbirds fairly upon his back. The pair lingered around their desecrated nest for several days, almost silent, and saddened by their loss, and then disappeared. They probably made another trial elsewhere.

The fish-crow only fishes when it has destroyed all the eggs and young birds it can find. It is the most despicable thief and robber among our feathered creatures. From May to August, it is gorged with the fledglings of the nest. It is fortunate that its range is so limited. In size it is smaller than the common crow, and is a much less noble and dignified bird. Its caw is weak and feminine—a sort of split and abortive caw, that stamps it the sneak-thief it is. This crow is common farther south, but is not found in this State, so far as I have observed, except in the valley of the Hudson.

One season a pair of them built a nest in a Norway Spruce that stood amid a dense growth of other ornamental trees near a large unoccupied house. They sat down amid plenty. The wolf established himself in the fold. The many birds—robins, thrushes, finches, vireos, pewees—that seek the vicinity of dwellings (especially of these large country residences with their many trees and park-like grounds), for the greater safety of their eggs and young, were the easy and convenient victims of these robbers. They plundered right and left, and were not disturbed till their young were nearly fledged, when some boys, who had long before marked them as their prize, rifled the nest.

The song-birds nearly all build low; their cradle is not upon the tree-top. It is only birds of prey that fear danger from below more than from above, and that seek the higher branches for their nests. A line five feet from the ground would run above more than half the nests, and one ten feet would bound more than three fourths of them. It is only the oriole and the wood pewee that, as a rule, go higher than this. The crows and jays and other enemies of the birds have learned to explore this belt pretty thoroughly. But the leaves and the protective coloring of most nests baffle them as effectually, no doubt as they do the professional oölogist. The nest of the red-eyed vireo is one of the most artfully placed in the wood. It is just beyond the point where the eye naturally pauses in its search; namely, on the extreme end of the lowest branch of the tree, usually four or five feet from the ground. One looks up and down through the tree,—shoots his eye-beams into it as he might discharge his gun at some game hidden there, but the drooping tip of that low horizontal branch—who would think of pointing his piece just there? If a crow or other marauder were to alight upon the branch or upon those above it, the nest would be screened from him by the large leaf that usually forms a canopy immediately above it. The nest-hunter standing at the foot of the tree and looking straight before him, might discover it easily, were it not for its soft, neutral gray tint which blends so thoroughly with the trunks and branches of trees. Indeed, I think there is no nest in the woods—no arboreal nest—so well concealed. The last one I saw was a pendent from the end of a low branch of a maple, that nearly grazed the clapboards of an unused hay-barn in a remote backwoods clearing. I peeped through a crack and saw the old birds feed the nearly fledged young within a few inches of my face. And yet the cow-bird finds this nest and drops her parasitical egg in it. Her tactics in this as in other cases are probably to watch the movements of the parent bird. She may often be seen searching anxiously through the trees or bushes for a suitable nest, yet she may still oftener be seen perched upon some good point of observation watching the birds as they come and go about her. There is no doubt that, in many cases, the cow-bird makes room for her own illegitimate egg in the nest by removing one of the bird's own. When the cow-bird finds two or more eggs in a nest in which she wishes to deposit her own, she will remove one of them. I found a sparrow's nest with two sparrow's eggs and one cow-bird's egg, another egg lying a foot or so below it on the ground. I replaced the ejected egg, and the next day found it again removed, and another cow-bird's egg in its place; I put it back the second time, when it was again ejected, or destroyed, for I failed to find it anywhere. Very alert and sensitive birds like the warblers often bury the strange egg beneath a second nest built on top of the old. A lady, living in the suburbs of an eastern city, one morning heard cries of distress from a pair of house-wrens that had a nest in a honeysuckle on her front porch. On looking out of the window, she beheld this little comedy—comedy from her point of view, but no doubt grim-tragedy from the point of view of the wrens; a cow-bird with a wren's egg in its beak running rapidly along the walk with the outraged wrens forming a procession behind it, screaming, scolding, and gesticulating as only these voluble little birds can. The cow-bird had probably been surprised in the act of violating the nest, and the wrens were giving her a piece of their minds.

Every cow-bird is reared at the expense of two or more song-birds. For every one of these dusky little pedestrians there amid the grazing cattle there are two more sparrows, or vireos, or warblers, the less. It is a big price to pay—two larks for a bunting—two sovereigns for a shilling; but Nature does not hesitate occasionally to contradict herself in just this way. The young of the cow-bird is disproportionately large and aggressive, one might say hoggish. When disturbed it will clasp the nest and scream, and snap its beak threateningly. One hatched out in a song-sparrow's nest which was under my observation, and would soon have overridden and overborne the young sparrow, which came out of the shell a few hours later, had I not interfered from time to time and lent the young sparrow a helping hand. Every day I would visit the nest and take the sparrow out from under the pot-bellied interloper and place it on top so that presently it was able to hold its own against its enemy. Both birds became fledged and left the nest about the same time. Whether the race was an even one after that, I know not.

I noted but two warblers' nests during that season, one of the black-throated blue-back and one of the redstart,—the latter built in an apple-tree but a few yards from a little rustic summer-house where I idle away many summer days. The lively little birds, darting and flashing about, attracted my attention for a week before I discovered their nest. They probably built it by working early in the morning, before I appeared upon the scene, as I never saw them with material in their beaks. Guessing from their movements that the nest was in a large maple that stood near by, I climbed the tree and explored it thoroughly, looking especially in the forks of the branches, as the authorities say these birds build in a fork. But no nest could I find. Indeed, how can one by searching find a bird's nest? I overshot the mark; the nest was much nearer me, almost under my very nose, and I discovered it, not by searching but by a casual glance of the eye, while thinking of other matters. The bird was just settling upon it as I looked up from my book and caught her in the act. The nest was built near the end of a long, knotty, horizontal branch of an apple-tree, but effectually hidden by the grouping of the leaves; it had three eggs, one of which proved to be barren. The two young birds grew apace, and were out of the nest early in the second week; but something caught one of them the first night. The other probably grew to maturity, as it disappeared from the vicinity with its parents after some days.

The blue-back's nest was scarcely a foot from the ground, in a little bush situated in a low, dense wood of hemlock and beech and maple, amid the Catskills,—a deep, massive, elaborate structure, in which the sitting bird sank till her beak and tail alone were visible above the brim. It was a misty, chilly day when I chanced to find the nest, and the mother-bird knew instinctively that it was not prudent to leave her four half incubated eggs uncovered and exposed for a moment. When I sat down near the nest she grew very uneasy, and after trying in vain to decoy me away by suddenly dropping from the branches and dragging herself over the ground as if mortally wounded, she approached and timidly and half doubtingly covered her eggs within two yards of where I sat. I disturbed her several times to note her ways. There came to be something almost appealing in her looks and manner, and she would keep her place on her precious eggs till my outstretched hand was within a few feet of her. Finally, I covered the cavity of the nest with a dry leaf. This she did not remove with her beak, but thrust her head deftly beneath it and shook it off upon the ground. Many of her sympathizing neighbors, attracted by her alarm note, came and had a peep at the intruder and then flew away, but the male bird did not appear upon the scene. The final history of this nest I am unable to give, as I did not again visit it till late in the season, when, of course, it was empty.

Years pass without my finding a brown-thrasher's nest; it is not a nest you are likely to stumble upon in your walk; it is hidden as a miser hides his gold, and watched as jealously. The male pours out his rich and triumphant song from the tallest tree he can find, and fairly challenges you to come and look for his treasures in his vicinity. But you will not find them if you go. The nest is somewhere on the outer circle of his song; he is never so imprudent as to take up his stand very near it. The artists who draw those cosy little pictures of a brooding mother-bird with the male perched but a yard away in full song, do not copy from nature. The thrasher's nest I found thirty or forty rods from the point where the male was wont to indulge in his brilliant recitative. It was in an open field under a low ground-juniper. My dog disturbed the sitting bird as I was passing near. The nest could be seen only by lifting up and parting away the branches. All the arts of concealment had been carefully studied. It was the last place you would think of looking, and, if you did look, nothing was visible but the dense green circle of the low-spreading juniper. When you approached, the bird would keep her place till you had begun to stir the branches, when she would start out, and, just skimming the ground, make a bright brown line to the near fence and bushes. I confidently expected that this nest would escape molestation, but it did not. Its discovery by myself and dog probably opened the door for ill luck, as one day, not long afterward, when I peeped in upon it, it was empty. The proud song of the male had ceased from his accustomed tree, and the pair were seen no more in that vicinity.

The phoebe-bird is a wise architect, and perhaps enjoys as great an immunity from danger, both in its person and its nest, as any other bird. Its modest, ashen-gray suit is the color of the rocks where it builds, and the moss of which it makes such free use gives to its nest the look of a natural growth or accretion. But when it comes into the barn or under the shed to build, as it so frequently does, the moss is rather out of place. Doubtless in time the bird will take the hint, and when she builds in such places will leave the moss out. I noted but two nests, the summer I am speaking of: one, in a barn, failed of issue, on account of the rats, I suspect, though the little owl may have been the depredator; the other, in the woods, sent forth three young. This latter nest was most charmingly and ingeniously placed. I discovered it while in quest of pond-lilies, in a long, deep level stretch of water in the woods. A large tree had blown over at the edge of the water, and its dense mass of up-turned roots, with the black, peaty soil filling the interstices, was like the fragment of a wall several feet high, rising from the edge of the languid current. In a niche in this earthy wall, and visible and accessible only from the water, a phoebe had built her nest, and reared her brood. I paddled my boat up and came alongside prepared to take the family aboard. The young, nearly ready to fly, were quite undisturbed by my presence, having probably been assured that no danger need be apprehended from that side. It was not a likely place for minks, or they would not have been so secure.

I noted but one nest of the wood pewee, and that, too, like so many other nests, failed of issue. It was saddled upon a small dry limb of a plane-tree that stood by the roadside, about forty feet from the ground. Every day for nearly a week, as I passed by I saw the sitting bird upon the nest. Then one morning she was not in her place, and on examination the nest proved to be empty—robbed, I had no doubt, by the red squirrels, as they were very abundant in its vicinity, and appeared to make a clean sweep of every nest. The wood pewee builds an exquisite nest, shaped and finished as if cast in a mould. It is modeled without and within with equal neatness and art, like the nest of the humming-bird and the little gray gnat-catcher. The material is much more refractory than that used by either of these birds, being, in the present case, dry, fine cedar twigs; but these were bound into a shape as rounded and compact as could be moulded out of the most plastic material. Indeed, the nest of this bird looks precisely like a large, lichen-covered, cup-shaped excrescence of the limb upon which it is placed. And the bird, while sitting, seems entirely at ease. Most birds seem to make very hard work of incubation. It is a kind of martyrdom which appears to tax all their powers of endurance. They have such a fixed, rigid, predetermined look, pressed down into the nest and as motionless as if made of cast-iron. But the wood pewee is an exception. She is largely visible above the rim of the nest. Her attitude is easy and graceful; she moves her head this way and that, and seems to take note of whatever goes on about her; and if her neighbor were to drop in for a little social chat, she could doubtless do her part. In fact, she makes light and easy work of what, to most other birds, is such a serious and engrossing matter. If it does not look like play with her, it at least looks like leisure and quiet contemplation.

There is no nest-builder that suffers more from crows and squirrels and other enemies than the wood-thrush. It builds as openly and unsuspiciously as if it thought the whole world as honest as itself. Its favorite place is the fork of a sapling, eight or ten feet from the ground, where it falls an easy prey to every nest-robber that comes prowling through the woods and groves. It is not a bird that skulks and hides, like the cat-bird, the brown-thrasher, the chat, or the cheewink, and its nest is not concealed with the same art as theirs. Our thrushes are all frank, open-mannered birds; but the veery and the hermit build upon the ground, where they at least escape the crows, owls, and jays, and stand a better chance to be overlooked, by the red squirrel and weasel also; while the robin seeks the protection of dwellings and out-buildings. For years I have not known the nest of a wood-thrush to succeed. During the season referred to I observed but two, both apparently a second attempt, as the season was well advanced, and both failures. In one case, the nest was placed in a branch that an apple-tree standing near a dwelling, held out over the highway. The structure was barely ten feet above the middle of the road, and would just escape a passing load of hay. It was made conspicuous by the use of a large fragment of newspaper in its foundation—an unsafe material to build upon in most cases. Whatever else the press may guard, this particular newspaper did not guard this nest from harm. It saw the egg and probably the chick, but not the fledgling. A murderous deed was committed above the public highway, but whether in the open day or under cover of darkness I have no means of knowing. The frisky red squirrel was doubtless the culprit. The other nest was in a maple sapling, within a few yards of the little rustic summer-house already referred to. The first attempt of the season, I suspect, had failed in a more secluded place under the hill; so the pair had come up nearer the house for protection. The male sang in the trees near by for several days before I chanced to see the nest. The very morning, I think, it was finished, I saw a red squirrel exploring a tree but a few yards away; he probably knew what the singing meant as well as I did. I did not see the inside of the nest, for it was almost instantly deserted, the female having probably laid a single egg, which the squirrel had devoured.

If I were a bird, in building my nest I should follow the example of the bobolink, placing it in the midst of a broad meadow, where there was no spear of grass, or flower or growth unlike another to mark its site. I judge that the bobolink escapes the dangers to which I have adverted as few or no other birds do. Unless the mowers come along at an earlier date than she has anticipated, that is, before July 1st, or a skunk goes nosing through the grass, which is unusual, she is as safe as bird well can be in the great open of nature. She selects the most monotonous and uniform place she can find amid the daisies or the timothy and clover, and places her simple structure upon the ground in the midst of it. There is no concealment, except as the great conceals the little, as the desert conceals the pebble, as the myriad conceals the unit. You may find the nest once, if your course chances to lead you across it and your eye is quick enough to note the silent brown bird as she darts quickly away; but step three paces in the wrong direction, and your search will probably be fruitless. My friend and I found a nest by accident one day, and then lost it again one minute afterward. I moved away a few yards to be sure of the mother-bird, charging my friend not to stir from his tracks. When I returned, he had moved two paces, he said (he had really moved four), and we spent a half hour stooping over the daisies and the buttercups, looking for the lost clew. We grew desperate, and fairly felt the ground all over with our hands, but without avail. I marked the spot with a bush, and came the next day, and with the bush as a centre, moved about it in slowly increasing circles, covering, I thought, nearly every inch of ground with my feet, and laying hold of it with all the visual power that I could command, till my patience was exhausted, and I gave up, baffled. I began to doubt the ability of the parent birds themselves to find it, and so secreted myself and watched. After much delay, the male bird appeared with food in his beak, and satisfying himself that the coast was clear, dropped into the grass which I had trodden down in my search. Fastening my eye upon a particular meadow-lily, I walked straight to the spot, bent down, and gazed long and intently into the grass. Finally my eye separated the nest and its young from its surroundings. My foot had barely missed them in my search, but by how much they had escaped my eye I could not tell. Probably not by distance at all, but simply by unrecognition. They were virtually invisible. The dark gray and yellowish brown dry grass and stubble of the meadow-bottom were exactly copied in the color of the half-fledged young. More than that, they hugged the nest so closely and formed such a compact mass, that though there were five of them, they preserved the unit of expression,—no single head or form was defined; they were one, and that one was without shape or color, and not separable, except by closest scrutiny, from the one of the meadow-bottom. That nest prospered, as bobolinks' nests doubtless generally do; for, notwithstanding the enormous slaughter of the birds during their fall migrations by Southern sportsmen, the bobolink appears to hold its own, and its music does not diminish in our Northern meadows.

Birds with whom the struggle for life is the sharpest seem to be more prolific than those whose nest and young are exposed to fewer dangers. The robin, the sparrow, the pewee, etc., will rear, or make the attempt to rear, two and sometimes three broods in a season; but the bobolink, the oriole, the kingbird, the goldfinch, the cedar-bird, the birds of prey, and the woodpeckers, that build in safe retreats, in the trunks of trees, have usually but a single brood. If the bobolink reared two broods, our meadows would swarm with them.

I noted three nests of the cedar-bird in August in a single orchard, all productive, but all with one or more unfruitful eggs in them. The cedar-bird is the most silent of our birds having but a single fine note, so far as I have observed, but its manners are very expressive at times. No bird known to me is capable of expressing so much silent alarm while on the nest as this bird. As you ascend the tree and draw near it, it depresses its plumage and crest, stretches up its neck, and becomes the very picture of fear. Other birds, under like circumstances, hardly change their expression at all till they launch into the air, when by their voice they express anger rather than alarm.

I have referred to the red squirrel as a destroyer of the eggs and young of birds. I think the mischief it does in this respect can hardly be over estimated. Nearly all birds look upon it as their enemy, and attack and annoy it when it appears near their breeding haunts. Thus, I have seen the pewee, the cuckoo, the robin, and the wood-thrush pursuing it with angry voice and gestures. A friend of mine saw a pair of robins attack one in the top of a tall tree so vigorously that they caused it to lose its hold, when it fell to the ground, and was so stunned by the blow as to allow him to pick it up. If you wish the birds to breed and thrive in your orchard and groves, kill every red squirrel that infests the place; kill every weasel also. The weasel is a subtle and arch enemy of the birds. It climbs trees and explores them with great ease and nimbleness. I have seen it do so on several occasions. One day my attention was arrested by the angry notes of a pair of brown-thrashers that were flitting from bush to bush along an old stone row in a remote field. Presently I saw what it was that excited them—three large red weasels, or ermines coming along the stone wall, and leisurely and half playfully exploring every tree that stood near it. They had probably robbed the thrashers. They would go up the trees with great ease, and glide serpent-like out upon the main branches. When they descended the tree they were unable to come straight down, like a squirrel, but went around it spirally. How boldly they thrust their heads out of the wall, and eyed me and sniffed me, as I drew near,—their round, thin ears, their prominent, glistening, bead-like eyes, and the curving, snake-like motions of the head and neck being very noticeable. They looked like blood-suckers and egg-suckers. They suggested something extremely remorseless and cruel. One could understand the alarm of the rats when they discover one of these fearless, subtle, and circumventing creatures threading their holes. To flee must be like trying to escape death itself. I was one day standing in the woods upon a flat stone, in what at certain seasons was the bed of a stream, when one of these weasels came undulating along and ran under the stone upon which I was standing. As I remained motionless, he thrust his wedge-shaped head, and turned it back above the stone as if half in mind to seize my foot; then he drew back, and presently went his way. These weasels often hunt in packs like the British stoat. When I was a boy, my father one day armed me with an old musket and sent me to shoot chipmunks around the corn. While watching the squirrels, a troop of weasels tried to cross a bar-way where I sat, and were so bent on doing it that I fired at them, boy-like, simply to thwart their purpose. One of the weasels was disabled by my shot, but the troop was not discouraged, and, after making several feints to cross, one of them seized the wounded one and bore it over, and the pack disappeared in the wall on the other side.

Let me conclude this chapter with two or three notes about this alert enemy of the birds and the lesser animals, the weasel.

A farmer one day heard a queer growling sound in the grass; on approaching the spot he saw two weasels contending over a mouse; each had hold of the mouse pulling in opposite directions, and were so absorbed in the struggle that the farmer cautiously put his hands down and grabbed them both by the back of the neck. He put them in a cage, and offered them bread and other food. This they refused to eat, but in a few days one of them had eaten the other up, picking his bones clean and leaving nothing but the skeleton.

The same farmer was one day in his cellar when two rats came out of a hole near him in great haste, and ran up the cellar wall and along its top till they came to a floor timber that stopped their progress, when they turned at bay, and looked excitedly back along the course they had come. In a moment a weasel, evidently in hot pursuit of them, came out of the hole, and seeing the farmer, checked his course and darted back. The rats had doubtless turned to give him fight, and would probably have been a match for him.

The weasel seems to track its game by scent. A hunter of my acquaintance was one day sitting in the woods, when he saw a red squirrel run with great speed up a tree near him, and out upon a long branch, from which he leaped to some rocks, and disappeared beneath them. In a moment a weasel came in full course upon his trail, ran up the tree, then out along the branch, from the end of which he leaped to the rocks as the squirrel did, and plunged beneath them.

Doubtless the squirrel fell a prey to him. The squirrel's best game would have been to have kept to the higher tree-tops, where he could easily have distanced the weasel. But beneath the rocks he stood a very poor chance. I have often wondered what keeps such an animal as the weasel in check, for weasels are quite rare. They never need go hungry, for rats and squirrels and mice and birds are everywhere. They probably do not fall a prey to any other animal, and very rarely to man. But the circumstances or agencies that check the increase of any species of animal are, as Darwin says, very obscure and but little known.

Chapter 12

On Dangerous Ground

Lamar Underwood

I wrote this piece of fiction for Sports Afield *after my years as chief editor there. I am including it here because I believe it is one of the best portraits of today's most dangerous situation in wilderness travel: a bear on a kill.*

The four rainbow trout finned easily to hold themselves suspended in the current, their shadows wavering over the brown pebbly streambed at a place where the Toubok River curved from the dark canyon of a spruce forest and clattered sunlit and sparkling through a field of low alder bushes. Pointed into the flow, the fish did not see or detect the enormous grizzly as it slowly emerged from the shadowed timber and walked across the sandbar to the shoals behind their position.

The great bear's muscles moved with fluid, rippling ease, so devoid of stiffness that the entire body seemed on the verge of collapse. Beneath the stumpy legs, the dry sand yielded to a depth of two inches as each footfall silently recorded the passage of the massive 1,500-pound creature. Its front feet, fifteen inches long by ten wide, bore claws that curved downward over the last half of their six-inch length. The rear feet were not as wide, their claws shorter. Tiny ears, a broad shelving forehead, and burly snout gave the bear's face a doglike appearance. The deeply dished eyes were devoid of malevolence, innocently unexpressive. Thicker and wider than the head itself, the neck led back to the prominent hump that seemed to float, unattached to the rest of the body, as the creature walked, the light upstream breeze stirring the outer frosting of silver hair and the dark brown pelt beneath.

When he reached the edge of the current, the grizzly waddled into the flow without pausing, heading directly across the rocky shoals. The trout shot upstream into a deeper pool, splinters of light as they flared through the clear water. Across the stream, the grizzly paused to shake itself. His legs and underbelly blurred with motion as luminous mist flew from the soaked fur. In a moment, he went on. Shouldering through the border of alders that grew down to the water's edge, he headed downstream.

As the great bear walked along the river, his presence had an immediate impact on the rhythm of the late-afternoon life sustained by the stream. On a hillside across the river, pine squirrels saw the bear and began to chirr in scolding, nervous alarm. A pair of ravens watched the beast approach, then flapped away, croaking as they flew. Peering from the uppermost snag of a lightning-killed white spruce, an osprey saw the bear wade directly through the bay-like depression where it had been fishing. The bird lifted into the air, caught a thermal, and circled away downstream. A hen mallard and a drake, floating on the current, bounced straight up and curved away over the spruce tops, their wings whispering.

All day the great bear had foraged opportunistically while wandering through the river valley. Once, when he was crossing a saddle of talus rock that bridged two ridges on the slopes above the stream, he had detected the powerful odor of prey in the mixture of scents his amazing nose sorted from the mountain air: dank rock, moss and lichen, wildflowers, rotting snow, pumice and sand.

For several yards he had coursed the trail over the stones like a bird dog, head down, wheezing as his nostrils flooded with scent. Rounding a rocky shoulder, he was enveloped by a cloud of odor the wind brought down from the ledges above. The bear looked up and instantly crouched into a stalk, as a band of Dall sheep ewes and lambs came into view, alert and tense, their superb vision focused on the menace before them. They watched, mesmerized for a moment, then bounded up the slope with a harsh rattling of hooves. The bear broke into a sprint for a few yards, then slowed and stopped as the weaving, bobbing forms disappeared over the ridge line. The grizzly watched the empty slope for a few moments, then turned and resumed his journey.

Later he spent two frustrating hours trying to dig a ground squirrel from its den. Barely larger than a mouse, the squirrel had screeched in mortal terror as the claws scratched and probed to within inches of its perch in a tunnel between two underground rocks. But the huge paws could not be forced into the tiny aperture. Finally, snorting with excitement, the grizzly began to dig for the tiny morsel. By the time he became bored with the pursuit and wandered on his way, the torn ground looked as if a bomb had struck.

Since copulating with a sow and then immediately leaving her two weeks before, the grizzly had become increasingly obsessed with feeding. He had been with the female for ten days, following her steady, aimless wanderings that are part of the great bears' courtship rituals, and the experience had burned away the last of the winter fat he had brought from his many weeks of semi-hibernation. Now his instincts had carried him down from the higher ranges to the fertile lower slopes, where he expected to find the tubers of wildflowers, seed pods, plant bulbs, and other growths that composed the greater part of his diet at this time of the year. There were pea vine roots to dig, horsetail and sourdock plants to chomp down. Also, another sense of need gripped the great bear, pulling him deeper into the river valley. Usually by this time every spring, the banks of the river had provided the special food that would satisfy the craving that gnawed at him. Carrion—a moose or caribou carcass, gift of the melting winter snows—would bring the strength and satisfaction the grizzly instinctively knew he needed. The memory of such rich feeding could not be obliterated by a diet of plants, and for days the grizzly's instincts had held him close to the river. Sometimes he wandered the nearby ridges for a while, but he always came back to the current, searching expectantly along the brushy shoreline.

The great bear continued downstream, slipping in and out of the alders like some enormous shadow. When the thicket began to thin, the grizzly stopped. Across a wide expanse of muskeg that came down to the edge of the stream, open country stretched away to a distant line of timber. Closer, on one side of the muskeg, a line of willows gave way to a belt of spruce on high ground.

The bear moved into the thicket, stopped again. In every direction, the willows had been heavily browsed, the ground scarred and trampled. The scent of the beast that had fed there permeated the air like fog. The bear stepped gingerly ahead, drinking in the smell, seeking a source for the diffused odor.

Twenty yards to one side, a thick clump of brush exploded with noise and movement. A cow moose crashed through the brush and headed across the clearing, trotting in a ragged gait.

Instantly the grizzly charged.

The moose bolted in panic, nostrils flaring, eyes bulging wildly. She looked back over her shoulder just as a paw smashed into the side of her neck, breaking it with a crack that resounded over the bear's roar and the collision of the massive bodies. The bear's bulk hurtled into the cow's shoulder, breaking bones and battering muscle and sinew into pulp. One of the cow's front legs snapped under the impact, and she was thrown forward and to one side, landing on her shoulder, her head and neck flopping limply as they thudded to the ground. The grizzly bit into the flesh, sinking his fangs deep into the blood-spurting neck, shaking his head as he tightened his grip.

Gradually, the grizzly sensed the lack of movement in his prey and relaxed his hold. He stood for a moment, watching the carcass. The cow's eyes stared ahead, wide and empty, the light inside extinguished since the initial blow to the neck.

The great bear circled, sniffing and watching. Finally, he bit into the base of the neck, braced his massive shoulders, and began to pull the cow along the ground. Despite his brute strength, the grizzly could only move the body a foot or so in one continuous pull. Stopping periodically to look around and sniff the air for intruders, then bending down to gain a new purchase on his prize, the bear worked for over an hour to move his kill twenty yards from the willows. The opening where he finally stopped was closer to the spruce trees and the river but was almost identical to the spot where the moose had been struck down.

For some strange reason, however, the grizzly's instincts were satisfied now. His paws resting on the carcass, he lifted his nose, inspecting the light currents of air.

Finally he began to feed.

A pair of magpies watched from a nearby branch, keeping their distance for now but knowing their turn would come.

"I'd feel a whole lot better about leaving you here if you'd take this." The pilot clicked back the hammer of the long-barreled .44 magnum revolver. "Hell, I'll even show you how to use it." He held the gun with a two-handed combat grip, steadied his feet on the pontoons of the floatplane, and aimed across the water.

To Sam Larkin, the metallic snap of the hammer falling on an empty chamber seemed a strange sound above the lapping of the gentle waves against the rocks. He glared silently at the plane as it floated over the sun-dappled shallows, some ten yards from the level slab of stone where he and his backpacks had just been put ashore. From far down the lake, the call of a loon echoed through the stillness. The cry was at once lilting and plaintive, a cry of wildness and solitude.

The pilot lowered the handgun, opened the action, and idly spun the empty cylinder. The holster belt that sagged from his waist was lined with blunt-nosed cartridges that gleamed dully. To Larkin, the idea of lugging that grim bulk and heaviness through the Alaska wilderness for the next ten days was too depressing to contemplate. He smiled at the pilot, trying to show appreciation for his offer.

"I'll be all right," Larkin said. "I've lived in New York City for seven years without a gun. That's more dangerous than being out here."

"No it ain't," the pilot answered.

Larkin studied the man's face for a sign of levity. The eyes were cold dark slits, the other features expressionless behind a heavy reddish beard and long hair that spilled from a baseball cap with a Cessna label on the front. Larkin suspected that the pilot was very young, but he could not be certain. Whatever his age, he had handled the plane well on the flight from Anchorage, setting the single-engined 182 on the small lake with a deftness and precision that Larkin had admired. Now the pilot had become an intruder. Larkin wanted him to be on his way.

"Wilderness grizzlies just want to be left alone," Larkin said. "They'll bugger off as long as you don't do something stupid, like surprise one."

"If this is your first trip to Alaska, how come you know so much about our bears?"

"I read a lot. I've been looking forward to this for a long time."

The pilot shrugged his shoulders. He unbuckled the gun, turned quickly, and eased gingerly along the pontoon to the cockpit. Larkin knelt on one knee and began checking the straps of his oversized backpack and a smaller shoulder pack.

The pilot carried a paddle as he came back to the front of the pontoon. Kneeling, he thrust the blade down against the brown-pebbled bottom and pushed hard to shove the plane out of the shallows. "You know," he called, "a lot of those writers have never seen a bear, 'cept in a zoo. What they write about is all made-up bullshit."

"Thanks for your help," Larkin called. "I'll be careful." He could imagine what the pilot was thinking: *This tenderfoot's gonna get his smart New York ass in deep-shit trouble.* Larkin realized that almost everything about his appearance looked new and untested: his khaki trousers and long-sleeve cotton jersey, his packs, even his boyish, lightly tanned face. His blond hair was cut short and neat. The only marks of backcountry experience about him were his well-worn boots, with leather uppers, rubber bottoms, and heavy-lugged Vibram soles—a perfect combination for the springy tundra and swampy lowlands, as well as the harder ground along the slopes of the ridges.

The plane was floating in deeper water. The pilot could no longer touch the bottom with his paddle. He stood and shouted to Larkin. "Okay, so don't surprise a grizzly. But, if you should happen to, do you know what to do?"

"Shout. Sing. Whistle. Anything to make noise and scare it away."

"No, that's all wrong!" The pilot waved his hand impatiently. "If you should happen up on a grizzly, say as close as I am to you right now, there's only one thing to do."

"What's that?" Larkin called, interested.

"The only thing you can do is to relax. Otherwise, you'll die all tensed up."

Larkin chuckled at the gag before he realized the pilot was not smiling.

"Rock Lake, ten days from now," Larkin called, getting back to business. "I'll be there."

"Don't eat all your food," the pilot shouted. "If the weather socks in, you'll have to camp at the lake till we can fly. Just sit tight."

The pilot climbed into the cockpit, slammed the door, and waved at Larkin as the electrical circuits hummed and the engine sputtered to life.

Larkin stood at the edge of the water and watched the plane taxi slowly downwind. Against the dark line of trees at the far end of the lake, the plane looked like a brightly painted toy. It made a slow U-turn and headed back toward Larkin, plowing quickly through the water. He could see white explosions of foam as the ship picked up speed. In a moment the roar of the engine was upon him and the pontoons were skimming the surface, throwing twin contrails of spray over their wakes. The plane rose slowly from the water and immediately leveled off, gathering speed. As the plane approached the shore it began to climb steeply, and was still climbing as it roared overhead and out of sight beyond the spruce hillside behind the edge of the lake.

Larkin looked at his watch. Eight p.m. here, midnight back in New York. He had left his Upper West Side apartment at six in the morning. Now, eighteen hours later, he was on a trail deep in the Alaska Range.

Larkin looked out across the water, listening for the call of the loon. Light breezes stroked the surface into wavelets that shimmered in the sunlight. Along the shoreline, the water was dark and smooth in the shadows of the low hills cupping the lake. The silence was like some strange new sound that rang in the ears. Then the loon's cry danced across the water again. Somewhere nearby, a fish swirled. Larkin felt a surge of pleasure. He was alone but not lonely.

He pulled a map from a side pocket of his backpack. The act of unfolding the map and checking his position was a formality. The curving patterns of brown, green, and blue lines had been engraved in his mind during the countless hours he had spent poring over the map in anticipation of the trip.

On the map, his landing spot was a tiny dot squeezed by flowing contour lines that marked the surrounding hills. A line indicating a trail wiggled away from where he stood and brought his finger to the serpentine course of the Toubok River, which flowed out of the Alaska Range. After hiking upstream along the river for a week, he intended to cut cross-country to Rock Lake, where the float plane would pick him up. He expected to do some superb fishing and hiking while enjoying grand views and ideal campsites all along the way. He slipped the map back into the backpack and weighed his next move. There was no need to hurry; even after the sun dipped below the horizon, it would rise again before full darkness descended. The demands that usually made him pressed for time were behind him now. Out here, he would let events flow along at their own pace. He would enjoy the view for a bit before moving toward the river to find a campsite. Despite the long hours of his journey, he felt only exhilaration.

He opened a flap of the shoulder pack and reached inside for his binoculars. He sat down on the rock shelf where the barren stone was splashed with color; lichens formed filigrees of purple, doughnuts of green, mushroom bursts of orange.

Larkin raised his knees and leaned forward to steady his elbows as he lifted the glasses. The compact but powerful 10 × 40 lenses bit into the distance and pulled startling detail into view.

Green and bright in the evening sunlight, the surrounding forest of spruce, birch, and cottonwood stretched away toward the ramparts of the Alaska Range. The spruce on the lower slopes of the mountains gave way to gulches of misty-green alder that crept up the ridges for a distance, then disappeared into the grayness of rock ledges and shale saddles. Shadowed canyons gaped alongside the slanting ridges.

Above, the snow line gradually began, first in scattered pockets where the sun never reached, then in blinding white couloirs flanked by hanging curtains of glacial ice. From this jumble of stone and icy blueness, the peaks themselves erupted into the skyline, hard-etched towers looming like sentinels on the edge of the earth.

Larkin lowered the binoculars, blinking. He felt he was on the brink of some secret Eden he would be the first to enter. No glitches on the trip, perfect weather on the trail. What more could he ask?

The question produced a sudden stab of disappointment. Ted Walsh wasn't here. Sam's friend and companion of many trails and campfires had been forced to drop out of the trip, despite the fact that this trek was to have been the greatest of them all. "The finale of the carefree years," Walsh called it. Larkin was getting married later that summer.

The decision to press on alone had been an easy one for Sam. He had realized for some time that he enjoyed going solo in the wilderness.

God, he had brought a lot of stuff, Larkin thought as he reached for his backpack. He had treated himself to a new expedition-type pack with state-of-the-art features. The freeze-dried food and gear he felt he would need brought the unit to nearly sixty pounds. He braced his legs and swung the pack up to rest on an extended knee. With a quick and practiced move, he brought the load up and onto his back, pushing his arms through the shoulder straps. He staggered slightly as he wiggled into the contours of the pack's frame and reached for his waist belt.

At that moment, Larkin could not help but think of the kidding he was being spared by Ted Walsh's absence. Walsh was the absolute master of reducing weight and bulk to gossamer. Ted's tricks—such as squeezing toothpaste from the tube and carrying it wrapped in light plastic—knew no limits. In his search for lightweight, efficient gadgets he was indefatigable.

Larkin swung the strap of the kit bag over his shoulder. The bag held his fishing gear: lures and flies, lightweight fly and spinning reels, and two pack rods that broke down into twelve-inch-long sections.

He was ready to begin his journey. He looked at the lake and wondered if he would see it again. Perhaps with Susan, his bride to be, or with their children someday.

He turned to the trail, a faint trace that led up along the slope of the hillside and out of sight through the scattered spruce trees. Leaning forward against the heft of the pack, he started up the ridge. Behind him, the loon was still calling from far out on the lake.

A sudden itching sensation on the backs of his hands interrupted the pleasure Larkin was feeling. Frowning at his oversight, he slapped at the mosquitoes and reached into the shoulder pack to get some repellent.

Even paradise had its pests.

The willow thicket was quiet in the evening shadows. The magpies had ceased their quarrelling over the tidbits of flesh they could find on the ground where the grizzly had killed the moose. Smaller birds were hushed as well, leaving only the rustles of hares and ground squirrels and the swirls of rising fish. The pulse of the river world seemed to have vanished.

The carcass of the moose was almost unrecognizable now. Except for one section where a leg and hoof angled out crazily, and another where a brown patch of head lay exposed to the sky, empty baleful eyes jutting outward, the entire body was crudely covered with an assortment of brush and clumps of mossy tundra.

The great bear sprawled belly down on top of his handiwork, his legs splayed out, his head resting on a hump pushed up by the curve of the cow's shoulder. He was asleep.

Suddenly his eyes flickered, then opened wide. Without moving his head, he flared his nostrils and lifted his ears. He detected nothing that alarmed him. Then a trace of wind stirred through the willows and died away.

The grizzly slipped down from the kill without a sound and tensed into a crouch, his head thrust forward, his legs poised like springs. The sound that had awakened him was gone again. The still air held no scents that were new or threatening.

He heard the noise again, more distinct now, getting closer. Still there was no scent to send alarm through his twenty-ounce brain. But even without the message of scent, this grizzly's instincts told him the noise represented danger. He eased toward the side of the clearing, where the willows were thicker and a stand of birch trees began.

The grizzly vanished into the cover, a shadow moving within shadows.

The magpies flew down to the abandoned kill.

Sam Larkin was frustrated. He had passed up two decent campsites when he had first hit the river. Now, nearly an hour later, he was slogging through a swamp-like area where the current was hemmed in by a thick growth of alders. Forced to wade in the shallows to make any progress at all, he was sweating heavily and achingly tired. He had broken out the repellent again, and his face, hands, and hair reeked of the clammy paste of medicine and perspiration. Clouds of mosquitoes hovered in the still air. The sun had dipped behind the hills, and the breeze had died with it. Footing was difficult in the heavy shadows, and he had tripped twice, staggering and barely avoiding a headlong fall.

You're getting sloppy, Sam told himself. This is exactly the kind of place where you have to worry about bears.

Everything he had read about the grizzly had stressed the point that the animal's relatively poor eyesight was more than offset by its superb hearing and remarkable nose. He remembered an Indian proverb from an article he had been reading on the plane only a few hours before. *The pine needle fell in the forest. The eagle saw it fall; the deer heard it fall; the bear smelled it fall.*

That was irony for you, Larkin thought. A grizzly on the cover of *In Wilderness* on the day I'm headed for Alaska.

In Wilderness was a new national magazine Ted Walsh had edited since its inception a year ago. Difficulties at the magazine had knocked Walsh out of the trip with Sam, despite the fact that Walsh had planned the entire venture. One of the magazine's regular contributors lived on the Toubok, and Walsh had mapped out a trek that would include a surprise visit to the writer's cabin, four days' hike upstream.

Even without Ted Walsh along, Sam had decided to stick to the original plan. He had always wanted to meet the writer, Jonathan Hill, whose article and photographs on the grizzly were the most recent in a series of pieces on Alaska.

Ahead, Sam could see a bend in the alders. The current was dark and smooth where it curved into view.

Okay, it's showtime, he told himself. He raised his voice in song. Bits and pieces of "Get Me to the Church on Time" filled the air as he waded on through the dark riffles.

He broke off in mid-note, laughing. His voice sounded absurdly loud and ridiculous above the murmur of the river.

"Instead of singing, I'll settle for talking to myself," Larkin mumbled. "It'll sound a helluva lot more pleasant.

"If there're any bears around here, I hope they hear me now!" Larkin called aloud. He shuddered at the alien sound of his own voice. "This is inane," he muttered.

Larkin sloshed on around the bend. The alders seemed to be thinning out, the terrain changing. Then he saw the river pouring straight at him from a stretch of open country where the muskeg plain and stands of spruce trees formed the horizon. Beyond a point of willows on the right bank, a ramp of dry, rocky soil slanted down from the higher ground.

Larkin's spirits soared. Camp at last!

The great bear crouched in the shadows, downwind of the willow thicket. The scent of the intruder flooded his nostrils now, triggering an instinctive force that compelled him to flee. But that force was only part of the complex emotions that stirred within him. The gamy odor of the moose kill made him confused and agitated.

He watched and waited.

Within moments, the scent of the intruder became overwhelming, raging toward the grizzly like a firestorm.

The smell of the moose kill mingled with the scent of the danger. The meat provided strength, an instinctive sense of well-being.

The great bear was afraid. Yet he did not flee.

Suddenly he spotted movement. The willow branches shook, then parted.

The puny two-legged menace stood in the clearing, looking off toward the river.

Larkin had been trying to hurry. His boots made loud sucking noises as he trudged along the muddy bank where the willows grew down to the water. He paused to study the last thirty yards that separated him from the far side of the willow thicket and the beginning of the open ground. The willows seemed to be thinner up away from the bank of the river. He could see gaps in the clumps of bushes and a few scattered birches on beyond. He headed that way, expecting firmer ground.

He had to use his arms and hands to ward the thick branches from his face. The green limbs he shoved aside immediately whipped back into place, snagging on his packs. He pressed on through the tangle with dogged determination.

In a moment he broke into a clearing. To his right, away from the stream, the willows gave way to a stand of birches. Straight ahead he could see the tops of the spruces, which marked the beginning of the tundra plain. That was the spot where he wanted to make camp.

The stillness was like a kind of vapor, and his breathing was labored, as if all oxygen had been squeezed out of the air.

He stepped ahead, then stopped, listening. He had heard something.

Faint and distant, the call of a loon broke through the stillness.

Was that what he had heard? Terrific! Music for his first camp. There must be a lake somewhere over there. Loons were not river birds.

He moved along a few paces, skirting the edges of a few willow clumps that loomed in the way.

Two magpies burst into flight from off to his left, squawking as they flapped on out over the river.

Larkin gasped, startled and shaken. A feverish chill swept over him, cutting through his general discomfort of fatigue, thirst, and hunger.

Come on, for Christ's sake, his thoughts urged. Let's get to camp.

He started again, then paused in midstep, staring at the place where the magpies had jumped, his mouth wide open.

The pile of brush that held his gaze was a haphazard mound of willow and spruce branches, bulging up waist-high. In the middle of the tangle, the head of a moose stared at him with vacant unseeing eyes, like some strange mounted trophy. A leg angled out of the brush to one side.

Larkin turned and looked around. The clearing was empty. The silence made the pounding of the blood in his temples feel like physical blows. He stood frozen to the spot, his mind trying to respond to a question he could not answer. *What in the name of God was going on?*

An explanation—logical and compelling—came to him in a burst of clarity.

A hunter! A goddamn poacher! Killed the moose out of season and covered the carcass to hide it.

Adrenaline surged through his body. Random ideas shot through his mind and disappeared.

Poachers hid their kills from game wardens. . . . The wardens used airplanes and helicopters. . . . Where was the poacher? Was he hidden nearby right now, watching? Poachers had been known to commit murder!

Larkin looked around again. The silence and empty clearing mocked him in his panic. Then he heard the loon calling from the distant lake.

A lake! Was the poacher there? With an airplane?

Mesmerized by the vision before him, he took a tentative step toward the brush pile. Then another.

He heard a heavy nasal *woof* and in the same instant he felt his backpack explode and he was hurtling forward through the air. The breath burst from his lungs as his stomach and face hit the ground, and he was engulfed in a storm of roars and massive, twisting muscle and flesh. His mind was swept clear of thought, except for one word that flared again and again.

Grizzly!

Grizzly . . . a searing pain across his buttocks, then fangs sinking into flesh . . . *grizzly* . . . a paw crushing his shoulder, claws raking his neck . . . *grizzly* . . . a slobbering mouth biting at his head, the fangs skidding and tearing across the flesh . . . *grizzly* . . . his hands afire with pain, his hands that he flapped feebly over the back of his head for protection . . . *grizzly* . . . his face pushing down into the moss, seeking refuge and finally finding oblivion.

He was swimming up through a murky sea, unable to hold the surface, gasping and floating for a second, then going under again. Gradually this thread of consciousness strengthened, and the lucid realization that he was still alive finally came—not from growing strength but from pain.

He tried to hang on to a simple thought: *The bear is gone—but I must not move! I'll have to play dead in case the beast is still nearby.*

His thoughts touched on the sources of his agony, one by one.

His buttocks were ripped. His shoulder was smashed, and his neck felt hot and wet. His head throbbed with pain, and blood filled his right eye. He could be blind in that eye. He could not tell. His ears and hands were numb.

Despite his injuries, he was totally conscious now. He was coming back! His heart was strong and he could live with the pain. Somehow, he was going to make it! What a story he would have to tell.

He remained frozen to the ground, trying to listen, but hearing nothing except his own thoughts. The first nauseating waves of shock swept over him, eroding the little strength he had left.

Dimly, through a smear of blood over his left eye, he could see the bottom of a willow bush. Vague shapes that he knew were stuff from his backpack were strewn over the ground.

The backpack had saved him, that was for sure, he thought. Without it, the grizzly's first blow would have killed him.

He decided the bear must be gone. Perhaps he had been unconscious a long time. There was no way to tell.

He moved his arm to bring his right hand down from the back of his head.

Nothing happened.

He tried to raise his hand so that he could see it. The bloody vision of his good eye cleared.

His fingers were gone. The hand was a bloody stump of bones and torn flesh.

Larkin screamed, a shrieking, unearthly cry of terror and pain.

His howl opened the earth. He was tumbling through the core of a roaring holocaust. Fangs found his face, and suddenly he was beyond any knowing.

The great bear raked at the corpse with a final desultory swipe. He trotted to the side of the clearing and turned, crouching, watching.

The body sprawled at the edge of the stream. A dark cloud of blood settled into an eddy, then was caught by the current and swept away.

The loon was still calling from the distant lake. The sound was like the cry of something that had come from far away and was lost and afraid in the vastness.

Chapter 13

Shipwreck of the Whaleship *Essex*

Owen Chase

If you've ever been inclined to think that the images of the great white whale Moby-Dick taking out the whaleship Pequod *with a slam-dunk move seemed a bit far-fetched, you might owe Mister Herman Melville an apology. As subsequent history has revealed, it seems old Herm got the original germ of the idea for his great novel from real life—a Nantucket whaleship named* Essex *that got the deep six in an attack by a sperm whale in the Pacific. Twenty men survived the sinking of the* Essex *by taking to three open lifeboats, but only eight of these shipwreck survivors lived to tell the story of what happened during the sea journey. For three months and three thousand miles, the whaling men suffered the worst ordeals of hunger and thirst imaginable in their epic journey of survival. One of the boats was lost at sea, and eventually the other two became separated. Before they reached the haven of rescue, the survivors resorted to cannibalism to sustain life.*

Owen Chase was the first mate of the Essex *and was one of the eight survivors. Twenty years after his narrative of the ordeal was originally published, Herman Melville borrowed a copy from Chase's son and read it while at sea on a whaling vessel in the South Pacific. "The reading of the wondrous story upon the landless sea and very close to the very latitude of the shipwreck had a surprising effect on me," Melville later wrote. He actually started writing* Moby-Dick *eight years after reading Chase's book.*

This excerpt of the Owen Chase narrative is from the edition published by the Lyons Press in 1999, with an introduction by Tim Cahill. Two separate sections are excerpted. The first describes the actual attack of the whale and the crew taking to the boats on November 20, 1820. As the second part of the excerpt begins, the whalers are struggling to stay alive on Henderson Island, deep in the South Pacific, far west of Easter Island and actually not too far from Pitcairn Island, famous as the last stop of the HMS Bounty. *When the men arrived on the island on December 20, they thought their prayers had been answered, but subsequent exploration has shown that the place is virtually barren of food and water. Thoughts of resuming their dreadful ocean voyage are rampant.*

I have not been able to recur to the scenes which are now to become the subject of description, although a considerable time has elapsed, without feeling a mingled emotion of horror and astonishment at the almost incredible destiny that has preserved me and my surviving companions from a terrible death. Frequently, in my reflections on the subject, even after this lapse of time, I find myself shedding tears of gratitude for our deliverance, and blessing God, by whose divine aid and protection we were conducted through a series of unparalleled suffering and distress, and restored to the bosoms of our families and friends. There is no knowing what a stretch of pain and misery the human mind is capable of contemplating, when it is wrought upon by the anxieties of preservation; nor what pangs and weaknesses the body is able to endure, until they are visited upon it; and when at last deliverance comes, when the dream of hope is realized, unspeakable gratitude takes possession of the soul, and tears of joy choke the utterance. We require to be taught in the school of some signal suffering, privation, and despair, the great lessons of constant dependence upon an almighty forbearance and mercy. In the midst of the wide ocean, at night, when the sight of the heavens was shut out, and the dark tempest came upon us, then it was that we felt ourselves ready to exclaim, "Heaven have mercy upon us, for nought but that can save us now." But I proceed to the recital.—On the 20th of November (cruising in latitude 0° 40′S., longitude 119° 0′W.), a shoal of whales was discovered off the lee-bow. The weather at this time was extremely fine and clear, and it was about 8 o'clock in the morning that the man at the mast-head gave the usual cry of, "There she blows." The ship was immediately put away, and we ran down in the direction for them. When we had got within half a mile of the place where they were observed, all our boats were lowered down, manned, and we started in pursuit of them. The ship, in the meantime, was brought to the wind, and the main-top-sail hove aback, to wait for us. I had the harpoon in the second boat; the captain preceded me in the first. When I arrived at the spot where we calculated they were, nothing was at first to be seen. We lay on our oars in anxious expectation of discovering them come up somewhere near us. Presently one rose, and spouted a short distance ahead of my boat; I made all speed towards it, came up with, and struck it; feeling the harpoon in him, he threw himself, in agony, over towards the boat (which at that time was up alongside of him), and, giving a severe blow with his tail, struck the boat near the edge of the water, amidships, and stove a hole in her. I immediately took up the boat hatchet, and cut the line, to disengage the boat from the whale, which by this time was running off with great velocity. I succeeded in getting clear of him, with the loss of the harpoon and line; and finding the water to pour fast in the boat, I hastily stuffed three or four of our jackets in the hole, ordered one man to keep constantly bailing, and the rest to pull immediately for the ship; we succeeded in keeping the boat free, and shortly gained the ship. The captain and the second mate, in the other two boats, kept up the pursuit, and soon struck another whale. They being at this time a considerable distance to leeward, I went forward, braced around the mainyard, and put the ship off in a direction for them; the boat which had been stove was immediately hoisted in, and after examining the hole, I found that I could, by nailing a piece of canvas over it, get her ready to join in a fresh pursuit, sooner than by lowering down the other remaining boat which belonged to the ship. I accordingly turned her over upon the quarter, and was in the act of nailing on the canvas, when I observed a very large spermaceti whale, as well as I could judge about eighty-five feet in length; he broke water about twenty rods off our weather-bow, and was lying quietly, with his head in a direction for the ship. He spouted two or three times, and then disappeared. In less than two or three seconds he came up again, about the length of the ship off, and made directly for us, at the rate of about three knots. The ship was then going with about the same velocity. His appearance and attitude gave us at first no alarm; but while I stood watching his movements, and observing him but a ship's length off, coming down for us with great celerity, I involuntarily ordered the boy at the helm to put it hard up; intending to sheer off and avoid him. The words were scarcely out of my mouth, before he came down upon us with full speed, and struck the ship with his head, just forward of the fore-chains; he gave us such an appalling and tremendous jar, as nearly threw us all on our faces. The ship brought up as suddenly and violently as if she had struck a rock, and trembled for a few seconds like a leaf. We looked at each other with perfect amazement, deprived almost of the power of speech. Many minutes elapsed before we were able to realize the dreadful accident; during which time he passed under the ship, grazing her keel as he went along, came up alongside of her to leeward, and lay on the top of the water (apparently stunned with the violence of the blow) for the space of a minute; he then suddenly started off, in a direction to leeward. After a few moments reflection, and recovering, in some measure, from the sudden consternation that had seized us, I of course concluded that he had stove a hole in the ship, and that it would be necessary to set the pumps going. Accordingly they were rigged, but had not been in operation more than one minute before I perceived the head of the ship to be gradually settling down in the water; I then ordered the signal to be set for the other boats, which, scarcely had I dispatched, before I again discovered the whale, apparently in convulsions, on the top of the water, about one hundred rods to leeward. He was enveloped in the foam of the sea, that his continual and violent thrashing about in the water had created around him, and I could distinctly see him smite his jaws together, as if distracted with rage and fury. He remained a short time in this situation, and then started off with great velocity, across the bows of the ship, to windward. By this time the ship had settled down a considerable distance in the water, and I gave her up for lost. I, however, ordered the pumps to be kept constantly going, and endeavoured to collect my thoughts for the occasion. I turned to the boats, two of which we then had with the ship, with an intention of clearing them away, and getting all things ready to embark in them, if there should be no other resource left; and while my attention was thus engaged for a moment, I was aroused with the cry of a man at the hatchway, "Here he is—he is making for us again." I turned around, and saw him about one hundred rods directly ahead of us, coming down apparently with twice his ordinary speed, and to me at that moment, it appeared with tenfold fury and vengeance in his aspect. The surf flew in all directions about him, and his course towards us was marked by a white foam of a rod in width, which he made with the continual violent thrashing of his tail; his head was about half out of water, and in that way he came upon, and again struck the ship. I was in hopes when I descried him making for us, that by a dexterous movement of putting the ship away immediately, I should be able to cross the line of his approach, before he could get up to us, and thus avoid what I knew, if he should strike us again, would prove our inevitable destruction. I bawled out to the helmsman, "Hard up!" but she had not fallen off more than a point, before we took the second shock. I should judge the speed of the ship to have been at this time about three knots, and that of the whale about six. He struck her to windward, directly under the cathead, and completely stove in her bows. He passed under the ship again, went off to leeward, and we saw no more of him. Our situation at this juncture can be more readily imagined than described. The shock to our feelings was such, as I am sure none can have an adequate conception of that were not there: the misfortune befell us at a moment when we least dreamt of any accident; and from the pleasing anticipations we had formed, of realizing the certain profits of our labour, we were dejected by a sudden, most mysterious, and overwhelming calamity. Not a moment, however, was to be lost in endeavouring to provide for the extremity to which it was now certain we were reduced. We were more than a thousand miles from the nearest land, and with nothing but a light open boat, as the resource of safety for myself and companions. I ordered the men to cease pumping, and every one to provide for himself; seizing a hatchet at the same time, I cut away the lashings of the spare boat, which lay bottom up across two spars directly over the quarter deck, and cried out to those near me to take her as she came down. They did so accordingly, and bore her on their shoulders as far as the waist of the ship. The steward had in the meantime gone down into the cabin twice, and saved two quadrants, two practical navigators, and the captain's trunk and mine; all which were hastily thrown into the boat, as she lay on the deck, with the two compasses which I snatched from the binnacle. He attempted to descend again; but the water by this time had rushed in, and he returned without being able to effect his purpose. By the time we had got the boat to the waist, the ship had filled with water, and was going down on her beam-ends: we shoved our boat as quickly as possible from the plank-shear into the water, all hands jumping in her at the same time, and launched off clear of the ship. We were scarcely two boat lengths distant from her, when she fell over to windward, and settled down in the water.

Amazement and despair now wholly took possession of us. We contemplated the frightful situation the ship lay in, and thought with horror upon the sudden and dreadful calamity that had overtaken us. We looked upon each other, as if to gather some consolatory sensation from an interchange of sentiments, but every countenance was marked with the paleness of despair. Not a word was spoken for several minutes by any of us; all appeared to be bound in a spell of stupid consternation; and from the time we were first attacked by the whale, to the period of the fall of the ship, and of our leaving her in the boat, more than ten minutes could not certainly have elapsed! God only knows in what way, or by what means, we were enabled to accomplish in that short time what we did; the cutting away and transporting the boat from where she was deposited would of itself, in ordinary circumstances, have consumed as much time as that, if the whole ship's crew had been employed in it. My companions had not saved a single article but what they had on their backs; but to me it was a source of infinite satisfaction, if any such could be gathered from the horrors of our gloomy situation, that we had been fortunate enough to have preserved our compasses, navigators, and quadrants. After the first shock of my feelings was over, I enthusiastically contemplated them as the probable instruments of our salvation; without them all would have been dark and hopeless. Gracious God! What a picture of distress and suffering now presented itself to my imagination. The crew of the ship were saved, consisting of twenty human souls. All that remained to conduct these twenty beings through the stormy terrors of the ocean, perhaps many thousand miles, were three open light boats. The prospect of obtaining any provisions or water from the ship, to subsist upon during the time, was at least now doubtful. How many long and watchful nights, thought I, are to be passed? How many tedious days of partial starvation are to be endured, before the least relief or mitigation of our sufferings can be reasonably anticipated. We lay at this time in our boat, about two ship lengths off from the wreck, in perfect silence, calmly contemplating her situation, and absorbed in our own melancholy reflections, when the other boats were discovered rowing up to us. They had but shortly before discovered that some accident had befallen us, but of the nature of which they were entirely ignorant. The sudden and mysterious disappearance of the ship was first discovered by the boat-steerer in the captain's boat, and with a horror-struck countenance and voice, he suddenly exclaimed, "Oh, my God! Where is the ship?" Their operations upon this were instantly suspended, and a general cry of horror and despair burst from the lips of every man, as their looks were directed for her, in vain, over every part of the ocean. They immediately made all haste towards us. The captain's boat was the first that reached us. He stopped about a boat's length off, but had no power to utter a single syllable: he was so completely overpowered with the spectacle before him that he sat down in his boat, pale and speechless. I could scarcely recognize his countenance, he appeared to be so much altered, awed, and overcome with the oppression of his feelings, and the dreadful reality that lay before him. He was in a short time however enabled to address the inquiry to me, "My God, Mr. Chase, what is the matter?" I answered, "We have been stove by a whale." I then briefly told him the story. After a few moment's reflection he observed that we must cut away her masts, and endeavour to get something out of her to eat. Our thoughts were now all accordingly bent on endeavours to save from the wreck whatever we might possibly want, and for this purpose we rowed up and got on to her. Search was made for every means of gaining access to her hold; and for this purpose the lanyards were cut loose, and with our hatchets we commenced to cut away the masts, that she might right up again, and enable us to scuttle her decks. In doing which we were occupied about three quarters of an hour, owing to our having no axes, nor indeed any other instruments, but the small hatchets belonging to the boat. After her masts were gone she came up about two-thirds of the way upon an even keel. While we were employed about the masts the captain took his quadrant, shoved off from the ship, and got an observation. We found ourselves in latitude 0° 40′S., longitude 119°W. We now commenced to cut a hole through the planks, directly above two large casks of bread, which most fortunately were between decks, in the waist of the ship, and which being in the upper side, when she upset, we had strong hopes was not wet. It turned out according to our wishes, and from these casks we obtained six hundred pounds of hard bread. Other parts of the deck were then scuttled, and we got without difficulty as much fresh water as we dared to take in the boats, so that each was supplied with about sixty-five gallons; we got also from one of the lockers a musket, a small canister of powder, a couple of files, two rasps, about two pounds of boat nails, and a few turtles. In the afternoon the wind came on to blow a strong breeze; and having obtained every thing that occurred to us could then be got out, we began to make arrangements for our safety during the night. A boat's line was made fast to the ship, and to the other end of it one of the boats was moored, at about fifty fathoms to leeward; another boat was then attached to the first one, about eight fathoms astern; and the third boat, the like distance astern of her. Night came on just as we had finished our operations; and such a night as it was to us! So full of feverish and distracting inquietude, that we were deprived entirely of rest. The wreck was constantly before my eyes. I could not, by any effort, chase away the horrors of the preceding day from my mind: they haunted me the live-long night. My companions—some of them were like sick women; they had no idea of the extent of their deplorable situation. One or two slept unconcernedly, while others wasted the night in unavailing murmurs. I now had full leisure to examine, with some degree of coolness, the dreadful circumstances of our disaster. The scenes of yesterday passed in such quick succession in my mind that it was not until after many hours of severe reflection that I was able to discard the idea of the catastrophe as a dream. Alas! It was one from which there was no awaking; it was too certainly true, that but yesterday we had existed as it were, and in one short moment had been cut off from all the hopes and prospects of the living! I have no language to paint out the horrors of our situation. To shed tears was indeed altogether unavailing, and withal unmanly; yet I was not able to deny myself the relief they served to afford me. After several hours of idle sorrow and repining I began to reflect upon the accident, and endeavoured to realize by what unaccountable destiny or design (which I could not at first determine) this sudden and most deadly attack had been made upon us: by an animal, too, never before suspected of premeditated violence, and proverbial for its insensibility and inoffensiveness. Every fact seemed to warrant me in concluding that it was anything but chance which directed his operations; he made two several attacks upon the ship, at a short interval between them, both of which, according to their direction, were calculated to do us the most injury, by being made ahead, and thereby combining the speed of the two objects for the shock; to effect which, the exact manoeuvres which he made were necessary. His aspect was most horrible, and such as indicated resentment and fury. He came directly from the shoal which we had just before entered, and in which we had struck three of his companions, as if fired with revenge for their sufferings. But to this it may be observed, that the mode of fighting which they always adopt is either with repeated strokes of their tails, or snapping of their jaws together; and that a case, precisely similar to this one, has never been heard of amongst the oldest and most experienced whalers. To this I would answer, that the structure and strength of the whale's head is admirably designed for this mode of attack; the most prominent part of which is almost as hard and as tough as iron; indeed, I can compare it to nothing else but the inside of a horse's hoof, upon which a lance or harpoon would not make the slightest impression. The eyes and ears are removed nearly one-third the length of the whole fish, from the front part of the head, and are not in the least degree endangered in this mode of attack. At all events, the whole circumstances taken together, all happening before my own eyes, and producing, at the time, impressions in my mind of decided, calculating mischief on the part of the whale (many of which impressions I cannot now recall) induce me to be satisfied that I am correct in my opinion. It is certainly, in all its bearings, a hitherto unheard of circumstance, and constitutes, perhaps, the most extraordinary one in the annals of the fishery.

As this section begins, the survivors of the Essex*'s sinking are on Henderson Island, where they landed on December 20, 1820. At this point in the narrative, it is obvious to them that the landfall they thought would be their salvation for food and water is not unlike a desert wasteland. They realize they will have to sail on . . . and keep hoping.*

December 23rd. At 11 o'clock a.m., we again visited our spring: the tide had fallen to about a foot below it, and we were able to procure, before it rose again, about twenty gallons of water. It was at first a little brackish, but soon became fresh, from the constant supply from the rock and the departure of the sea. Our observations this morning tended to give us every confidence in its quantity and quality, and we, therefore, rested perfectly easy in our minds on the subject, and commenced to make further discoveries about the island. Each man sought for his own daily living, on whatsoever the mountains, the shore, or the sea, could furnish him with; and every day, during our stay there, the whole time was employed in roving about for food. We found, however, on the twenty-fourth, that we had picked up, on the island, every thing that could be got at, in the way of sustenance; and, much to our surprise, some of the men came in at night and complained of not having gotten sufficient during the day to satisfy the cravings of their stomachs. Every accessible part of the mountain, contiguous to us, or within the reach of our weak enterprise, was already ransacked, for birds' eggs and grass, and was rifled of all that they contained: so that we began to entertain serious apprehensions that we should not be able to live long here; at any rate, with the view of being prepared, as well as possible, should necessity at any time oblige us to quit it, we commenced, on the twenty-fourth, to repair our boats, and continued to work upon them all that and the succeeding day. We were enabled to do this, with much facility, by drawing them up and turning them over on the beach, working by spells of two or three hours at a time, and then leaving off to seek for food. We procured our water daily, when the tide would leave the shore: but on the evening of the twenty-fifth, found that a fruitless search for nourishment had not repaid us for the labors of a whole day. There was no one thing on the island upon which we could in the least degree rely, except the peppergrass, and of that the supply was precarious, and not much relished without some other food. Our situation here, therefore, now became worse than it would have been in our boats on the ocean; because, in the latter case, we should be still making some progress towards the land, while our provisions lasted, and the chance of falling in with some vessel be considerably increased. It was certain that we ought not to remain here unless upon the strongest assurances in our own minds, of sufficient sustenance, and that, too, in regular supplies, that might be depended upon. After much conversation amongst us on this subject, and again examining our navigators, it was finally concluded to set sail for Easter Island, which we found to be E.S.E. from us in latitude 27° 9′S., longitude 109° 35′W. All we knew of this island was that it existed as laid down in the books; but of its extent, productions, or inhabitants, if any, we were entirely ignorant; at any rate, it was nearer by eight hundred and fifty miles to the coast, and could not be worse in its productions than the one we were about leaving.

The twenty-sixth of December was wholly employed in preparations for our departure; our boats were hauled down to the vicinity of the spring, and our casks, and everything else that would contain it, filled with water.

There had been considerable talk between three of our companions about their remaining on this island, and taking their chance both for a living, and an escape from it; and as the time drew near at which we were to leave, they made up their minds to stay behind. The rest of us could make no objection to their plan, as it lessened the load of our boats, allowed us their share of the provisions, and the probability of their being able to sustain themselves on the island was much stronger than that of our reaching the mainland. Should we, however, ever arrive safely, it would become our duty, and we so assured them, to give information of their situation, and make every effort to procure their removal from thence; which we accordingly afterwards did.

Their names were William Wright of Barnstable, Massachusetts, Thomas Chapple of Plymouth, England, and Seth Weeks of the former place. They had begun, before we came away, to construct a sort of habitation, composed of the branches of trees, and we left with them every little article that could be spared from the boats. It was their intention to build a considerable dwelling, that would protect them from the rains, as soon as time and materials could be provided. The captain wrote letters, to be left on the island, giving information of the fate of the ship, and that of our own; and stating that we had set out to reach Easter Island, with further particulars, intended to give notice (should our fellow sufferers die there, and the place be ever visited by any vessel) of our misfortunes. These letters were put in a tin case, enclosed in a small wooden box, and nailed to a tree, on the west side of the island, near our landing place. We had observed, some days previously, the name of a ship, *The Elizabeth*, cut out in the bark of this tree, which rendered it indubitable that one of that name had once touched here. There was, however, no date to it, or anything else, by which any further particulars could be made out.

December 27th. I went, before we set sail this morning, and procured for each boat a flat stone, and two armfuls of wood, with which to make a fire in our boats, should it become afterwards necessary in the further prosecution of our voyage; as we calculated we might catch a fish, or a bird, and in that case be provided with the means of cooking it; otherwise, from the intense heat of the weather, we knew they could not be preserved from spoiling. At ten o'clock a.m., the tide having risen far enough to allow our boats to float over the rocks, we made all sail, and steered around the island, for the purpose of making a little further observation, which would not detain us any time, and might be productive of some unexpected good fortune. Before we started we missed our three companions, and found they had not come down, either to assist us to get off, nor to take any kind of leave of us. I walked up the beach towards their rude dwelling, and informed them that we were then about to set sail, and should probably never see them more. They seemed to be very much affected, and one of them shed tears. They wished us to write to their relations, should Providence safely direct us again to our homes, and said but little else. They had every confidence in being able to procure a subsistence there as long as they remained: and, finding them ill at heart about taking any leave of us, I hastily bid them "good-bye," hoped they would do well, and came away. They followed me with their eyes until I was out of sight, and I never saw more of them.

On the N.W. side of the island we perceived a fine white beach, on which we imagined we might land, and in a short time ascertain if any further useful discoveries could be effected, or any addition made to our stock of provisions; and having set ashore five or six of the men for this purpose, the rest of us shoved off the boats and commenced fishing. We saw a number of sharks, but all efforts to take them proved ineffectual; and we got but a few small fish, about the size of a mackerel, which we divided amongst us. In this business we were occupied for the remainder of the day, until six o'clock in the afternoon, when the men, having returned to the shore from their search in the mountains, brought a few birds, and we again set sail and steered directly for Easter Island. During that night, after we had got quite clear of the land, we had a fine strong breeze from the N.W.; we kept our fires going, and cooked our fish and birds, and felt our situation as comfortable as could be expected. We continued on our course, consuming our provisions and water as sparingly as possible, without any material incident, until the thirtieth, when the wind hauled out E.S.E. directly ahead, and so continued until the thirty-first, when it again came to the northward, and we resumed our course.

On the third of January we experienced heavy squalls from the W.S.W. accompanied with dreadful thunder and lightning, that threw a gloomy and cheerless aspect over the ocean, and incited a recurrence of some of those heavy and desponding moments that we had before experienced. We commenced from Ducie's Island to keep a regular reckoning, by which, on the fourth of January, we found we had got to the southward of Easter Island, and the wind prevailing E.N.E. we should not be able to get on to the eastward, so as to reach it. Our birds and fish were all now consumed, and we had begun again upon our short allowance of bread. It was necessary, in this state of things, to change our determination of going to Easter Island, and shape our course in some other direction, where the wind would allow of our going. We had but little hesitation in concluding, therefore, to steer for the island of Juan Fernandez, which lay about E.S.E. from us, distant two thousand five hundred miles. We bent our course accordingly towards it, having for the two succeeding days very light winds, and suffering excessively from the intense heat of the sun. The seventh brought us a change of wind to the northward, and at twelve o'clock we found ourselves in latitude 30° 18′S., longitude 117° 29′W. We continued to make what progress we could to the eastward.

January 10th. Matthew P. Joy, the second mate, had suffered from debility, and the privations we had experienced, much beyond any of the rest of us, and was on the eighth removed to the captain's boat, under the impression that he would be more comfortable there, and more attention and pains be bestowed in nursing and endeavouring to comfort him. This day being calm, he manifested a desire to be taken back again; but at 4 o'clock in the afternoon, after having been, according to his wishes, placed in his own boat, he died very suddenly after his removal. On the eleventh, at six o'clock in the morning, we sewed him up in his clothes, tied a large stone to his feet, and, having brought all the boats to, consigned him in a solemn manner to the ocean. This man did not die of absolute starvation, although his end was no doubt very much hastened by his sufferings. He had a weak and sickly constitution, and complained of being unwell the whole voyage. It was an incident, however, which threw a gloom over our feelings for many days. In consequence of his death, one man from the captain's boat was placed in that from which he died, to supply his place, and we stood away again on our course.

On the 12th of January we had the wind from the N.W. which commenced in the morning, and came on to blow before night a perfect gale. We were obliged to take in all sail and run before the wind. Flashes of lightning were quick and vivid, and the rain came down in cataracts. As, however, the gale blew us fairly on our course, and our speed being great during the day, we derived, I may say, even pleasure from the uncomfortableness and fury of the storm. We were apprehensive that in the darkness of this night we should be separated, and made arrangements, each boat to keep an E.S.E. course all night. About eleven o'clock my boat being ahead a short distance of the others, I turned my head back, as I was in the habit of doing every minute, and neither of the others were to be seen. It was blowing and raining at this time as if the heavens were separating, and I knew not hardly at the moment what to do. I hove my boat to the wind, and lay drifting about an hour, expecting every moment they would come up with me, but not seeing anything of them, I put away again, and stood on the course agreed upon, with strong hopes that daylight would enable me to discover them again. When the morning dawned, in vain did we look over every part of the ocean for our companions; they were gone! And we saw no more of them afterwards. It was folly to repine at the circumstance; it could neither be remedied, nor could sorrow secure their return; but it was impossible to prevent ourselves feeling all the poignancy and bitterness that characterizes the separation of men who have long suffered in each other's company, and whose interests and feelings fate had so closely linked together. By our observation, we separated in latitude 32° 16′S., longitude 112° 20′W. For many days after this accident, our progress was attended with dull and melancholy reflections. We had lost the cheering of each other's faces, that which strange as it is, we so much required in both our mental and bodily distresses. The 14th January proved another very squally and rainy day. We had now been nineteen days from the island, and had only made a distance of about 900 miles: necessity began to whisper us, that still further reduction of our allowance must take place, or we must abandon altogether the hopes of reaching the land, and rely wholly on the chance of being taken up by a vessel. But how to reduce the daily quantity of food, with any regard to life itself, was a question of the utmost consequence. Upon our first leaving the wreck, the demands of the stomach had been circumscribed to the smallest possible compass; and subsequently before reaching the island, a diminution had taken place of nearly one-half; and it was now, from a reasonable calculation, become necessary even to curtail that at least one-half; which must, in a short time, reduce us to mere skeletons again. We had a full allowance of water, but it only served to contribute to our debility; our bodies deriving but the scanty support which an ounce and a half of bread for each man afforded. It required a great effort to bring matters to this dreadful alternative, either to feed our bodies and our hopes a little longer, or in the agonies of hunger to seize upon and devour our provisions, and coolly await the approach of death.

We were as yet, just able to move about in our boats, and slowly perform the necessary labors appertaining to her; but we were fast wasting away with the relaxing effects of the water, and we daily almost perished under the torrid rays of a meridian sun; to escape which, we would lie down in the bottom of the boat, cover ourselves over with the sails, and abandon her to the mercy of the waves. Upon attempting to rise again, the blood would rush into the head, and an intoxicating blindness come over us, almost to occasion our suddenly falling down again. A slight interest was still kept up in our minds by the distant hopes of yet meeting with the other boats, but it was never realized. An accident occurred at night, which gave me a great cause of uneasiness, and led me to an unpleasant rumination upon the probable consequences of a repetition of it. I had laid down in the boat without taking the usual precaution of securing the lid of the provision chest, as I was accustomed to do, when one of the white men awoke me, and informed me that one of the blacks had taken some bread from it. I felt at the moment the highest indignation and resentment at such conduct in any of our crew and immediately took my pistol in my hand, and charged him if he had taken any, to give it up without the least hesitation, or I should instantly shoot him!—He became at once very much alarmed, and trembling, confessed the fact, pleading the hard necessity that urged him to it: he appeared to be very penitent for his crime, and earnestly swore that he would never be guilty of it again. I could not find it in my soul to extend towards him the least severity on this account, however much, according to the strict imposition which we felt upon ourselves, it might demand it. This was the first infraction; and the security of our lives, our hopes of redemption from our sufferings, loudly called for a prompt and signal punishment; but every humane feeling of nature plead in his behalf, and he was permitted to escape, with the solemn injunction that a repetition of the same offence would cost him his life.

I had almost determined upon this occurrence to divide our provisions, and give to each man his share of the whole stock; and should have done so in the height of my resentment had it not been for the reflection that some might, by imprudence, be tempted to go beyond the daily allowance, or consume it all at once, and bring on a premature weakness or starvation: this would of course disable them for the duties of the boat, and reduce our chances of safety and deliverance.

On the 15th of January, at night, a very large shark was observed swimming about us in a most ravenous manner, making attempts every now and then upon different parts of the boat, as if he would devour the very wood with hunger; he came several times and snapped at the steering oar, and even the stern-post. We tried in vain to stab him with a lance, but we were so weak as not to be able to make any impression upon his hard skin; he was so much larger than an ordinary one, and manifested such a fearless malignity, as to make us afraid of him; and our utmost efforts, which were at first directed to kill him for prey, became in the end self-defense. Baffled however in all his hungry attempts upon us, he shortly made off.

On the 16th of January, we were surrounded with porpoises in great numbers, that followed us nearly an hour, and which also defied all manoeuvres to catch them. The 17th and 18th proved to be calm; and the distresses of a cheerless prospect and a burning hot sun were again visited upon our devoted heads.

We began to think that Divine Providence had abandoned us at last; and it was but an unavailing effort to endeavour to prolong a now tedious existence. Horrible were the feelings that took possession of us!—The contemplation of a death of agony and torment, refined by the most dreadful and distressing reflections, absolutely prostrated both body and soul. There was not a hope now remaining to us but that which was derived from a sense of the mercies of our Creator. The night of the 18th was a despairing era in our sufferings; our minds were wrought up to the highest pitch of dread and apprehension for our fate, and all in them was dark, gloomy, and confused. About 8 o'clock, the terrible noise of whale spouts near us sounded in our ears: we could distinctly hear the furious thrashing of their tails in the water, and our weak minds pictured out their appalling and hideous aspects. One of my companions, the black man, took an immediate fright, and solicited me to take out the oars, and endeavour to get away from them. I consented to his using any means for that purpose; but alas! It was wholly out of our power to raise a single arm in our own defense. Two or three of the whales came down near us, and went swiftly off across our stern, blowing and spouting at a terrible rate; they, however, after an hour or two disappeared, and we saw no more of them. The next day, the 19th of January, we had extremely boisterous weather, with rain, heavy thunder and lightning, which reduced us again to the necessity of taking in all sail and lying to. The wind blew from every point of the compass within the twenty-four hours, and at last towards the next morning settled at E.N.E. a strong breeze.

January 20th. The black man, Richard Peterson, manifested today symptoms of a speedy dissolution; he had been lying between the seats in the boat, utterly dispirited and broken down, without being able to do the least duty, or hardly to place his hand to his head for the last three days, and had this morning made up his mind to die rather than endure further misery: he refused his allowance; said he was sensible of his approaching end, and was perfectly ready to die: in a few minutes he became speechless, the breath appeared to be leaving his body without producing the least pain, and at four o'clock he was gone. I had two days previously conversations with him on the subject of religion on which he reasoned very sensibly, and with much composure; and begged me to let his wife know his fate, if ever I reached home in safety. The next morning we committed him to the sea, in latitude 35° 07′S., longitude 105° 46′W. The wind prevailed to the eastward until the

24th of January, when it again fell calm. We were now in a most wretched and sinking state of debility, hardly able to crawl around the boat, and possessing but strength enough to convey our scanty morsel to our mouths. When I perceived this morning that it was calm, my fortitude almost forsook me. I thought to suffer another scorching day, like the last we had experienced, would close before night the scene of our miseries; and I felt many a despairing moment that day, that had well nigh proved fatal. It required an effort to look calmly forward, and contemplate what was yet in store for us, beyond what I felt I was capable of making; and what it was that buoyed me above all the terrors which surrounded us, God alone knows. Our ounce and a half of bread, which was to serve us all day, was in some cases greedily devoured, as if life was to continue but another moment; and at other times, it was hoarded up and eaten crumb by crumb, at regular intervals during the day, as if it was to last us for ever. To add to our calamities, biles began to break out upon us, and our imaginations shortly became as diseased as our bodies. I laid down at night to catch a few moments of oblivious sleep, and immediately my starving fancy was at work. I dreamt of being placed near a splendid and rich repast, where there was every thing that the most dainty appetite could desire; and of contemplating the moment in which we were to commence to eat with enraptured feelings of delight; and just as I was about to partake of it, I suddenly awoke to the cold realities of my miserable situation. Nothing could have oppressed me so much. It set such a longing frenzy for victuals in my mind, that I felt as if I could have wished the dream to continue for ever, that I never might have awoke from it. I cast a sort of vacant stare about the boat, until my eyes rested upon a bit of tough cowhide, which was fastened to one of the oars; I eagerly seized and commenced to chew it, but there was no substance in it, and it only served to fatigue my weak jaws, and add to my bodily pains. My fellow sufferers murmured very much the whole time, and continued to press me continually with questions upon the probability of our reaching land again. I kept constantly rallying my spirits to enable me to afford them comfort. I encouraged them to bear up against all evils, and if we must perish, to die in our own cause, and not weakly distrust the providence of the Almighty by giving ourselves up to despair. I reasoned with them, and told them that we would not die sooner by keeping up our hopes; that the dreadful sacrifices and privations we endured were to preserve us from death, and were not to be put in competition with the price which we set upon our lives, and their value to our families: it was, besides, unmanly to repine at what neither admitted of alleviation nor cure; and withal, that it was our solemn duty to recognize in our calamities an overruling divinity, by whose mercy we might be suddenly snatched from peril, and to rely upon him alone, "Who tempers the wind to the shorn lamb."

The three following days, the 25th, 26th, and 27th, were not distinguished by any particular circumstances. The wind still prevailed to the eastward, and by its obduracy, almost tore the very hopes of our hearts away: it was impossible to silence the rebellious repinings of our nature, at witnessing such a succession of hard fortune against us. It was our cruel lot not to have had one bright anticipation realized—not one wish of our thirsting souls gratified. We had, at the end of these three days, been urged to the southward as far as latitude 36° into a chilly region, where rains and squalls prevailed; and we now calculated to tack and stand back to the northward:

after much labor, we got our boat about; and so great was the fatigue attending this small exertion of our bodies, that we all gave up for a moment and abandoned her to her own course.—Not one of us had now strength sufficient to steer, or indeed to make one single effort towards getting the sails properly trimmed, to enable us to make any headway. After an hour or two of relaxation, during which the horrors of our situation came upon us with a despairing force and effect, we made a sudden effort and got our sails into such a disposition as that the boat would steer herself; and we then threw ourselves down, awaiting the issue of time to bring us relief, or to take us from the scene of our troubles. We could now do nothing more; strength and spirits were totally gone; and what indeed could have been the narrow hopes, that in our situation, then bound us to life?

January 28th. Our spirits this morning were hardly sufficient to allow of our enjoying a change of the wind, which took place to the westward.—It had nearly become indifferent to us from what quarter it blew: nothing but the slight chance of meeting a vessel remained to us now: it was this narrow comfort alone that prevented me from lying down at once to die. But fourteen days stinted allowance of provisions remained, and it was absolutely necessary to increase the quantity to enable us to live five days longer: we therefore partook of it, as pinching necessity demanded, and gave ourselves wholly up to the guidance and disposal of our Creator.

The 29th and 30th of January, the wind continued west, and we made considerable progress until the 31st, when it again came ahead, and prostrated all our hopes. On the 1st of February, it changed again to the westward, and on the 2nd and 3rd blew to the eastward; and we had it light and variable until the 8th of February. Our sufferings were now drawing to a close; a terrible death appeared shortly to await us; hunger became violent and outrageous, and we prepared for a speedy release from our troubles; our speech and reason were both considerably impaired, and we were reduced to be at this time certainly the most helpless and wretched of the whole human race. Isaac Cole, one of our crew, had the day before this, in a fit of despair, thrown himself down in the boat, and was determined there calmly to wait for death. It was obvious that he had no chance; all was dark he said in his mind, not a single ray of hope was left for him to dwell upon; and it was folly and madness to be struggling against what appeared so palpably to be our fixed and settled destiny. I remonstrated with him as effectually as the weakness both of my body and understanding would allow of; and what I said appeared for a moment to have a considerable effect: he made a powerful and sudden effort, half rose up, crawled forward and hoisted the jib, and firmly and loudly cried that he would not give up; that he would live as long as the rest of us—but alas! This effort was but the hectic fever of the moment, and he shortly again relapsed into a state of melancholy and despair. This day his reason was attacked, and he became about 9 o'clock in the morning a most miserable spectacle of madness: he spoke incoherently about everything, calling loudly for a napkin and water, and then, lying stupidly and senselessly down in the boat again, would close his hollow eyes, as if in death. About 10 o'clock, we suddenly perceived that he became speechless; we got him as well as we were able upon a board, placed on one of the seats of the boat, and covering him up with some old clothes, left him to his fate. He lay in the greatest pain and apparent misery, groaning piteously until four o'clock, when he died, in the most horrid and frightful convulsions I ever witnessed. We kept his corpse all night, and in the morning my two companions began as a course to make preparations to dispose of it in the sea; when after reflecting on the subject all night, I addressed them on the painful subject of keeping the body for food!! Our provisions could not possibly last us beyond three days, within which time, it was not in any degree probable that we should find relief from our present sufferings, and that hunger would at last drive us to the necessity of casting lots. It was without any objection agreed to, and we set to work as fast as we were able to prepare it so as to prevent its spoiling. We separated his limbs from his body, and cut all the flesh from the bones; after which, we opened the body, took out the heart, and then closed it again—sewed it up as decently as we could, and committed it to the sea. We now first commenced to satisfy the immediate cravings of nature from the heart, which we eagerly devoured, and then ate sparingly of a few pieces of the flesh; after which we hung up the remainder, cut in thin strips about the boat, to dry in the sun: we made a fire and roasted some of it, to serve us during the next day. In this manner did we dispose of our fellow sufferer; the painful recollection of which brings to mind at this moment, some of the most disagreeable and revolting ideas that it is capable of conceiving. We knew not then to whose lot it would fall next, either to die or be shot, and eaten like the poor wretch we had just dispatched. Humanity must shudder at the dreadful recital. I have no language to paint the anguish of our souls in this dreadful dilemma. The next morning, the 10th of February, we found that the flesh had become tainted, and had turned of a greenish color upon which we concluded to make a fire and cook it at once, to prevent its becoming so putrid as not to be eaten at all: we accordingly did so, and by that means preserved it for six or seven days longer; our bread during the time remained untouched; as that would not be liable to spoil, we placed it carefully aside for the last moments of our trial. About three o'clock this afternoon a strong breeze set in from the N.W. and we made very good progress, considering that we were compelled to steer the boat by management of the sails alone: this wind continued until the thirteenth, when it changed again ahead. We contrived to keep soul and body together by sparingly partaking of our flesh, cut up in small pieces and eaten with salt water. By the fourteenth, our bodies became so far recruited, as to enable us to make a few attempts at guiding our boat again with the oar; by each taking his turn, we managed to effect it, and to make a tolerable good course. On the fifteenth, our flesh was all consumed, and we were driven to the last morsel of bread, consisting of two cakes; our limbs had for the last two days swelled very much, and now began to pain us most excessively. We were still, as near as we could judge, three hundred miles from the land, and but three days of our allowance on hand. The hope of a continuation of the wind, which came out at west this morning, was the only comfort and solace that remained to us: so strong had our desires at last reached in this respect, that a high fever had set in, in our veins, and a longing that nothing but its continuation could satisfy. Matters were now with us at their height; all hope was cast upon the breeze; and we tremblingly and fearfully awaited its progress, and the dreadful development of our destiny. On the sixteenth, at night, full of the horrible reflections of our situation, and panting with weakness, I laid down to sleep, almost indifferent whether I should ever see the light again. I had not lain long, before I dreamt I saw a ship at some distance off from us, and strained every nerve to get to her, but could not. I awoke almost overpowered with the frenzy I had caught in my slumbers, and stung with the cruelties of a diseased and disappointed imagination. On the seventeenth, in the afternoon, a heavy cloud appeared to be settling down in an E. by N. direction from us, which in my view, indicated the vicinity of some land, which I took for the island of Mas Afuera. I concluded it could be no other; and immediately upon this reflection, the life blood began to flow again briskly in my veins. I told my companions that I was well convinced it was land, and if so, in all probability we should reach it before two days more. My words appeared to comfort them much; and by repeated assurances of the favourable appearance of things, their spirits acquired even a degree of elasticity that was truly astonishing. The dark features of our distress began now to diminish a little, and the countenance, even amid the gloomy bodings of our hard lot, to assume a much fresher hue. We directed our course for the cloud, and our progress that night was extremely good. The next morning, before daylight, Thomas Nicholson, a boy about seventeen years of age, one of my two companions who had thus far survived with me, after having bailed the boat, laid down, drew a piece of canvas over him, and cried out that he then wished to die immediately. I saw that he had given up, and I attempted to speak a few words of comfort and encouragement to him, and endeavoured to persuade him that it was a great weakness and even wickedness to abandon a reliance upon the Almighty, while the least hope, and a breath of life remained; but he felt unwilling to listen to any of the consolatory suggestions which I made to him; and, notwithstanding the extreme probability which I stated there was of our gaining the land before the end of two days more, he insisted upon lying down and giving himself up to despair. A fixed look of settled and forsaken despondency came over his face: he lay for some time silent, sullen, and sorrowful—and I felt at once satisfied that the coldness of death was fast gathering upon him: there was a sudden and unaccountable earnestness in his manner that alarmed me, and made me fear that I myself might unexpectedly be overtaken by a like weakness, or dizziness of nature, that would bereave me at once of both reason and life; but Providence willed it otherwise.

At about seven o'clock this morning, while I was lying asleep, my companion who was steering, suddenly and loudly called out "*There's a Sail!*" I know not what was the first movement I made upon hearing such an unexpected cry: the earliest of my recollections are that immediately I stood up, gazing in a state of abstraction and ecstasy upon the blessed vision of a vessel about seven miles off from us; she was standing in the same direction with us, and the only sensation I felt at the moment was, that of a violent and unaccountable impulse to fly directly towards her. I do not believe it is possible to form a just conception of the pure, strong feelings, and the unmingled emotions of joy and gratitude, that took possession of my mind on this occasion: the boy, too, took a sudden and animated start from his despondency, and stood up to witness the probable instrument of his salvation. Our only fear was now that she would not discover us, or that we might not be able to intercept her course: we, however, put our boat immediately, as well as we were able, in a direction to cut her off; and found, to our great joy, that we sailed faster than she did. Upon observing us, she shortened sail, and allowed us to come up to her. The captain hailed us, and asked who we were. I told him we were from a wreck, and he cried out immediately for us to come alongside the ship. I made an effort to assist myself along to the side, for the purpose of getting up, but strength failed me altogether, and I found it impossible to move a step further without help. We must have formed at that moment, in the eyes of the captain and his crew, a most deplorable and affecting picture of suffering and misery. Our cadaverous countenances, sunken eyes, and bones just starting through the skin, with the ragged remnants of clothes stuck about our sun burnt bodies, must have produced an appearance to him affecting and revolting in the highest degree. The sailors commenced to remove us from our boat, and we were taken to the cabin, and comfortably provided for in every respect. In a few minutes we were permitted to taste of a little thin food, made from tapioca, and in a few days, with prudent management, we were considerably recruited. This vessel proved to be the brig *Indian*, Captain William Crozier, of London; to whom we are indebted for every polite, friendly, and attentive disposition towards us, that can possibly characterize a man of humanity and feeling. We were taken up in latitude 33° 45′S., longitude 81° 03′W. At twelve o'clock this day we saw the island of Mas Afuera, and on the 25th of February, we arrived at Valparaiso in utter distress and poverty. Our wants were promptly relieved there.

Chapter 14

To Build a Fire

Jack London

Cast your mind back over time for a moment, if you will, and try to recall the coldest weather you've ever experienced. Well, it's about to get a lot colder. Jack London (1876–1916) was an extraordinary man, whose life has always reminded me of a shooting star, brilliant, irresistible, suddenly gone. Not only did he write volumes of wonderful prose created from his seafaring and wilderness trail adventures, but he was also a true champion of the weak and the poor, the abused people of his time. What a man he was. And what a writer! Perhaps this is the classic of all survival tales. You can throw all the adjectives you wish at it, and they will all stick: gripping, stirring, surprising . . . the list would be endless.

Day had broken cold and gray, exceedingly cold and gray, when the man turned aside from the main Yukon trail and climbed the high earth-bank, where a dim and little-travelled trail led eastward through the fat spruce timberland. It was a steep bank, and he paused for breath at the top, excusing the act to himself by looking at his watch. It was nine o'clock. There was no sun nor hint of sun, though there was not a cloud in the sky. It was a clear day, and yet there seemed an intangible pall over the face of things, a subtle gloom that made the day dark, and that was due to the absence of sun. This fact did not worry the man. He was used to the lack of sun. It had been days since he had seen the sun, and he knew that a few more days must pass before that cheerful orb, due south, would just peep above the skyline and dip immediately from view.

The man flung a look back along the way he had come. The Yukon lay a mile wide and hidden under three feet of ice. On top of this ice were as many feet of snow. It was all pure white, rolling in gentle undulations where the ice jams of the freeze-up had formed. North and south, as far as his eye could see, it was unbroken white, save for a dark hairline that curved and twisted from around the spruce-covered island to the south, and that curved and twisted away into the north, where it disappeared behind another spruce-covered island. This dark hairline was the trail—the main trail—that led south five hundred miles to the Chilcoot Pass, Dyea, and salt water; and that led north seventy miles to Dawson, and still on to the north a thousand miles to Nulato, and finally to St. Michael, on Bering Sea, a thousand miles and half a thousand more.

But all this—this mysterious, far-reaching hairline trail, the absence of sun from the sky, the tremendous cold, and the strangeness and weirdness of it all—made no impression on the man. It was not because he was long used to it. He was a newcomer in the land, a *chechaquo,* and this was his first winter. The trouble with him was that he was without imagination. He was quick and alert in the things of life, but only in things, and not in the significances. Fifty degrees below zero meant eighty-odd degrees of frost. Such fact impressed him as being cold and uncomfortable, and that was all. It did not lead him to meditate upon his frailty as a creature of temperature, and upon man's frailty in general, able only to live within certain narrow limits of heat and cold; and from there on it did not lead him to the conjectural field of immortality and man's place in the universe. Fifty degrees below zero stood for a bite of frost that hurt and that must be guarded against by use of mittens, ear flaps, warm moccasins, and thick socks. Fifty degrees below zero was to him just precisely fifty degrees below zero. That there should be anything more to it than that was a thought that never entered his head.

As he turned to go, he spat speculatively. There was a sharp, explosive crackle that startled him. He spat again. And again, in the air, before it could fall to the snow, the spittle crackled. He knew that at fifty below spittle crackled on the snow, but this spittle had crackled in the air. Undoubtedly it was colder than fifty below—how much colder he did not know. But the temperature did not matter. He was bound for the old claim on the left fork of Henderson Creek, where the boys were already. They had come over across the divide from the Indian Creek country, while he had come the roundabout way to take a look at the possibilities of getting out logs in the spring from the islands in the Yukon. He would be in to camp by six o'clock; a bit after dark, it was true, but the boys would be there, a fire would be going, and a hot supper would be ready. As for lunch, he pressed his hand against the protruding bundle under his jacket. It was also under his shirt, wrapped up in a handkerchief and lying against the naked skin. It was the only way to keep the biscuits from freezing. He smiled agreeably to himself as he thought of those biscuits, each cut open and sopped in bacon grease, and each enclosing a generous slice of fried bacon.

He plunged in among the big spruce trees. The trail was faint. A foot of snow had fallen since the last sled had passed over, and he was glad he was without a sled, travelling light. In fact, he carried nothing but the lunch wrapped in the handkerchief. He was surprised, however, at the cold. It certainly was cold, he concluded, as he rubbed his numb nose and cheekbones with his mittened hand. He was a warm-whiskered man, but the hair on his face did not protect the high cheekbones and the eager nose that thrust itself aggressively into the frosty air.

At the man's heels trotted a dog, a big native husky, the proper wolf dog, gray-coated and without any visible or temperamental difference from its brother, the wild wolf. The animal was depressed by the tremendous cold. It knew that it was no time for travelling. Its instinct told it a truer tale than was told to the man by the man's judgment. In reality, it was not merely colder than fifty below zero; it was colder than sixty below, than seventy below. It was seventy-five below zero. Since the freezing point is thirty-two above zero, it meant that one hundred and seven degrees of frost obtained. The dog did not know anything about thermometers. Possibly in its brain there was no sharp consciousness of a condition of very cold such as was in the man's brain. But the brute had its instinct. It experienced a vague but menacing apprehension that subdued it and made it slink along at the man's heels, and that made it question eagerly every unwonted movement of the man as if expecting him to go into camp or to seek shelter somewhere and build a fire. The dog had learned fire, and it wanted fire, or else to burrow under the snow and cuddle its warmth away from the air.

The frozen moisture of its breathing had settled on its fur in a fine powder of frost, and especially were its jowls, muzzle and eyelashes whitened by its crystalled breath. The man's red beard and mustache were likewise frosted, but more solidly, the deposit taking the form of ice and increasing with every warm, moist breath he exhaled. Also, the man was chewing tobacco, and the muzzle of ice held his lips so rigidly that he was unable to clear his chin when he expelled the juice. The result was that a crystal beard of the color and solidity of amber was increasing its length on his chin. If he fell down it would shatter itself, like glass, into brittle fragments. But he did not mind the appendage. It was the penalty all tobacco chewers paid in that country, and he had been out before in two cold snaps. They had not been so cold as this, but by the spirit thermometer at Sixty-Mile he knew that they had been registered at fifty below and at fifty-five.

He held on through the level stretch of woods for several miles, crossed a wide flat of nigger heads, and dropped down a bank to the frozen bed of a small stream. This was Henderson Creek, and he knew he was ten miles from the forks. He looked at his watch. It was ten o'clock. He was making four miles an hour, and he calculated that he would arrive at the forks at half-past twelve. He decided to celebrate that event by eating his lunch there.

The dog dropped in again at his heels, with a tail drooping discouragement, as the man swung along the creek bed. The furrow of the old sled trail was plainly visible, but a dozen inches of snow covered the marks of the last runners. In a month no man had come up or down that silent creek. The man held steadily on. He was not much given to thinking, and just then particularly he had nothing to think about save that he would eat lunch at the forks and that at six o'clock he would be in camp with the boys. There was nobody to talk to; and, had there been, speech would have been impossible because of the ice muzzle on his mouth. So he continued monotonously to chew tobacco and to increase the length of his amber beard.

Once in a while the thought reiterated itself that it was very cold and that he had never experienced such cold. As he walked along he rubbed his cheekbones and nose with the back of his mittened hand. He did this automatically, now and again changing hands. But, rub as he would, the instant he stopped his cheekbones went numb, and the following instant the end of his nose went numb. He was sure to frost his cheeks; he knew that, and experienced a pang of regret that he had not devised a nose strap of the sort Bud wore in cold snaps. Such a strap passed across the cheeks, as well, and saved them. But it didn't matter much, after all. What were frosted cheeks? A bit painful, that was all; they were never serious.

Empty as the man's mind was of thoughts, he was keenly observant, and he noticed the changes in the creek, the curves and bends and timber jams, and always he sharply noted where he placed his feet. Once, coming around a bend he shied abruptly, like a startled horse, curved away from the place where he had been walking, and retreated several paces back along the trail. The creek he knew was frozen clear to the bottom—no creek could contain water in that arctic winter—but he knew also that there were springs that bubbled out from the hillsides and ran along under the snow and on top the ice of the creek. He knew that the coldest snaps never froze these springs, and he knew likewise their danger. They were traps. They hid pools of water under the snow that might be three inches deep, or three feet. Sometimes a skin of ice half an inch thick covered them, and in turn was covered by the snow. Sometimes there were alternate layers of water and ice skin, so that when one broke through he kept on breaking through for a while, sometimes wetting himself to the waist.

That was why he had shied in such panic. He had felt the give under his feet and heard the crackle of a snow-hidden ice skin. And to get his feet wet in such a temperature meant trouble and danger. At the very least it meant delay, for he would be forced to stop and build a fire, and under its protection to bare his feet while he dried his socks and moccasins. He stood and studied the creek bed and its banks, and decided that the flow of water came from his right. He reflected awhile, rubbing his nose and cheeks, then skirted to the left, stepping gingerly and testing the footing for each step. Once clear of the danger, he took a fresh chew of tobacco and swung along at his four-mile gait.

In the course of the next two hours he came upon several similar traps. Usually the snow above the hidden pools had a sunken, candied appearance that advertised the danger. Once again, however, he had a close call; and once, suspecting danger, he compelled the dog to go on in front. The dog did not want to go. It hung back until the man shoved it forward, and then it went quickly across the white, unbroken surface. Suddenly it broke through, floundered to one side, and got away to firmer footing. It had wet its forefeet and legs, and almost immediately the water that clung to it turned to ice. It made quick efforts to lick the ice off its legs, then dropped down in the snow and began to bite out the ice that had formed between the toes. This was a matter of instinct. To permit the ice to remain would mean sore feet. It did not know this. It merely obeyed the mysterious prompting that arose from the deep crypts of its being. But the man knew, having achieved a judgment on the subject, and he removed the mitten from his right hand and helped tear out the ice particles. He did not expose his fingers more than a minute, and was astonished at the swift numbness that smote them. It certainly was cold. He pulled on the mitten hastily, and beat the hand savagely across his chest.

At twelve o'clock the day was at its brightest. Yet the sun was too far south on its winter journey to clear the horizon. The bulge of the earth intervened between it and Henderson Creek, where the man walked under a clear sky at noon and cast no shadow. At half-past twelve, to the minute, he arrived at the forks of the creek. He was pleased at the speed he had made. If he kept it up, he would certainly be with the boys by six. He unbuttoned his jacket and shirt and drew forth his lunch. The action consumed no more than a quarter of a minute, yet in that brief moment the numbness laid hold of the exposed fingers. He did not put the mitten on, but, instead, struck the fingers a dozen sharp smashes against his leg. Then he sat down on a snow-covered log to eat. The sting that followed upon the striking of his fingers against his leg ceased so quickly that he was startled. He had had no chance to take a bite of biscuit. He struck the fingers repeatedly and returned them to the mitten, baring the other hand for the purpose of eating. He tried to take a mouthful, but the ice muzzle prevented. He had forgotten to build a fire and thaw out. He chuckled at his foolishness, and as he chuckled he noted the numbness creeping into the exposed fingers. Also, he noted that the stinging which had first come to his toes when he sat down was already passing away. He wondered whether the toes were warm or numb. He moved them inside the moccasins and decided that they were numb.

He pulled the mitten on hurriedly and stood up. He was a bit frightened. He stamped up and down until the stinging returned into the feet. It certainly was cold, was his thought. That man from Sulphur Creek had spoken the truth when telling how cold it sometimes got in the country. And he had laughed at him at the time! That showed one must not be too sure of things. There was no mistake about it, it *was* cold. He strode up and down, stamping his feet and threshing his arms, until reassured by the returning warmth. Then he got out matches and proceeded to make a fire. From the undergrowth, where high water of the previous spring had lodged a supply of seasoned twigs, he got his firewood. Working carefully from a small beginning, he soon had a roaring fire, over which he thawed the ice from his face and in the protection of which he ate his biscuits. For the moment the cold of space was outwitted. The dog took satisfaction in the fire, stretching out close enough for warmth and far enough away to escape being singed.

When the man had finished, he filled his pipe and took his comfortable time over a smoke, then he pulled on his mittens, settled the ear flaps of his cap firmly about his ears, and took the creek trail up the left fork. The dog was disappointed and yearned back towards the fire. This man did not know cold. Possibly all the generations of his ancestry had been ignorant of cold, of real cold, of cold one hundred and seven degrees below freezing point. But the dog knew; all its ancestry knew, and it had inherited the knowledge. And it knew that it was not good to walk abroad in such fearful cold. It was the time to lie snug in a hole in the snow and wait for a curtain of cloud to be drawn across the face of outer space whence this cold came. On the other hand, there was no keen intimacy between the dog and the man. The one was the toil slave of the other, and the only caresses it had ever received were the caresses of the whip lash and of harsh and menacing throat sounds that threatened the whip lash. So the dog made no effort to communicate its apprehension to the man. It was not concerned in the welfare of the man; it was for its own sake that it yearned back toward the fire. But the man whistled, and spoke to it with the sound of whip lashes, and the dog swung in at the man's heels and followed after.

The man took a chew of tobacco and proceeded to start a new amber beard. Also, his moist breath quickly powdered with white his mustache, eyebrows, and lashes. There did not seem to be so many springs on the left fork of the Henderson, and for half an hour the man saw no signs of any. And then it happened. At a place where there were no signs, where the soft, unbroken snow seemed to advertise solidity beneath, the man broke through. It was not deep. He wet himself halfway to the knees before he floundered out to the firm crust.

He was angry, and cursed his luck aloud. He had hoped to get into camp with the boys at six o'clock, and this would delay him an hour, for he would have to build a fire and dry out his footgear. This was imperative at that low temperature—he knew that much; and he turned aside to the bank, which he climbed. On top, tangled in the underbrush about the trunks of several small spruce trees, was a high-water deposit of dry firewood—sticks and twigs, principally, but also larger portions of seasoned branches and fine, dry, last year's grasses. He threw down several large pieces on top of the snow. This served for a foundation and prevented the young flame from drowning itself in the snow it otherwise would melt. The flame he got by touching a match to a small shred of birch bark that he took from his pocket. This burned even more readily than paper. Placing it on the foundation, he fed the young flame with wisps of dry grass and with the tiniest dry twigs.

He worked slowly and carefully, keenly aware of his danger. Gradually, as the flame grew stronger, he increased the size of the twigs with which he fed it. He squatted in the snow, pulling the twigs out from their entanglement in the brush and feeding directly to the flame. He knew there must be no failure. When it is seventy-five below zero, a man must not fail in his first attempt to build a fire—that is, if his feet are wet. If his feet are dry, and he fails, he can run along the trail for half a mile and restore his circulation. But the circulation of wet and freezing feet cannot be restored by running when it is seventy-five below. No matter how fast he runs, the wet feet will freeze the harder.

All this the man knew. The old-timer on Sulphur Creek had told him about it the previous fall, and now he was appreciating the advice. Already all sensation had gone out of his feet. To build the fire he had been forced to remove his mittens, and the fingers had quickly gone numb. His pace of four miles an hour had kept his heart pumping blood to the surface of his body and to all the extremities. But the instant he stopped, the action of the pump eased down. The cold of space smote the unprotected tip of the planet, and he, being on that unprotected tip, received the full force of the blow. The blood of his body recoiled before it. The blood was alive, like the dog, and like the dog it wanted to hide away and cover itself up from the fearful cold. So long as he walked four miles an hour, he pumped the blood, willy-nilly, to the surface; but now it ebbed away and sank down into the recesses of his body. The extremities were the first to feel its absence. His wet feet froze the faster, and his exposed fingers numbed the faster, though they had not yet begun to freeze. Nose and cheeks were already freezing, while the skin of all his body chilled as it lost its blood.

But he was safe. Toes and nose and cheeks would be only touched by the frost, for the fire was beginning to burn with strength. He was feeding it with twigs the size of his finger. In another minute he would be able to feed it with branches the size of his wrist, and then he could remove his wet footgear, and, while it dried, he could keep his naked feet warm by the fire, rubbing them at first, of course, with snow. The fire was a success. He was safe. He remembered the advice of the old-timer on Sulphur Creek, and smiled. The old-timer had been very serious in laying down the law that no man must travel alone in the Klondike after fifty below. Well, here he was; he had had the accident; he was alone; and he had saved himself. Those old-timers were rather womanish, some of them, he thought. All a man had to do was to keep his head, and he was all right. Any man who was a man could travel alone. But it was surprising, the rapidity with which his cheeks and nose were freezing. And he had not thought his fingers could go lifeless in so short a time. Lifeless they were, for he could scarcely make them move together to grip a twig, and they seemed remote from his body and from him. When he touched a twig, he had to look and see whether or not he had hold of it. The wires were pretty well down between him and his finger ends.

All of which counted for little. There was the fire, snapping and crackling and promising life with every dancing flame. He started to untie his moccasins. They were coated with ice; the thick German socks were like sheaths of iron halfway to the knees; and the moccasin strings were like rods of steel all twisted and knotted as by some conflagration. For a moment he tugged with his numb fingers, then, realizing the folly of it, he drew his sheath knife.

But before he could cut the strings, it happened. It was his own fault or, rather, his mistake. He should not have built the fire under the spruce tree. He should have built it in the open. But it had been easier to pull the twigs from the brush and drop them directly on the fire. Now the tree under which he had done this carried a weight of snow on its boughs. No wind had blown for weeks, and each bough was full freighted. Each time he had pulled a twig he had communicated a slight agitation to the tree—an imperceptible agitation, so far as he was concerned, but an agitation sufficient to bring about the disaster. High up in the tree one bough capsized its load of snow. This fell on the boughs beneath, capsizing them. This process continued, spreading out and involving the whole tree. It grew like an avalanche, and it descended upon the man and the fire, and the fire was blotted out! Where it had burned was a mantle of fresh and disordered snow.

The man was shocked. It was as though he had just heard his own sentence of death. For a moment he sat and stared at the spot where the fire had been. Then he grew very calm. Perhaps the old-timer on Sulphur Creek was right. If he had only had a trail mate he would have been in no danger now. The trail mate could have built the fire. Well, it was up to him to build the fire over again, and this second time there must be no failure. Even if he succeeded, he would most likely lose some toes. His feet must be badly frozen by now, and there would be some time before the second fire was ready.

Such were his thoughts, but he did not sit and think them. He was busy all the time they were passing through his mind. He made a new foundation for a fire, this time out in the open, where no treacherous tree could blot it out. Next he gathered dry grasses and tiny twigs from the high-water flotsam. He could not bring his fingers together to pull them out, but he was able to gather them by the handful. In this way he got many rotten twigs and bits of green moss that were undesirable, but it was the best he could do. He worked methodically, even collecting an armful of larger branches to be used later when the fire gathered strength. And all the while the dog sat and watched him, a certain wistfulness in its eyes, for it looked upon him as the fire provider, and the fire was slow in coming.

When all was ready, the man reached in his pocket for a second piece of birch bark. He knew the bark was there, and though he could not feel it with his fingers, he could hear its crisp rustling as he fumbled for it. Try as he would, he could not clutch hold of it. And all the time, in his consciousness, was the knowledge that each instant his feet were freezing. This thought tended to put him in a panic, but he fought against it and kept calm. He pulled on his mittens with his teeth, and threshed his arms back and forth, beating his hands with all his might against his sides. He did this sitting down, and he stood up to do it; and all the while the dog sat in the snow, its wolf brush of a tail curled around warmly over its forefeet, its sharp wolf ears pricked forward intently as it watched the man. And the man, as he beat and threshed with his arms and hands, felt a great surge of envy as he regarded the creature that was warm and secure in its natural covering.

After a time he was aware of the first faraway signals of sensations in his beaten fingers. The faint tingling grew stronger till it evolved into a stinging ache that was excruciating, but which the man hailed with satisfaction. He stripped the mitten from his right hand and fetched forth the birch bark. The exposed fingers were quickly going numb again. Next he brought out his bunch of sulphur matches. But the tremendous cold had already driven the life out of his fingers. In his effort to separate one match from the others, the whole bunch fell into the snow. He tried to pick it out of the snow, but failed. The dead fingers could neither clutch nor touch. He was very careful. He drove the thought of his freezing feet, and nose, and cheeks, out of his mind, devoting his whole soul to the matches. He watched, using the sense of vision in place of that of touch, and when he saw his fingers on each side the bunch, he closed them—that is, he willed to close them, for the wires were down, and the fingers did not obey. He pulled the mitten on the right hand, and beat it fiercely against his knee. Then, with both mittened hands, he scooped the bunch of matches, along with much snow, into his lap. Yet he was no better off.

After some manipulation he managed to get the bunch between the heels of his mittened hands. In this fashion he carried it to his mouth. The ice crackled and snapped when by a violent effort he opened his mouth. He drew the lower jaw in, curled the upper lip out of the way and scraped the bunch with his upper teeth in order to separate a match. He succeeded in getting one, which he dropped on his lap. He was no better off. He could not pick it up. Then he devised a way. He picked it up in his teeth and scratched it on his leg. Twenty times he scratched before he succeeded in lighting it. As it flamed he held it with his teeth to the birch bark. But the burning brimstone went up his nostrils and into his lungs, causing him to cough spasmodically. The match fell into the snow and went out.

The old-timer on Sulphur Creek was right, he thought in the moment of controlled despair that ensued: after fifty below, a man should travel with a partner. He beat his hands, but failed in exciting any sensation. Suddenly he bared both hands, removing the mittens with his teeth. He caught the whole bunch between the heels of his hands. His arm muscles not being frozen enabled him to press the hand heels tightly against the matches. Then he scratched the bunch along his leg. It flared into flame, seventy sulphur matches at once! There was no wind to blow them out. He kept his head to one side to escape the strangling fumes, and held the blazing bunch to the birch bark. As he so held it, he became aware of sensation in his hand. His flesh was burning. He could smell it. Deep down below the surface he could feel it. The sensation developed into pain that grew acute. And still he endured it, holding the flame of the matches clumsily to the bark that would not light readily because his own burning hands were in the way, absorbing most of the flame.

At last, when he could endure no more, he jerked his hands apart. The blazing matches fell sizzling into the snow, but the birch bark was alight. He began laying dry grasses and the tiniest twigs on the flame. He could not pick and choose, for he had to lift the fuel between the heels of his hands. Small pieces of rotten wood and green moss clung to the twigs, and he bit them off as well as he could with his teeth. He cherished the flame carefully and awkwardly. It meant life, and it must not perish. The withdrawal of blood from the surface of his body now made him begin to shiver, and he grew more awkward. A large piece of green moss fell squarely on the little fire. He tried to poke it out with his fingers, but his shivering frame made him poke too far, and he disrupted the nucleus of the little fire, the burning grasses and the tiny twigs separating and scattering. He tried to poke them together again, but in spite of the tenseness of the effort, his shivering got away with him, and the twigs were hopelessly scattered. Each twig gushed a puff of smoke and went out. The fire provider had failed. As he looked apathetically about him, his eyes chanced on the dog, sitting across the ruins of the fire from him, in the snow, making restless, hunching movements, slightly lifting one forefoot and then the other, shifting its weight back and forth on them with wistful eagerness.

The sight of the dog put a wild idea into his head. He remembered the tale of the man, caught in a blizzard, who killed a steer and crawled inside the carcass, and so was saved. He would kill the dog and bury his hands in the warm body until the numbness went out of them. Then he could build another fire. He spoke to the dog, calling it to him; but in his voice was a strange note of fear that frightened the animal, who had never known the man to speak in such a way before. Something was the matter, and its suspicious nature sensed danger—it knew not what danger, but somewhere, somehow, in its brain arose an apprehension of the man. It flattened its ears down at the sound of the man's voice, and its restless, hunching movements and the liftings and shiftings of its forefeet became more pronounced; but it would not come to the man. He got on his hands and knees and crawled toward the dog. This unusual posture again excited suspicion, and the animal sidled mincingly away.

The man sat up in the snow for a moment and struggled for calmness. Then he pulled on his mittens, by means of his teeth, and got upon his feet. He glanced down at first in order to assure himself that he was really standing up, for the absence of sensation in his feet left him unrelated to the earth. His erect position in itself started to drive the webs of suspicion from the dog's mind; and when he spoke peremptorily, with the sound of whip lashes in his voice, the dog rendered its customary allegiance and came to him. As it came within reaching distance, the man lost his control. His arms flashed out to the dog, and he experienced genuine surprise when he discovered that his hands could not clutch, that there was neither bend nor feeling in his fingers. He had forgotten for the moment that they were frozen and that they were freezing more and more. All this happened quickly, and before the animal could get away, he encircled its body with his arms. He sat down in the snow, and in this fashion held the dog, while it snarled and whined and struggled.

But it was all he could do, hold its body encircled in his arms and sit there. He realized that he could not kill the dog. There was no way to do it. With his helpless hands he could neither draw nor hold his sheath knife nor throttle the animal. He released it, and it plunged wildly away, with tail between its legs, and still snarling. It halted forty feet away and surveyed him curiously, with ears sharply pricked forward.

The man looked down at his hands in order to locate them, and found them hanging on the ends of his arms. It struck him as curious that one should have to use his eyes in order to find out where his hands were. He began threshing his arms back and forth, beating the mittened hands against his sides. He did this for five minutes, violently, and his heart pumped enough blood up to the surface to put a stop to his shivering. But no sensation was aroused in his hands. He had an impression that they hung like weights on the ends of his arms, but when he tried to run the impression down, he could not find it.

A certain fear of death, dull and oppressive, came to him. This fear quickly became poignant as he realized that it was no longer a mere matter of freezing his fingers and toes, or of losing his hands and feet, but that it was a matter of life and death with the chances against him. This threw him into a panic, and he turned and ran along the old, dim trail. The dog joined in behind and kept up with him. He ran blindly, without intention, in fear such as he had never known in his life. Slowly, as he plowed and floundered through the snow, he began to see things again—the banks of the creek, the old timber jams, the leafless aspens, and the sky. The running made him feel better. He did not shiver. Maybe, if he ran on, his feet would thaw out; and, anyway, if he ran far enough, he would reach camp and the boys. Without doubt he would lose some fingers and toes and some of his face; but the boys would take care of him, and save the rest of him when he got there. And at the same time there was another thought in his mind that said he would never get to the camp and the boys; that he would soon be stiff and dead. This thought he kept in the background and refused to consider. Sometimes it pushed itself forward and demanded to be heard, but he thrust it back and strove to think of other things.

It struck him as curious that he could run at all on feet so frozen that he could not feel them when they struck the earth and took the weight of his body. He seemed to himself to skim along above the surface, and to have no connection with the earth. Somewhere he had once seen a winged Mercury, and he wondered if Mercury felt as he felt when skimming over the earth.

His theory of running until he reached camp and the boys had one flaw in it: he lacked the endurance. Several times he stumbled, and finally he tottered, crumpled up, and fell. When he tried to rise, he failed. He must sit and rest, he decided, and next time he would merely walk and keep on going. As he sat and regained his breath, he noted that he was feeling quite warm and comfortable. He was not shivering, and it even seemed that a warm glow had come to his chest and trunk. And yet, when he touched his nose or cheeks, there was no sensation. Running would not thaw them out. Nor would it thaw out his hands and feet. Then the thought came to him that the frozen portions of his body must be extending. He tried to keep this thought down, to forget it, to think of something else; he was aware of the panicky feeling that it caused, and he was afraid of the panic. But the thought asserted itself, and persisted, until it produced a vision of his body totally frozen. This was too much, and he made another wild run along the trail. Once he slowed down to a walk, but the thought of the freezing extending itself made him run again.

And all the time the dog ran with him, at his heels. When he fell down a second time, it curled its tail over its forefeet and sat in front of him, facing him, curiously eager and intent. The warmth and security of the animal angered him, and he cursed it till it flattened down its ears appeasingly. This time the shivering came more quickly upon the man. He was losing in his battle with the frost. It was creeping into his body from all sides. The thought of it drove him on, but he ran no more than a hundred feet, when he staggered and pitched headlong. It was his last panic. When he had recovered his breath and control, he sat up and entertained in his mind the conception of meeting death with dignity. However, the conception did not come to him in such terms. His idea of it was that he had been making a fool of himself, running around like a chicken with its head cut off—such was the simile that occurred to him. Well, he was bound to freeze anyway, and he might as well take it decently. With this newfound peace of mind came the first glimmerings of drowsiness. A good idea, he thought, to sleep off to death. It was like taking an anesthetic. Freezing was not so bad as people thought. There were lots worse ways to die.

He pictured the boys finding his body the next day. Suddenly he found himself with them, coming along the trail and looking for himself. And, still with them, he came around a turn in the trail and found himself lying in the snow. He did not belong with himself any more, for even then he was out of himself, standing with the boys and looking at himself in the snow. It certainly was cold, was his thought. When he got back to the States he could tell the folks what real cold was. He drifted on from this to a vision of the old-timer on Sulphur Creek. He could see him quite clearly, warm and comfortable, and smoking a pipe.

"You were right, old hoss; you were right," the man mumbled to the old-timer of Sulphur Creek.

Then the man drowsed off into what seemed to him the most comfortable and satisfying sleep he had ever known. The dog sat facing him and waiting. The brief day drew to a close in a long, slow twilight. There were no signs of a fire to be made, and, besides, never in the dog's experience had it known a man to sit like that in the snow and make no fire. As the twilight drew on, its eager yearning for the fire mastered it, and with a great lifting and shifting of forefeet, it whined softly, then flattened its ears down in anticipation of being chidden by the man. But the man remained silent. Later the dog whined loudly. And still later it crept close to the man and caught the scent of death. This made the animal bristle and back away. A little longer it delayed, howling under the stars that leaped and danced and shone brightly in the cold sky. Then it turned and trotted up the trail in the direction of the camp it knew, where there were other food providers and fire providers.

Sources

"Run for the Trees," by Lamar Underwood, originally appeared in *American Frontiersman* magazine. Reprinted by permission of Lamar Underwood.

"Terror at Land's End," by George Reiger, is an excerpt from George Reiger's book *Wanderer on My Native Shore* (Simon & Schuster, 1983). Reprinted by permission of George Reiger.

"When Lewis and Clark First Met Grizzlies!" is from *The Journals of Lewis and Clark*.

"A Grip on Death," by Archibald Rutledge, was originally published in *Field & Stream* magazine in 1936 and was included in the anthology *The Field and Stream Reader* (1946). The original title was "Milstead Ropes One."

"Tembo!," by Carl Akeley, is excerpted from his book *In Brightest Africa* (Doubleday, 1923).

"The Tsavo Man-Eaters," by Lt. Col. John Henry Patterson, is excerpted from the original book *The Man-Eaters of Tsavo* (1907).

"An Adventure with a Dog and a Glacier," by John Muir, is excerpted from his book *Travels in Alaska* (1915).

"Love of Life," by Jack London, is excerpted from his book *Love of Life and Other Stories* (Macmillan, 1918).

"The Midwinter Beach," by Henry Beston, is excerpted from his book *The Outermost House* (Doubleday, 1929).

"The Tragedies of the Nests," by John Burroughs, is excerpted from his book *Birds and Bees, Sharp Eyes and Other Papers*, first published in the early 1900s.

"On Dangerous Ground," by Lamar Underwood, is excerpted from his novel (Doubleday, 1989). Reprinted by permission of Lamar Underwood.

"Shipwreck of the Whaleship Essex," by Owen Chase, is excerpted from his book of the same title, first published in 1921 by W. B. Gilley.

"To Build a Fire," by Jack London, is excerpted from his book *Lost Face* (Mills and Boon Ltd., 1916).

www.ingramcontent.com/pod-product-compliance
Lightning Source LLC
Chambersburg PA
CBHW020053050826
49324CB00034B/316
9781493096046